The Failure of Risk Management

The Failure of Risk Management:

Why It's Broken and How to Fix It

Douglas W. Hubbard

John Wiley & Sons, Inc.

Published by John Wiley & Sons, Inc., Hoboken, New Jersey.

Published simultaneously in Canada.

For general information on our other products and services, or technical support, please contact our Customer Care Department within the United States at 800-762-2974, outside the United States at 317-572-3993 or fax 317-572-4002.

Wiley also publishes its books in a variety of electronic formats. Some content that appears in print may not be available in electronic books.

For more information about Wiley products, visit our web site at www.wiley.com.

Library of Congress Cataloging-in-Publication Data

Hubbard, Douglas W., 1962-
The failure of risk management : why it's broken and how to fix it / Douglas W. Hubbard.
p. cm.
Includes bibliographical references and index.
ISBN 978-0-470-38795-5 (cloth)
1. Risk management. I. Title.
HD61.H76 2009
658.15'5–dc22

2008052147

Printed in the United States of America

10 9 8 7 6 5 4 3 2 1

I dedicate this book to my entire support staff: my wife, Janet, and our children, Evan, Madeleine, and Steven.

Contents

Preface

I started writing this book in early 2008, well before the most serious period of the financial crisis. The original plan was to turn in my manuscript in December but, as the economic crisis developed, the publisher saw that a book about the failure of risk management might become more relevant to many readers. So, at my editor's urging, instead of writing a 50,000-word manuscript due by December, I wrote an 80,000-word manuscript by the end of October.

Although the financial crisis becomes an important backdrop for a book about risk management, I still wanted to write a much broader book than a reaction to the most recent disaster. This book should be just as relevant after the next big natural disaster, major product safety recall, or catastrophic industrial accident. Better yet, I hope readers see this book as a resource they need *before* those events occur. Risk management that simply reacts to yesterday's news is not risk management at all.

I addressed risk in my first book, *How to Measure Anything: Finding the Value of Intangibles in Business.* Risk struck me as one of those items that is consistently perceived as an *intangible* by management. In a way, they are right. A risk that something could occur—the probability of some future event—is not *tangible* in the same way as progress on a construction project or the output of a power plant. But it is every bit as measurable. Two entire chapters in the first book focused just on the measurement of uncertainty and risks.

Unfortunately, risk management based on actual measurements of risks is not the predominant approach in most industries. I see solutions for managing the risks of some very important problems that are in fact no better than astrology. And this is not a controversial position I'm taking. The flaws in these methods are widely known to the researchers who study them. The message has simply not been communicated to the larger audience of managers.

In 1994, I developed a method I called *Applied Information Economics*, in part for the same reason that I wrote this and the previous book. I have watched consultants come up with a lot of half-baked schemes for assessing risks, measuring performance, and prioritizing portfolios with no apparent foundation in statistics or decision science. Arbitrary scoring schemes have virtually taken over some aspects of formalized decision-making processes in management. In other areas, some methods that do have a sound scientific and mathematical basis are consistently misunderstood and misapplied.

Of all the good, solid academic research and texts on risk analysis, risk management, and decision science, none seem to be directly addressing the problem of the apparently unchecked spread of pseudoscience in this field. In finance, Nassim Taleb's popular books, *Fooled by Randomness* and *The Black Swan*, have pointed out the existence of serious problems. But in those cases, there was not much practical advice for risk managers and very little information about assessing risks outside of finance. There is a need to point out these problems to a wide audience for a variety of different risks.

This book is somewhat more confrontational than my first one. No doubt, some proponents of widely used methods—some of which have been codified in international standards—might feel offended by some of the positions I am taking in this book. As such, I've taken care that each of the key claims I make about the weaknesses of some methods is supported by the thorough research of others, and not just my own opinion. The research is overwhelmingly conclusive—much of what has been done in risk management, when measured objectively, has added no value to the issue of managing risks. It may actually have made things worse.

Although the solution to better risk management is, for most, better quantitative analysis, a specialized mathematical text on the analysis and management of risks would not reach a wide enough audience. The numerous such texts already published haven't seemed to penetrate the management market, and I have no reason to believe that mine would fare any better. The approach I take here is to provide my readers with just enough technical information that they can make a 180-degree turn in risk management. They can stop using the equivalent of astrology in risk management and at least start down the path of the better methods. For risk managers, mastering those methods will become part of a longer career and a study that goes beyond this book. This is more like a first book in astronomy for recovering astrologers—we have to debunk the old and introduce the new.

Douglas W. Hubbard

Acknowledgments

Many people helped me with this book in many ways. Some I have interviewed for this book, some have provided their own research (even some prior to publication), and others have spent time reviewing my manuscript and offering many suggestions for improvement. In particular, I would like to thank Dr. Sam Savage of Stanford University, who has been extraordinarily helpful on all these counts.

Daniel Kahneman
Tony Cox
Christopher "Kip" Bohn
Jim Deloach
Stephen Wolfram
Bob Clemen
Robin Dillon-Merrill
Karen Jenni
Rick Julien
David Budescu
Ray Covert
David Bearden
Jim Franklin
John Schuyler
Dennis William Cox
Jim Dyer
Steve Hoye
John Spangenberg
Jason Mewes
Dan Garrow
Reed Augliere
Fiona MacMillan
Bill Panning
Yook Seng Kong
Allen Kubitz
Andrew Braden
Rob Donat
Diana Del Bel Belluz
Andrew Freeman
Thompson Terry
Vic Fricas
Dr. Sam Savage
David Hubbard

An Introduction to the Crisis

CHAPTER 1

Healthy Skepticism for Risk Management

It is far better to grasp the universe as it really is than to persist in delusion, however satisfying and reassuring.

—Carl Sagan

Everything's fine today, that is our illusion.

—Voltaire

Any new and rapidly growing trend in management methods should be considered with healthy skepticism, especially when that method is meant to help direct and protect major investments and inform key public policy. It is time to apply this skepticism to the "risk management" methods meant to assess and then mitigate major risks of all sorts. Many of these methods are fairly new and are growing in popularity. Some are well-established and highly regarded. Some take a very soft, qualitative approach and others are rigorously quantitative. But for all of these methods, we have to ask the same, basic questions:

- Do any of these risk management methods work?
- Would anyone in the organization even know if they didn't work?
- If they didn't work, what would be the consequences?

For most organizations, the answers to these questions are all bad news. Natural, geopolitical, and financial disasters in the first few years of the 21st century have, perhaps only temporarily, created a new awareness of risk among the public, businesses, and lawmakers. This has spurred the development of several risk management methods, in both financial and non-financial sectors. Unfortunately, when these methods are measured rigorously, they don't appear to work. Most of the new non-financial methods are not based on any previous theories of risk analysis and there is no real, scientific evidence that they result in a measurable reduction in risk or improvement in decisions. Where scientific data does exist, the data shows that most methods fail to account for known sources of error in the analysis of risk or, worse yet, add error of their own. Even in the financial sector and other areas that use the most sophisticated, quantitative methods, there is a growing realization that certain types of systematic errors have undermined the validity of their analysis for years.

The answer to the second question (whether anyone would know that the risk management system has failed) is also *no*; most managers would not know what they need to look for to evaluate a risk management method and, more likely than not, can be fooled by a kind of "placebo effect"[1] and groupthink about the method. Even under the best circumstances, where the effectiveness of the risk management method itself was tracked closely and measured objectively, adequate evidence may not be available for some time. A more typical circumstance, however, is that the risk management method itself has no performance measures at all, even in the most diligent, metrics-oriented organizations. This widespread inability to make the sometimes-subtle differentiation between methods that work and methods that don't work means that ineffectual methods are likely to spread. Ineffectual methods may even be touted as "best practices" and, like a dangerous virus with a long incubation period, are passed from company to company with no early indicators of ill effects until it's too late.

Common Mode Failure

Finally, to answer the question about the consequences of unsound risk management methods, I'll use an example from a historic air-travel disaster to explain a concept called *common mode failure* (a concept from one of the more scientific approaches to risk analysis). In July 1989, I was the commander of the Army Reserve unit in Sioux City, Iowa. It was the first day of our two-week annual training and I had already left for Fort McCoy, Wisconsin, with a small group of support staff (the "advance party"). The convoy of the rest of the unit was going to leave that afternoon, about five hours behind us. But just before the main body was ready to leave for annual training, the unit was deployed for a major local emergency.

United Airlines flight 232 to Philadelphia was being redirected to the small Sioux City airport because of serious mechanical difficulties. It crashed, killing 111 passengers and crew. Fortunately, the large number of emergency workers available and the heroic airmanship of the crew helped make it possible to save 185 onboard. Most of my unit spent the first day of our annual training collecting the dead from the tarmac and the nearby cornfields.

During the flight, the DC-10's tail-mounted engine failed catastrophically, causing the fast-spinning turbine blades to fly out like shrapnel in all directions. The debris from the turbine managed to cut the lines to *all three* redundant hydraulic systems, making the aircraft nearly uncontrollable. Although the crew was able to guide the aircraft in the direction of the airport by varying thrust to the two remaining wing-mounted engines, the lack of tail control made a normal landing impossible.

Aviation officials would refer to this as a "one-in-a-billion" event[2] and the media repeated this claim. But since mathematical misconceptions are common, if someone tells you that something that just occurred had merely a one-in-a-billion chance of occurrence, you should consider the possibility that they calculated the odds incorrectly.

The type of event that caused the crash is called a *common mode failure*, because a single event caused the failure of multiple components in a system. If they had failed independently of each other, the failure of all three would be extremely unlikely. But because all three hydraulic systems had lines near the tail engine, a single event could damage all of them. The common mode failure wiped out the benefits of redundancy.

Now consider that the cracks in the turbine blades would have been detected except for what the National Transportation Safety Board (NTSB) called "inadequate consideration given to human factors" in the turbine blade inspection process. Is human error more likely than one in a billion? Absolutely; in a way, that was an *even more common* common mode failure in the system.

But the common mode failure hierarchy could be taken even further. Suppose that the risk management method itself was fundamentally flawed. If that were the case, then perhaps problems in design and inspection procedures would be very hard to discover and much more likely to materialize. Now suppose that the risk management methods not just in one airline but in most organizations in most industries were flawed. The effects of disasters like Katrina and the financial crisis of 2008/9 could be inadequately planned for simply because the methods used to assess the risk were misguided. Ineffective risk management methods that somehow manage to become standard spread this vulnerability to everything they touch.

The ultimate common mode failure would be a failure of risk management itself. A weak risk management approach is effectively the biggest risk in the organization.

If the initial assessment of risk is not based on meaningful measures, the risk mitigation methods—even if they could have worked—are bound to address the wrong problems. If risk assessment is a failure, then the best case is that the risk management effort is simply a waste of time and money because decisions are ultimately unimproved. In the worst case, the erroneous conclusions lead the organization down a more dangerous path that it would probably not have otherwise taken.

The financial crisis occurring while I wrote this book was another example of a common mode failure that traces its way back to the failure of risk management of firms like AIG, Lehman Brothers, Bear Stearns, and the federal agencies appointed to oversee them. Previously loose credit practices and overly leveraged positions combined with an economic downturn to create a cascade of loan defaults, tightening credit among institutions, and further economic downturns. If that weren't bad enough, poor risk management methods are used in government and business to make decisions that not only guide risk decisions involving billions—or trillions—of dollars, but are also used to affect decisions that impact human health and safety.

What happened is history. But here are just a few more examples of major, risky decisions currently made with questionable risk assessment methods, some of which we will discuss in more detail later. Any of these, and many more, could reveal themselves only after a major disaster in a business, government program, or even your personal life:

- The approval and prioritization of investments and project portfolios in major U.S. companies
- The evaluation of major security threats for business and government
- The decision to launch the space shuttle
- The approval of government programs worth many billions of dollars
- The determination of when additional maintenance is required for old bridges
- The evaluation of patient risks in health care
- The identification of supply chain risks due to pandemic viruses
- The decision to outsource pharmaceutical production to China

Clearly, getting any of these risks wrong would lead to major problems—as has already happened in some cases. The individual method used may have been sold as "formal and structured" and perhaps it was even claimed to be "proven." Surveys of organizations even show a significant percentage of managers who will say the risk management program was "successful" (more on this to come). Perhaps success was claimed for the reason that it helped to "build consensus," "communicate risks," or "change the culture."

Since the methods used did not actually measure these risks in a mathematically and scientifically sound manner, management doesn't even have the basis for determining whether a method works. Surveys about the adoption and success of risk management initiatives are almost always self-assessments by the surveyed organizations. They are not independent, objective measures of success in reducing risks. If the process doesn't correctly assess and mitigate risks, then what is the value of building consensus about it, communicating it, or changing the culture about it? Even if harmony were achieved, perhaps communicating and building consensus on the wrong solution will merely ensure that one makes the big mistakes faster and more efficiently.

Fortunately, the cost to fix the problem is almost always a fraction of a percent of the size of what is being risked. For example, a more realistic evaluation of risks in a large IT portfolio worth over a hundred million dollars would not have to cost more than half a million—probably a lot less. Unfortunately, the adoption of a more rigorous and scientific management of risk is still not widespread. And for major risks such as those in the previous list, that is a big problem for corporate profits, the economy, public safety, national security, and you.

What Counts as Risk Management

There are numerous topics in the broad category of *risk management* but it is often used in a much narrower sense than it should be. When the term is used too narrowly, it is either because *risk* is used too narrowly, *management* is used too narrowly, or both.

If you start looking for definitions of *risk*, you will find many wordings that add up to the same thing, and a few versions that are fundamentally different. For now, I'll skirt some of the deeper philosophical issues about what it means (yes, there are some, but that will come later) and I'll avoid some of the definitions that seem to be unique to specialized uses. Chapter 5 is devoted to why the definition I am going to propose is preferable to various mutually-exclusive alternatives that each have proponents who assume their's is the "one true" definition.

For now, I'll focus on a definition that, although it contradicts some definitions, best represents the one used by well-established, mathematical treatments of the term (e.g. actuarial science), as well as any English dictionary or even how the lay-public uses the term (see the box below).

DEFINITION OF *RISK*

Long definition: The probability and magnitude of a loss, disaster, or other undesirable event

Shorter (equivalent) definition: Something bad could happen

The second definition is more to the point, but the first definition gives us an indication of how to quantify a risk. First, we can state a probability that the undesirable event will occur. Also, we need to measure the magnitude of the loss from this event in terms of financial losses, lives lost, and so on.

The undesirable event could be just about anything, including natural disasters, a major product recall, the default of a major debtor, hackers releasing sensitive customer data, political instability around a foreign office, workplace accidents resulting in injuries, or a pandemic flu virus disrupting supply chains. It could also mean personal misfortunes, such as a car accident on the way to work, loss of a job, a heart attack, and so on. Almost anything that could go wrong is a risk.

Since risk *management* generally applies to a management process in an organization, I'll focus a bit less on personal risks. Of course, my chance of having a heart attack is an important personal risk to assess and I certainly try to manage that risk. But when I'm talking about the failure of risk management—as the title of this book indicates—I'm not really focusing on whether individuals couldn't do a better job of managing personal risks like losing weight to avoid heart attacks (certainly, most should). I'm talking about major organizations that have adopted what is ostensibly some sort of formal risk management approach that they use to make critical business and public policy decisions.

Now, let us discuss the second half of the phrase *risk management.* Again, as with *risk*, I find multiple, wordy definitions for *management*, but here is one that seems to represent and combine many good sources:

DEFINITION OF MANAGEMENT

Long definition: The planning, organization, coordination, control, and direction of resources toward defined objective(s)

Shorter, folksier definition: Using what you have to get what you need

There are a couple of qualifications that, while they should be extremely obvious, are worth mentioning when we put *risk* and *management* together. Of course, when an executive wants to manage risks, he or she actually wishes to reduce it or at least not unduly increase it in pursuit of better opportunities. And since the current amount of risk and its sources are not immediately apparent, an important part of reducing or minimizing risks is figuring out where the risks are. Also, risk management must accept that risk is inherent in business and risk reduction is practical only up to a point. Like any other management program, risk management has to make effective use of limited resources. Putting all of that together, here is a definition (again, not too different in spirit from the myriad definitions found in other sources):

DEFINITION OF RISK MANAGEMENT

Long definition: The identification, assessment, and prioritization of risks followed by coordinated and economical application of resources to minimize, monitor, and control the probability and/or impact of unfortunate events

Shorter definition: Being smart about taking chances

Risk management methods come in many forms, but the ultimate goal is to minimize risk in some area of the firm relative to the opportunities being sought, given resource constraints. Some of the names of these efforts have become terms of art in virtually all of business. A popular, and laudable, trend is to put the word *enterprise* in front of *risk management* to indicate that it is a comprehensive approach to risk for the firm. *Enterprise risk management (ERM)* is one of the headings under which many of the trends in risk management appear. I'll call ERM a type of risk management *program*, because this is often the banner under which risk management is known. I will also distinguish programs from actual methods since ERM could be implemented with entirely different methods, either soft or quantitative.

The following are just a few examples of various management programs to manage different kinds of risks (*Note:* Some of these can be components of others and the same program can contain a variety of different methods):

- Enterprise risk management (ERM)
- Portfolio management or project portfolio management (PPM)
- Disaster recovery and business continuity planning (DR/BCP)
- Project risk management (PRM)
- Governance risk and compliance (GRC)
- Emergency/crisis management processes

Risk management includes analysis and mitigation of risks related to physical security, product liability, information security, various forms of insurance, investment volatility, regulatory compliance, actions of competitors, workplace safety, getting vendors or customers to share risks, political risks in foreign governments, business recovery from natural catastrophes, or any other uncertainty that could result in a significant loss.

Anecdote: The Risk of Outsourcing Drug Manufacturing

At a conference organized by the Consumer Health Products Association (a pharmaceutical industry association), I witnessed a chemical engineer describing a new risk management process he had developed for his firm. The risk analysis method was meant to assess an important and emerging risk in this field.

To control costs, this large pharmaceutical manufacturer was more frequently outsourcing certain batch processes to China. Virtually all of this manufacturer's competition was doing the same. But while the costs were significantly lower, they had a concern that batches from China might have additional quality control issues over and above those of batches manufactured here in the United States. These concerns were entirely justified.

The conference was in October 2007, and earlier that year there had already been several widely publicized product safety incidents with goods produced in China. In June, there was a toxin found in toothpaste and lead found in toys produced in China. Then there was tainted pet food that killed as many as 4,000 pets. There was even the disturbing case of "Aqua Dots," the children's craft-beads that stuck together to make different designs. The coating of these beads could metabolize in the stomach to produce gamma hydroxy butyrate—the chemical used in date-rape drugs.

Except for me, almost all of the audience were chemists, chemical engineers, and industrial engineers. They were previously listening to extremely technical sessions on sheer stress of particles in various processing equipment, yield curves, and mechanical details of drug packaging. There was no shortage of scientific thinkers and, from what I could tell, no timidity about mathematical models.

Yet, when the presenter was explaining the details of his company's new method for analyzing the risk of batches outsourced to China, I saw none of the hard science and skeptical peer-review that seemed common in the other sessions. He was describing a method based on a subjective "weighted score."[3] In it, several "risk indicators" were each scored on a scale of 1 to 5. For example, if the manufacturer already produces a similar, but not identical, drug, it might get a low risk score of 2 on the indicator called "proven technical proficiency." If it was inspected by and got a positive evaluation from the Chinese health agency, but was not yet inspected by the Food and Drug Administration, then it might get a 4 on the "formal inspections" indicator. If the components of the drug required certain special safety controls that would be harder to outsource, then it might score as a higher risk in other areas. Each of these scores was based on the judgments of a team assembled to make these evaluations.

Then these scores were each multiplied by a weight of somewhere between 0.1 and 1.0 and then all of the weighted scores were totaled. The total of the weighted score might be 17.5 for one outsourcing strategy, 21.2 for another, and so on. The team that chose the scores also chose the weights and, again, it was based only on subjective judgments. The team further separated the resulting scores into various stratifications of risk that would, apparently, have some bearing on the decision to use a particular China-based source for a drug. For example, risk scores of over 20 might mean "Extremely high risk: Find an alternative"; 10 to 19 might mean "High risk: Proceed only with increased quality assurance," and so on.

When the engineer had finished describing the approach, I noticed that several heads in the room turned to me expecting some response. Earlier that day, I had given the keynote address describing, among other things, how risk can be quantified in a mathematically and scientifically meaningful way. Perhaps some were implementing something similar in their firms and were curious to see whether I would endorse it, but I suspect it was more likely they were expecting a criticism.

I neither endorsed nor rejected the approach outright. To be perfectly fair, neither position could yet be positively justified at that point without knowing a few more details (although there is a good chance it shared the flaws of many weighted scores, which I discuss later). I simply asked, "How do you know it works?" This is the most important question we could ask about a risk analysis and risk management approach. Once I knew the answer to that question, then I could legitimately take a position.

There was a long pause. It was obvious that they hadn't even considered how to answer that question. So I thought it would be helpful (if a bit leading) to prompt them with another question: "Would you call this approach *scientific*?" After another pause, I asked, "Do you see how an actuary or statistician might not call this a *risk analysis*?" At this point, I sensed the questions were more like brow-beating than being helpful.

I then suggested to the presenter that the engineers in this field could be as scientific in their approach to this problem as they are in any other aspect of their profession. I pointed out that, for one, there was no need to start from scratch. If they were developing a new process for pharmaceutical manufacture, I'm sure they would examine existing research in the area. Likewise, there is quite a lot of literature in the general area of assessing risks in a mathematically and scientifically sound manner. It would be helpful to know that they don't have to reinvent any of the fundamental concepts when it comes to measuring risks.

Then I pointed out that in the design of processes in drug production, once they had thoroughly reviewed the literature on a topic, no doubt they would design empirical tests of various components in the process, and measure them in a way that would satisfy the peer-reviewed journals and the FDA inspectors alike. Again, this same philosophy can apply to risk.

In fact, a much more sophisticated method is often already used to assess a different risk in the drug industry. "Stop-gate" analysis is used to determine whether a candidate for a new product should advance from formulation to animal testing, then from animal testing to human trials, until finally they decide whether to go to market. Many drug companies use proven statistical methods at each step in the stop-gate analysis. But, somehow, none of the basic concepts of stop-gate analysis were built upon to assess the risks of outsourcing production to China.

My questions to the presenter were rhetorical. I was already fairly sure that they had no objective measure for the effectiveness of this method. If they had known to create such measures, they would probably have been inclined to create a very different approach in the first place. When it came to designing a method for assessing and managing risks, these scientists and engineers developed an approach with no more scientific rigor behind it than an ancient shaman reading goat entrails to determine where to hunt. While the lack of such rigor would be considered negligent in most of their work, it was acceptable to use a risk assessment method with no scientific backing at all.

In effect, they didn't think of this new risk in the same way as they thought of the substances and processes they use to manufacture drugs in a highly regulated industry. The chemicals they process and the vessels they use are concrete, tangible things and, to the engineers, risk might seem like an abstraction. Even the methods they use in stop-gate analysis might take on an air of concreteness simply because, by now, they have a lot of data on the problem. Perhaps, to them, the process of managing an unfamiliar risk seems like an intangible thing that doesn't lend itself to the same methods of validation that a drug manufacturing process would have to undergo for FDA approval. Applying the type of scientific reasoning and testing they use on the production of a drug to the risk analysis of producing that same drug in China is a leap they had not considered.

The presenter and the audience felt that the weighted scoring method they described was something close to "best practices" for the industry. When I asked, nobody in the room claimed to have an approach that was any more sophisticated. Most had no risk analysis at all on this problem.

Fortunately for the company that was presenting its risk management solution, it had not yet seen the worst-case scenarios that might result from unsound risk analysis. But with an entire industry approaching the outsourcing problem with either unscientific risk analysis methods or none at all, the worst case was inevitable. Just a few months after the conference, another major drug company using similarly subjective risk management methods on this problem would discover exactly how much was being risked by the outsourcing decisions (and the meager risk analysis applied to it).

Baxter International, Inc. was receiving reports of dangerous adverse reactions to its Chinese-manufactured blood-thinning drug called heparin. To its credit, by mid-January 2008, Baxter had voluntarily recalled some lots of the multidose vials of the drug. By then, the FDA was considering a mandatory recall but had not yet done so because they believed other suppliers might not be able to meet demand for this critical drug. The FDA reasoned that this additional risk to patients requiring heparin therapy would be higher (I have no idea how much risk analysis went into *that* decision).

By February, the FDA had determined that the supply of heparin by other manufacturers was adequate and that Baxter should proceed with the recall of various types of heparin products. At the beginning of the recall in February, the FDA had linked four deaths to the Chinese-manufactured heparin and by March the number had grown to 19 deaths. By May 2008, the FDA had "clearly linked" a total of 81 deaths and 785 severe allergic reactions to the drug. Of course, chances are the various individual and class action lawsuits (just beginning as this book was written) will argue a much larger number.

The risks of outsourcing drug production to China always were high and the fact that some firms were at least attempting to develop a risk management method—regardless of its effectiveness—indicates that the industry was at least aware of the risk. The FDA is entrusted to inspect the operations of any drug manufacturer selling products in the United States, including foreign-based factories but, by March 2008, the FDA had inspected just 16 of the 566 Chinese drug manufacturers. The United States gets approximately 40% of its drugs from abroad. The scale of the problem easily justifies the very best risk analysis available.

Obviously, we can't be certain with only this information that the industry's lack of more sophisticated risk management for overseas drug manufacturing was the direct cause of the heparin incident. If the industry had used more sophisticated methods such as it already uses for stop-gate analysis, we could not be certain that some similar problem would not still have occurred. And, since the entire industry was unsophisticated in this area of risk management, there is certainly no reason to single out Baxter as particularly bad. This anecdote, by definition, is merely a single sample of the types of events that can occur and, by itself, is not sufficient to draw scientifically justified conclusions.

For any risk management method used in the pharmaceutical industry or any other industry, we must ask, again, "How do we know it works?" If we can't answer that question, then our most important risk management strategy should be to find a way to answer it and adopt a risk assessment and risk mitigation method that does work.

What Failure Means

At the beginning of this chapter, we defined *risk* and *risk management.* Now we need to discuss what I mean by the *failure* of risk management. With some exceptions, it may not be very obvious. And that is part of the problem.

First, a couple of points about the anecdotes I just used. I believe United Airlines was probably applying what it believed to be a prudent level of risk management. I also believe the entire pharmaceutical industry and Baxter in particular were making a well-intentioned effort to manage the risks of outsourcing to China. When I refer to the "failure of risk management," I do not just refer to outright negligence. Failing to employ the accounting controls that would have avoided Enron's demise, for example, are not the kind of failures I examine the most in this book. I will concentrate more on the failure of sincere efforts to manage risks, as I will presume is the case with many organizations—even though we know the possible lawsuits must argue otherwise. I'm focusing on those organizations that believe they have adopted an effective risk management method and are unaware that they haven't improved their situation one iota.

Second, I used these anecdotes in part to make a point about the limits of anecdotes when it comes to showing the failure or success of risk management. The single event of tainted blood thinner does not necessarily constitute a failure of risk management. Nor would a lucky streak of zero disasters have indicated that the risk management was working. At best, the pharmaceutical outsourcing anecdote shows one scenario of what could happen.

I think this is a departure from some approaches to the discussion of risk management. I have heard some entertaining speakers talk about various anecdotal misfortunes of companies as evidence that risk management failed. I have to admit, these stories are often fascinating, especially where the circumstances are engaging and the outcome was particularly disastrous. But I think the details of the mortgage crisis, 9/11, rogue traders, Hurricane Katrina, or Three Mile Island feed a kind of morbid curiosity more than they inform about risk management. Perhaps the stories made managers feel a little better about the fact they hadn't (yet) made such a terrible blunder.

I will continue to use examples like this because that is part of what it takes to help people connect with the concepts. But we need a better measure of the success or failure of risk management than single anecdotes. In most cases regarding risk management, an anecdote should be used only to *illustrate* a point, not to prove a point.

So, when I claim that risk management has failed, I'm not necessarily basing that on individual anecdotes of unfortunate things happening. It is possible, after all, that organizations where a disaster didn't occur were just lucky. They may have been doing nothing substantially different from organizations where disasters did occur. When I say that risk management has failed, it is for at least one of three reasons, all of which are independent of individual anecdotes: (1) the failure to measure and validate methods as a whole or in part; (2) the use of components that are known not to work; and (3) the lack of use of components that are known to work.

1. *Except for certain quantitative methods in certain industries, the effectiveness of risk management is almost never measured.* The biggest failure of risk management is that there is almost no experimentally verifiable evidence that the methods used improve on the assessment and mitigation of risks, especially for the softer (and much more popular) methods. If the only "evidence" is a subjective perception of success by the very managers who championed the method in the first place, then we have no reason to believe that the risk management method does not have a negative return. For a critical issue like risk management, we should require positive proof that it works—not just the lack of proof that it doesn't. Part of the success of any initiative is the measurable evidence of its success. It is a failure of risk management to know nothing of its own risks. It is also an avoidable risk that risk management, contrary to its purpose, fails to avoid.
2. *Some parts that have been measured don't work.* The experimental evidence that does exist for some aspects of risk management indicates the existence of some serious errors and biases. Since many risk management methods rely on human judgment, we should consider the research that shows how humans misperceive and systematically underestimate risks. If these problems are not identified and corrected, then they will invalidate any risk management method based even in part on human assessments. Other methods add error through arbitrary scales or the naïve use of historical data. Even

some of the most quantitatively rigorous methods fail to produce results that compare well with historical observations.

3. *Some parts that do work aren't used.* There are methods that are proven to work both in controlled laboratory settings and in the real world, but are not used in most risk management processes. These are methods that are entirely practical in the real world and, although they may be more elaborate, are easily justified for the magnitude of the decisions risk management will influence. Falling far short of what one could reasonably be expected to do is another form of failure.

In total, these failures add up to the fact that we still take unnecessary risks within risk management itself. Now it is time to measure risk management itself in a meaningful way so we can identify more precisely where risk management is broken and how to fix it.

Scope and Objectives of This Book

My objectives with this book are (1) to reach the widest possible audience among managers and analysts, (2) to give them enough information to quit using ineffective methods, and (3) to get them started on better solutions.

The first objective, reaching a wide audience, requires that I don't treat risk management myopically from the point of a given industry. There are many existing risk management texts that I consider important classics, but I see none that map the breadth of the different methods and the problems and advantages of each. There are financial risk assessment texts written specifically for financial analysts and economists. There are engineering and environmental risk texts for engineers and scientists. There are multiple risk management methods written for managers of software projects, computer security, or disaster recovery. Many of these sources seem to talk about risk management as if their methods comprised the entire subject. None seems entirely aware of the others.

The "wide audience" objective also means that I can't write just about the latest disaster. A reader picking up this book in 2009 may think the risk I'm talking about is a financial risk. If I had written this just after Katrina, risk might have meant something very different. But risk is not selective in that way and the best methods are not specific to one category of risks.

Thinking about risks means thinking about events that have not yet occurred, not just last year's news.

Finally, reaching a wide audience requires that I don't just write another esoteric text on quantitative methods for a small community of experts. Of those, there are already some excellent sources that I will not attempt to reproduce. A couple of slightly technical issues will be discussed, but only enough to introduce the important concepts.

The last two objectives, to get managers to quit using ineffectual methods and start them on a better path, are also satisfied by a "just technical enough" approach to the problem. This book won't make most managers masters of more quantitative and scientific methods of risk management. I merely want to convince them to make a radical change of direction from the methods they are most likely using now.

To accomplish these objectives, the remainder of this book is divided along the lines implied by the title:

- *Part One: An Introduction to the Crisis.* This first chapter introduced the problem and its seriousness. Chapter 2 outlines the diversity of approaches to assess and mitigate risks and discusses how managers rate their own firms in these areas. Chapter 3 examines how we should evaluate risk management methods.
- *Part Two: Why It's Broken.* After an introduction to four basic schools of thought about risk management, we will discuss the confusing differences in basic terminology among different areas of risk management. Then we will introduce several sources of fundamental errors in popular methods that remain unaddressed. We will list several fallacies that keep some from adopting better methods. Finally, this part of the text will outline some significant problems with even the most quantitative methods being used.
- *Part Three: How to Fix It.* This final part will introduce methods for addressing each of the previously discussed sources of error in risk management methods. We will talk about the basic concepts behind better methods, including how to think about probabilities and how to introduce scientific methods and measurements into risk management. Finally, we will talk about some of the issues involved in creating a culture in organizations and governments that would facilitate and incentivize better risk management.

Throughout this book, I will offer those who require more hands-on examples sample spreadsheets on this book's website at www.howtofixriskmgt.com. Those who prefer the "10,000-foot view" can still get a good idea of the issues without feeling dragged down by some technical details, whereas those who prefer to get more information can get specific example calculations. The website will also give all readers access to information on risks that evolve after this book has been published as well as a way to interact with other risk managers.

See this book's website at www.howtofixriskmgt.com for detailed examples from the book, discussion groups, and up-to-date news on risk management.

NOTES

1. My use of "placebo effect" requires a qualification. The placebo effect in medicine is the tendency among patients to experience both subjective and in some cases objectively observable improvements in health after receiving treatment that should be inert. This is a purely psychological effect but the improvements could be in objectively measurable ways—such as reducing blood pressure or cholesterol. However, when I refer to a placebo effect I mean that there literally is no improvement other than the subjective impression of an improvement.
2. Capt. A.C. Haynes "United 232: Coping With the 'One-in-a-Billion' Loss of All Flight Controls," *Accident Prevention* Volume 48, June 1991.
3. Some of the details of this are modified to protect the confidentiality of the firm that presented the method in this closed session, but the basic approach used was still a subjective weighted score.

CHAPTER 2

Risk Management: A Very Short Introduction to Where We've Been and Where (We Think) We Are

People who don't take risks generally make about two big mistakes a year. People who do take risks generally make about two big mistakes a year.

—Peter Drucker

Risk management is a very old idea that has relatively recently taken on somewhat of a new character. The history of any idea brings its own baggage that, whether we want it to or not, often limits our current thinking on the concept—and risk management is no exception. Institutions evolve, standards are codified, and professions mature in such a way that it causes all of us to think in more limited ways than we need to. We don't have to dispose of all these conventions, but we do need to be aware of why they were there in the first place.

The Entire History of Risk Management (in 800 Words or Less)

Organizational risk management could be said to have existed at least as early as the first time a king or chieftain decided to fortify walls, make security alliances, or store extra provisions in case of famine. Even more formalized risk management by agreement among parties seems to be a feature of the earliest civilizations. Since ancient Babylon, traders managed the risks of transporting goods great distances by having the buyers provide loans to the sellers that would be repaid with interest only when the goods arrived safely. A Babylonian king wrote in the Code of Hammurabi certain compensations or indemnifications for those harmed by bandits or floods. Babylon was also the birthplace of banking, where lenders managed risks starting with the careful selection of debtors.

But throughout most of human history, we were dealing with only half of the risk management problem, at most. From Babylon through the Middle Ages, risk management was an unguided mitigation of risks. Choosing what risks to prepare for was always a matter of gut feel. What differentiates risk management since the start of the Age of Enlightenment is in part a more systematic approach to assessing the risk. The development of probability theory and statistics in the 17th century allowed for risk to be quantified in a meaningful way. However, these powerful new tools would be adopted only in select industries for select applications.

From the 18th century to well into the 20th century, the quantitative assessment of risk was exemplified in—and largely limited to—insurance, banking, financial markets, and perhaps certain government agencies dealing with public health. For most of that period, the idea of a retailer or manufacturer using similar methods to assess risk in operations, new products, marketing campaigns, or major acquisitions was not seriously considered. For this reason, the executives in many firms may have treated risk management as synonymous with insurance or financial portfolio management (and many still do today).

By the 1940s, more sophisticated risk assessments were applied to and even further developed by nuclear power and oil exploration. This was facilitated by the emergence of computers and the ability to generate thousands of random scenarios with quantitative models. But until the end of the 20th century, risk management still wasn't even on the radar for most organizations.

The "new character" of risk management I mentioned in the first sentence of this chapter refers to the new set of pressures to adopt formal risk management methods and the spate of solutions developed by a wide variety of standards organizations and firms. The disappointing outcomes of investments in new technologies, the distribution of operations to global partners, the failures of some major corporations, 9/11, and general economic unease have driven boards and management to try to get a handle on risks. And, if they needed any more incentive, a new wave of regulatory mandates would provide the extra push. Sarbanes-Oxley is the most significant corporate reform since the creation of the Securities and Exchange Commission. The Basel II Accord created new international standards and requirements for risk management in banking. In the U.S. government, the President's Management Agenda (PMA), under Bush stated sweeping requirements for risk analysis of all major government programs. Even firms not directly affected by the legal mandates of these standards were caught up in a new awareness of a "risk culture."

In response, several of the major consulting firms and international standards organizations have charged in with a variety of "formal methodologies" for risk management. Many companies just decided to make up their own approaches. Even the established, "more sophisticated" risk management methods used in finance revealed cracks under the light of the 2008/9 financial crisis and several previous financial crises.

And the most popular, newer methods don't necessarily build on the foundation of earlier methods that have stood up to scientific and historical scrutiny. It's more like the rapid construction of mining towns in the American West during the Gold Rush, where nice facades are quickly erected with minimal attention to structural quality in the rest of the building. And anybody can put up a shingle saying he is a risk management expert.

So let's try to map out this rapidly expanding, "Wild West" frontier of risk management solutions. Things are moving fast, so this description will probably soon be incomplete. For now, we can examine how risk management is adopted in the modern organization, the risk assessment methods used, and the types of risk mitigation methods used.

Methods of Assessing Risks

The *weighted score* approach to assessing risk, as was used by some pharmaceutical manufacturers on the issue of outsourcing, is just one of many methods used in assessing risks. I suspect that some portion of readers of this book picked it up thinking I would talk about concepts like *modern portfolio theory*, *value at risk*, or *options theory*. Others picked it up thinking I was going to talk about the "risk maps" used in IT security or some strategic planners. Others will think of risk management without any connection to any of the above. But I'm not going to be exclusive.

I've come to the party ready to introduce you all to each other. You may not have known of the existence of these other approaches or you may be aware of them but find them to be ludicrous. Or you may just believe that the other methods, although valid in their own world, don't apply to you at all. But almost everyone has something to learn from a completely different school of risk management than their own. The following methods make up virtually all of the risk analysis methods used in business and government and, as I'll argue, each of them is flawed in some important way and most of them are no better than astrology. Obviously, if risks are not properly analyzed, then they can't be properly managed.

Note that some of these methods have also been used for problems that are not limited to *risk analysis* or *risk management* but, since they have been applied to those problems, I'll evaluate them in this context. Also, keep in mind that some of the items on the list that follows are not mutually exclusive and that many of the risk management solutions proposed by consulting firms and standards organizations involve some combination of these. But all of the following methods are used by somebody, and I know some to have passionate followers who swear that their solution is the only solution. And for every one of those I also find equally passionate detractors.

The following is a partial map of methods for risk management:

- *Expert intuition.* This is a sort of baseline of risk management methods. This is pure gut feel unencumbered by structured rating or evaluation systems of any kind. There are no points, probabilities, scales, or even standardized categories. In order for other methods to be of any value at all, they must show a measurable improvement on gut feel.

- *An expert audit.* This builds on the gut feel, but is more systematic. Experts, usually outside of the firm, try to develop comprehensive checklists and may or may not use the formal scoring or stratification methods discussed below.
- *Simple stratification methods.* These use "green-yellow-red" or "high-medium-low" rating scales on a variety of risky endeavors. Such terms might be used to independently assess likelihood and consequence so that risks can be displayed on a two-dimensional map. This map is sometimes called a *heat map* (where color-coding is used and red is the hottest) or sometimes a *risk matrix*, *risk map*, and so on. Sometimes a point scale (e.g., 1–5, where 5 is the highest) is used to assess likelihood and consequence so that the two values can be multiplied together to get a "risk score." (See Exhibit 2.1 for an example of a risk map for both verbal categories and numerical scores.)
- *Weighted scores.* There are also more elaborate scoring methods with dozens of "risk indicators," each on some scale, which are then multiplied by some "weight" so they can be added up to a "weighted risk score."
- *Traditional financial analysis (i.e., without using probabilities).* There are sometimes attempts to capture risk analysis within the bounds of conventional financial analysis tools. For example, a "discount rate" is used to adjust future cash flows to reflect the lower value of risky investments. One might also work out "best case" and "worst case" for costs and benefits of various decisions.

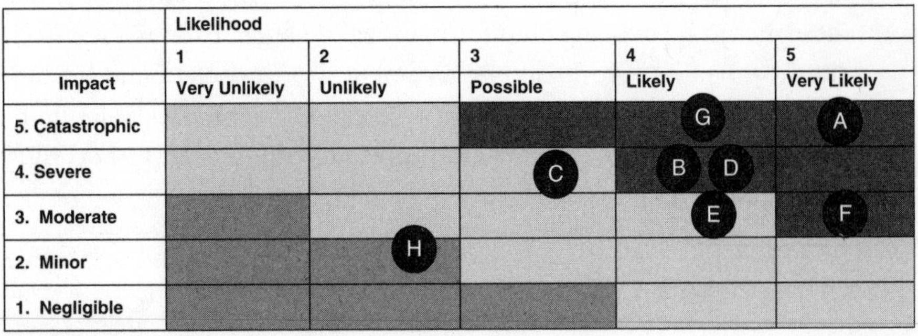

	Likelihood				
	1	2	3	4	5
Impact	Very Unlikely	Unlikely	Possible	Likely	Very Likely
5. Catastrophic				G	A
4. Severe			C	B D	
3. Moderate				E	F
2. Minor		H			
1. Negligible					

EXHIBIT 2.1 **Does This Work? One Version of a Risk Map Using Either Numerical or Verbal Scales**

- *A calculus of preferences*. Methods such as *multi-attribute utility theory (MAUT), multi-criteria decision making (MCDM), and analytic hierarchy process (AHP)* are more structured than the weighted score but ultimately still rely on the judgments of experts. In the case of AHP, a more sophisticated method is used to determine whether the expert judgments are at least *internally* consistent. As with the other methods listed so far, these have been used on lots of decision analysis problems that might not strictly be risk assessments. But they are included here because they have been used to evaluate decisions according to their risks.
- *Probabilistic models*. The most sophisticated risk analysts will eventually use some form of probabilistic models where the odds of various losses and their magnitudes are computed mathematically. It is the basis for modeling risk in the insurance industry and much of the financial industry. It has its own flaws but just as Newton was a starting point for Einstein, it is the best opportunity for continued improvement. It could use subjective inputs as do the other methods, but it is also well-suited to accept historical data or the results of empirical measurements. This includes the "probabilistic risk analysis" used in engineering as well as quantitative methods used in finance and insurance. Although this is merely one category in this list, it has enough substance to allow for a much more detailed taxonomy all by itself.

If these methods were used for no more than assessing corporate art for the reception area or where to have the company picnic, then the urgency of this evaluation would not be nearly as high. But as I have already pointed out, these methods are being used for many of the biggest and riskiest decisions in the corporate world and government. Fortunately, some of these can be modified to produce an approach that can be shown to be a significant improvement on the baseline condition of "winging it." Others must be scrapped entirely.

Risk Mitigation

To *mitigate* a risk is to moderate or alleviate a risk—to lessen it in some way. Higher risks may be deliberately accepted for bigger opportunities but even in those cases decision makers will not want to accept more risk than is necessary. It is common in risk management circles to think of a choice among four basic alternatives for managing a given risk:

1. *Avoid.* We can choose not to take an action that would create an exposure of some kind. We can avoid the merger, the new technology investment, the subprime mortgage market, and so on. This effectively makes that particular risk zero, but might increase risks in other areas (e.g., the lack of taking risks in R&D investments might make a firm less competitive).
2. *Reduce.* The manager goes ahead with the investment or other endeavor that has some risks, but takes steps to lessen them. The manager can decide to invest in the new chemical plant but implement better fire-safety systems to address a major safety risk.
3. *Transfer.* The manager can give the risk to someone else. Insurance is the best example of this. The manager can buy insurance without necessarily taking other steps to lessen the risk of the event (e.g., buying fire insurance instead of investing in advanced fire-prevention systems). Risk can also be transferred to customers or other stakeholders by contract (e.g., a contract that states, "The customer agrees that the company is not responsible for . . .").
4. *Retain.* This is the default choice for any risk management. You simply accept the risk as it is.

I, and some risk managers I know, find the boundaries between these a little murky. A transfer of risk is a reduction or avoidance of risk to the person transferring it away. A reduction in risk is really the avoidance of particular risks that are components of a larger risk. Even the retention of a risk can lead to the overall reduction in total risks if we are thinking of a portfolio of investments where some risks cancel out others. The ultimate objective of risk management should be, after all, the reduction of the total risk to the firm for a given expected return, whether through the transfer or avoidance of risks or the reduction of specific risks. If total risk is merely retained, then it is no different from not managing risks at all.

RISK "FILTERS" AT THE HAVI GROUP

Y.S. Kong is the treasurer and chief strategic planner at the HAVI Group in Illinois, a consortium of major distribution service companies operating in 40 countries. Y.S. prefers to categorize risk management activities by specific risk mitigation actions he calls *risk filters.* "We have four sequential 'risk filters': transference, operational, insurance, and retention," explains Kong. The first preference is to *transfer* risks to customers or suppliers through their contracts. The second filter, *operational,* is to address risks through better systems, procedures, roles, and so on. The third filter is to *insure* the risk (technically, this is also transferring risks). Finally, the *retention* of risk is not so much a filter, but where the other risks land if they don't get filtered out earlier. Even so, Y.S. as the treasurer is tasked with ensuring they have an adequate asset position to absorb any risk that ends up in this final bucket.

The treasurer at the HAVI Group prefers a taxonomy more oriented around specific actions he calls *risk filters* (see the box above). In the following list, I added a couple of items to his list and expanded on each of them to make it as general as possible. Unlike HAVI's risk filters, the order of this list does not imply a prescribed priority.

The following is a long, but still partial, list of risk mitigation alternatives:

- *Selection processes for major exposures.* This is the analysis of decisions that create new sources of potential losses to ensure that the risk being taken is justified by the expected reward. For example:
  - ☐ Risk/return analysis of major investments technology, new products, and so on
  - ☐ Selection of loan risks for banks; accounts receivable risks for other types of firms

- *Insurance.* This comes in dozens of specialized categories, but here are a few of the many general groups:
    - ☐ Insurance against loss of specific property and other assets, including fire, flood, and so on
    - ☐ Various liabilities, including product liability
    - ☐ Insurance for particular trades or transportation of goods, such as marine insurance or the launch of a communications satellite
    - ☐ Life insurance for key officers
    - ☐ Reinsurance, generally purchased by insurance companies, to help risks that may be concentrated in certain areas (hurricane insurance in Florida, earthquake insurance in California, etc.)
- *Contractual risk transfer.* Business contracts include various clauses such as "X agrees the company is not responsible for Y," including contracts with suppliers, customers, employees, partners, or other stakeholders.
- *Operational risk reduction.* This includes everything a firm might do internally through management initiatives to reduce risks, including:
    - ☐ Safety procedures
    - ☐ Training
    - ☐ Security procedures and systems
    - ☐ Emergency/contingency planning
    - ☐ Investments in redundant and/or high-reliability processes, such as multiple IT operations sites, new security systems, and so on
    - ☐ Organizational structures or roles defining clear responsibilities for and authority over certain types of risks (a shift safety officer, a chief information security officer, etc.)
- *Liquid asset position.* This is the approach to addressing the retention of risk but still attempting to absorb some consequences by using liquid reserves (i.e., cash, some inventory, etc.) to ensure losses would not be ruinous to the firm.
- *Compliance remediation.* This is not so much its own category of risk mitigation, since it can involve any combination of the previously mentioned items. But it is worth mentioning simply because it is a key driver for so much of current risk mitigation. This is, in part, a

matter of "crossing the *t*'s and dotting the *i*'s" in the growing volume of regulatory requirements.

- *Legal structure.* This is the classic example of limiting liability of owners by creating a corporation. But risk mitigation can take this further even for existing firms by compartmentalizing various risks into separate corporate entities as subsidiaries, or for even more effective insulation from legal liability, as completely independent spinoffs.
- *Activism.* This is probably the rarest form of risk mitigation since it is practical for relatively few firms, but it is important. Successful efforts to limit liabilities for companies in certain industries have been won by advocating new legislation. Examples are the Private Securities Litigation Reform Act of 1995, which limits damage claims against securities firms, Michigan's 1996 "FDA Defense" law, which limits product liability for drugs that were approved by the FDA, and the Digital Millennium Copyright Act of 1998, which limits the liability of firms that provide a conduit for the transmission of data from damages that may be caused by the sources of the data.

As always, an informed risk mitigation starts with an identification and then some kind of assessment of risks. Once a risk manager knows what

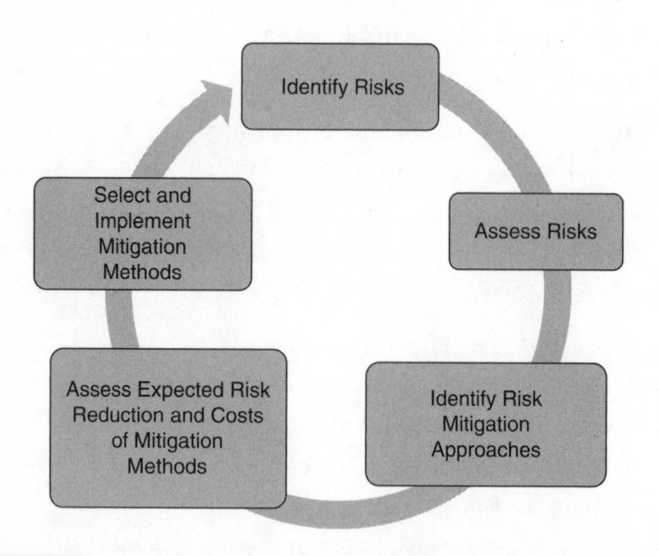

EXHIBIT 2.2 **A (Simplified) Risk Management Cycle**

the risks are, steps can be taken to address them in some way. It might seem that some extremely obvious risks can be managed without much of an assessment effort (e.g., implementing full backup and recovery at a data center that doesn't have it, installing security systems at a major jewelry store, etc.). But in most environments there are numerous risks, each with one or more potential risk mitigation strategies and a limited number of resources. We have to assess not only the initial risks but how much the risk would change if various precautions were taken. Then those risk mitigation efforts, once chosen, have to be monitored in the same fashion and the risk management cycle can begin again. (See Exhibit 2.2.) Notice that the assessment of risks appears prior to and as part of the selection of risk mitigation methods.

The State of Risk Management According to Surveys

Contrary to the claims of some vendors or consulting firms, neither the methods of risk assessment nor the methods of risk mitigation have evolved much for several decades. Some methods look new but simply repackage basic tools that have been around for quite awhile. It might be the case that some methods are only recently being used more often, but, with only a few exceptions, the underlying methods are often older than the management of the firm. What has changed—and continues to change rapidly—is the role of risk management in the firm.

Which risk assessment or risk mitigation strategies are used often depends on where risk management sits in the organization. In some firms, risk management is part of finance and sometimes even legal or human resources. The position of risk management within the firm tells us what that firm thinks *risk mitigation* means and the methods used are limited by this presumption of scope. The level of influence of the risk manager also dictates how or whether the recommendations of the risk manager are used by the firm.

To get a finger on the pulse of how the role of risk management has changed, several firms conduct regular surveys of risk management. Three of the major sources of these surveys in 2007 included a well-known business periodical, and two major firms that specialize in risk management:

1. The insurance brokerage and risk management firm Aon Corporation surveyed 320 organizations from 29 countries, each with over $1 billion in annual revenue.[1] Aon also conducted a separate survey of 103 individual risk managers or executives that focused on *enterprise risk management (ERM)*. It describes ERM as a business approach that "takes a comprehensive perspective of corporate operations, broadening the typical risk management focus."[2]
2. The risk management consulting firm Protiviti conducted a survey of 150 C-level individuals (CEO's, CFO's, etc.), half of which were from the Fortune 1,000 and all of which were among the Fortune 2,000.[3]
3. The Economist Intelligence Unit (a research arm of *The Economist* magazine) conducted an international survey of 218 executives, mostly C-level.[4]

The surveys, of course, were worded differently, the categories of risks were organized differently, and the samples of participating organizations were not exactly the same, so we should expect to see some differences in their results. Still, there are some interesting consistencies. Here is a summary of some of the points from the four surveys (including both surveys from Aon):

- The main threats addressed by risk management vary among the surveys. But for many firms the reason for having risk management is because they are told they are *required* to have it.
    - The single top-ranked risk was different in every survey (Aon: damage to reputation; *The Economist*: human capital risks; Protiviti: competitor risks).
    - Even though the exact order of top-ranked risks varied significantly, risks related to loss of reputation, regulatory environment, market volatility, and human capital were considered to be high-priority risks in all of the surveys.
    - Even though it was not the top-ranked risk in any of the surveys, regulatory risks appear to be the highest-ranked risk on average across all surveys. *The Economist* and Protiviti rank regulatory pressures as the second and third most important risks, respectively. The Aon study ranks regulatory risk only at sixth place among major risks but, tellingly, shows regulatory compliance as

the second highest priority for risk management—after adopting better risk analysis methods but ahead of loss prevention and an enterprise-wide view of risk.

- Risk management is already common and growing in use, scope of risks addressed, and visibility and authority within the organization.
  - A significant and growing number of organizations are implementing what they believe to be formal risk management processes. The Aon study finds that 90% of all firms responding said they had some form of a risk management function. The percentage is slightly higher in the Americas and Europe but only 68% in Asia.
  - More organizations are appointing specific risk management positions such as chief risk officer (CRO) but reports disagree on the extent. The EUI report states that 60% of their respondents have or plan to have a CRO, whereas the Aon report shows that only 35% have or plan to have a CRO. The Aon report further indicates that only in insurance, banking, investment finance, and utilities do most organizations have a CRO, but mentions that the CRO role "is slowly gaining ground outside of these sectors."
  - The Aon ERM survey finds that 50% of firms reported having an ERM function now and another 19% plan on adding one.
  - The visibility of risk management has reached the board level. The Aon report also looked at board involvement in risk management. It reports that 88% of surveyed firms stated that the board is "engaged in the review of risk management issues" and 78% said the board has "established policies on risk oversight." In companies over $25B, 52% say their board "systematically participates."
- Among those firms using risk management, a large and growing share of them believe they are doing well at it.
  - Two of the three surveys asked respondents how effective they felt their organizations were at risk management. The Protiviti survey indicates that about half state they are "very effective" at risk management and finds there is a clear "year-over-year improvement in perceived effectiveness in risk management." *The Economist* found that about half would rate themselves effective or very effective in a variety of risk management categories.

- In the Protiviti survey, 57% of Fortune 1,000 organizations said they quantify risks "to the fullest extent possible," up from 41% in 2006.
- For 8 out of the top 10 risks identified in the Aon survey, the majority of firms felt they were "prepared to manage" the risk.

In summary, while often prodded by regulatory necessity, most firms are adopting or plan to adopt risk management and most feel they are relatively successful in doing so. Certainly, a lot of time and effort has gone into creating these roles, functions, and processes related to risk management in these firms. And, given the visibility risk management now appears to have, the recommendations of this function seem to be influencing major decisions in the firm.

The report done by *The Economist* seems to draw the most confidence from the self-assessment of risk management effectiveness. They go so far as to say that the survey results suggest that risk management has become "a key contributor to market advantage." This is definitely consistent with the hype of the growing risk management industry.

But this claim by *The Economist* doesn't seem supported by its findings. In order to show that risk management was a "key contributor to market advantage," we should expect to see data that shows a relationship between the use of risk management methods and external performance measures such as shareholder return, market share, and so on. *The Economist* report does not attempt to show any such data, and neither do the other reports. Aon and Protiviti, in contrast, are much more cautious in their conclusions. Neither of the later reports have claimed that the survey results are evidence that risk management really has contributed to some larger measure of corporate performance. Protiviti makes it clear that the effectiveness results are merely self-assessments. Aon doesn't ask for a self-assessment at all and sticks to questions of what firms are actually doing.

It really comes down to more than whether self-assessments are honest. Knowing whether a risk management program is "successful" depends on whether firms can measure the success. This is not the same as asking whether they meet regulatory requirements, but I'm sure this is what some firms mean by saying their risk management was successful. Complying with regulations alone is important, of course, but the measure of success we need is whether risk was actually reduced or at least minimized through the efforts of risk management.

The requirements in regulations are sometimes vague on the methods and no regulations explicitly define quantitative measures of risk reduction. If all risk management does is show that minimum regulatory standards are met, without measurably mitigating risks, then it is nothing but a mere formality of getting the proper rubberstamp approval from the right authorities. Investors, employees, customers, and taxpayers (who need to periodically bail out some firms) would be mistaken to confuse regulatory compliance with an actual improvement in risk management.

NOTES

1. "Global Risk Management Survey '07," Aon Corporation, 2007
2. "Enterprise Risk Management: The Full Picture," Aon Corporation, 2007
3. "2007 U.S. Risk Barometer: Survey of C-Level Executives with the Nation's Largest Companies," Protiviti, 2007
4. "Best Practice in Risk Management: A Function Comes of Age," Economist Intelligence Unit, 2007

CHAPTER 3

How Do We Know What Works?

Leaders get out in front and stay there by raising the standards by which they judge themselves—and by which they are willing to be judged.

—Fredrick Smith, CEO, FedEx

"How do we know our risk management efforts work?" should be the single most persistent question of all those who manage risks. If they can't answer that question, then they have no reason to believe that efforts to manage risks are working or, for that matter, are even focusing on the right risks. The standard must be some objective measure that could be verified by other stakeholders in the organization or outside auditors.

If our question were instead "Do you feel your risk management has been successful?" then the evidence shown in the previous chapter would tell us that risk management is generally successful, at least half the time. So let's look at why self-assessments tell us so little, some possible objective measures we might use instead, and what we should be prepared to discover if we use objective measures.

An Assessment of Self-Assessments

Skepticism about what gains can be attributed to popular management tools is not only justified, but a requirement of good management. And self-assessed results of implementing these methods should be considered with even more suspicion. Such suspicions are sometimes tested and sometimes confirmed. In July 2003, *Harvard Business Review (HBR)* published the results of a study involving 160 organizations to measure the effectiveness of over 200 popular management tools, like TQM, ERP, and so on.[1] Independent external reviews of the degree of implementation of the various management tools were compared to shareholder return over a five-year period. In the article titled "What Really Works," the authors wrote:

> Our findings took us quite by surprise. Most of the management tools and techniques we studied had no direct causal relationship to superior business performance.

Even if a management tool could have been effective, studies based on self-assessments present other problems. Not surprisingly, there is a tendency for most of us to have at least a slightly inflated opinion of ourselves (friends and family will confirm that I'm no exception). For example, 87 percent of Stanford MBA students rate their academic performance to be in the top half of their class.[2] Other surveys show that a clear majority of people rate themselves as being more popular,[3] better looking,[4] healthier,[5] and better drivers[6] than at least half of the population.

Cornell psychologists Justin Kruger and David Dunning published their research in the area of self-assessments in the harshly titled article, "Unskilled and Unaware of It: How Difficulties in Recognizing One's Own Incompetence Lead to Inflated Self-Assessments." They show that about two-thirds of the entire population will rate themselves as better than most in reasoning skills, humor, and grammar. While the last few studies I just mentioned are not focused on management, if you think that C-level management and trained business professionals are more realistic and their confidence is more justified, wait until you read Chapter 6.

One test of whether self-assessments of effectiveness are realistic is the extent to which *measurements* are involved in risk management. There is an old management adage that says, "You can't manage what you can't measure." (This is often misattributed to W.E. Deming, but is a truism, nonetheless.) Management guru Peter Drucker considered measurement to be the "fourth basic element in the work of the manager." Since the key objective of risk management—risk reduction or at least a minimized risk for a given opportunity—may not exactly be obvious to the naked eye, only deliberate measurements could even detect it. The organizations that report they are "very effective" at risk management, must, presumably, be measuring risk very well.

But, to risk professionals from Protiviti and Aon (two of the firms that conducted the surveys in the previous chapter), something isn't adding up. Jim DeLoach, a Protiviti managing director, was skeptical of the self-assessments in the survey: "The number of organizations saying they were 'very effective' at managing risks was much higher than we expected." DeLoach points out that the study shows that of those who put themselves in the "very effective" group, 63 percent claim to quantify risks "to the fullest extent possible." Yet this is not what DeLoach observes first-hand when he examines risk management in various organizations. "Our experience is that most firms aren't quantifying risks. . . . I just have a hard time believing they are quantifying risks as they reported."

Christopher (Kip) Bohn, an actuary, fellow of the Casualty Actuarial Society and director at Aon Global Risk Consulting, is equally cautious about interpreting the findings of the Aon Global Risk Survey. Nearly half of all companies surveyed claim to use some form of quantitative analysis in risk management and more than half among those with an annual revenue of over $25 billion. But, like DeLoach, Bohn's personal observations are different: "For most organizations, the state of the art is a qualitative analysis. They do surveys and workshops and get a list of risks on the board. They come up with a ranking system with a frequency and impact, each valued on a scale of, for example, one to five." This is not exactly what an actuary like Bohn considers to be quantitative analysis of risk.

My own experience seems to agree more with the personal observations of DeLoach and Bohn than the results of the self-assessment surveys. Whenever I give a speech about risk management to a large group of managers, I ask those who have a defined approach for managing risks to raise their hands. A lot of hands go up, maybe half on average. I then ask them to keep their hands up only if they measure risks. Many of the hands go down. Then I ask them to keep their hands up only if probabilities are used in their measurements of risks (note how essential this is, given the definition of risk we stated). More hands go down and, maybe, one or two remain up. Then I ask them to keep their hands up if they think their measures of probabilities and losses are in any way based on statistical analysis or methods used in actuarial science. After that, all the hands are down. It's not that the methods I'm proposing are not practical. I have used them routinely on a variety of problems (I'll argue in more detail later against the myth that such methods aren't practical).

Of course, some managers have argued that the standards I suggest for evaluating risk management are unfair and they will still argue that their risk management program was a success. When asked for specifics about the evidence of success, I find they will produce an interesting array of defenses for a method they currently use in risk management. However, among these defenses will be quite a few things that do *not* constitute evidence that a particular method is working. I have reason to believe that these defenses are common, not only because I've heard them frequently but because many were cited as benefits of risk management in the surveys by Aon, *The Economist*, and Protiviti.

The following are some common, but invalid, claims given as evidence that a risk management process is successful:

- When asked, the managers will say that the other stakeholders involved in the process will claim that the effort was a success. They may even have conducted a formal internal survey. But, as the previous studies show, self-assessments are not reliable. Furthermore, without an independent, objective measure of risk management, the perception of any success may merely be a kind of placebo effect. That is, they might feel better about their situation just by virtue of the fact that they perceive they are doing something about it.
- The proponents of the method will point out that the method was "structured." There are a lot of structured methods that are proven not to work. (Astrology, for example, is structured.)
- Often, a "change in culture" is cited as a key benefit of risk management. This, by itself, is not an objective of risk management—even though some of the risk management surveys show that risk managers considered it to be one of the main benefits of the risk management effort. But does the type of change matter? Does it matter if the culture doesn't really lead to reduced risks or measurably better decisions? Of course it matters.
- The proponents will argue that the method "helped to build consensus." This is a curiously common response, as if the consensus itself were the goal and not actually better analysis and management of risks. An exercise that builds consensus to go down a completely

disastrous path probably ensures only that the organization goes down the wrong path even faster.

- The proponents will claim that the underlying theory is mathematically proven. Since the users of the method usually cannot test this for themselves, it is often no better than the medical claims offered by snake-oil salesmen. I find that most of the time when this claim is used, the person claiming this cannot actually produce or explain the mathematical proof, nor can the person they heard it from. In many cases, it appears to be something passed on without question. Even if the method is based on a widely recognized theory, such as options theory (for which the creators were awarded the Nobel in 1997) or modern portfolio theory (the Nobel in 1990), it is very common for mathematically sound methods to be misapplied. And those famous methods themselves have some important shortcomings that all risk managers should know about.
- The vendor of the method will claim that the mere fact that other organizations bought it, and resorted to one or more of the above arguments, is proof that it worked. I call this the "testimonial proof." But if the previous users of the method evaluated it using criteria no better than those listed above, then the testimonial is not evidence of effectiveness.
- The final and most desperate defense is the claim, "But at least we are doing *something*." I'm amazed at how often I hear this, as if it were irrelevant whether the "something" makes things better or worse. Imagine a patient complains of an earache and a doctor, unable to solve the problem, begins to saw off the patient's foot. "At least I am doing something," the doctor says in defense.

With some exceptions (e.g., insurance, some financial management, etc.), risk management is not an evolved profession with standardized certification requirements and methods originally developed with rigorous scientific testing or mathematical proof. So we can't be certain that everyone answering the surveys of the previous chapter is really using a valid standard to rate their success. But even if risk managers had some uniform type of professional quality assurance, surveys of risk managers would still not be a valid measure of risk management effectiveness. That would be like measuring the effectiveness of aspirin by a survey of family practice doctors instead of a clinical trial. What we need are objective measures of the success of risk management.

Potential Objective Evaluations of Risk Management

If self-assessments don't suffice, then what objective measures are possible for risk management? At its root, the objective measure of risk management should be based on the whether and how much risk was actually reduced or whether risk was acceptable for a given payoff. In order to do that, the risk management method should have an approach for properly assessing the risks. In order to measure the effectiveness of risk management, we have to measure risk itself.

Recall from Chapter 1 that risk can be measured by the probability of an event and its severity. Of the two, severity is slightly more straightforward, especially after the fact. If, say, the recall of a defective product occurs, many of the costs would be directly observable. The original costs of manufacturing the recalled product and the original costs of distribution are now wasted money. Then there is the cost of recovering the defective product, possibly involving an ad campaign. The less obvious costs, like the loss of reputation, might be estimated by the cost of a subsequent loss of market share or the costs of the marketing efforts to offset it. The measure of the severity could have a lot of error and still seem more *tangible* than probability.

Measuring a *probability* is where many people, including many risk managers, seem to have some difficultly. This is not something we directly touch and feel; it is an abstraction that confuses many people. All we can do is use *indirect* measures of a probability, like observing how frequently the event occurs under certain conditions. The probability is easy to measure if the event in question is so common that a change can be detected in a short period of time. If a large retailer is trying to reduce the risk of loss due to shoplifting (an event that may occur more than a hundred times per month per store), then one inventory before the improved security efforts and another a month after would suffice to detect a change.

But a risk manager isn't usually concerned with very high-frequency and low-cost events such as shoplifting. Remember, a risk has to have a component of uncertainty as well as a cost. In a retailer like Sears or

Wal-Mart, theft should be so common that it becomes more of a fully anticipated cost than a risk. Similarly, the "risks" of running out of 60W GE incandescent bulbs or mislabeling a price on a single item are, correctly, not usually the types of risks we think of as foremost in the minds of risk managers. The biggest risks tend to be those things that are more rare but potentially disastrous—perhaps even events that have not yet occurred in this organization.

Suppose, for example, a major initiative is undertaken by the retailer's IT department to make point-of-sale and inventory management systems more reliable. If the chance of these systems being down for an hour or more were reduced from 20% per year to 5% per year, how would they know just by looking at the first year? The probability of an event occurring is not as easily observable as the cost of the event once it occurs.

Fortunately, there are some methods of determining effectiveness in risk management. These four should work even if the risks being managed are fairly rare:

1. *Statistical inferences based on large samples:* This is the hard way unless there is already published research on the same process.
2. *Direct evidence of cause and effect:* This is great if we can find it, but may still require statistical verification.
3. *Component testing of risk management:* This allows us to use existing research on parts of the risk management method, some of which have been thoroughly tested for decades.
4. *A "check of completeness":* This is simply comparing the items evaluated in a risk management system against a list of known risks for a company. It helps us determine whether risk management is too narrowly focused.

Statistical Inferences Based on Large Samples

First, let's talk about the "hard way" to measure the effectiveness of risk management. If risk management is supposed to, for example, reduce the risk of events that are so rare that actual results alone would be insufficient to draw conclusions, then we can't just use the short-term history of one organization. Even if improved risk management has a significant effect on reducing losses from various risks, it may take a large number of samples to be confident that the risk management is working. This is similar to the *HBR* study that evaluated the effectiveness of various management fads by attempting to correlate them to shareholder returns in a large number of firms over a long period. (A study such as the *HBR* study is what would really have been required to support a claim such as the one made by the report of *The Economist*—that risk management had become a key contributor to market advantage.)

To build on the earlier pharmaceutical outsourcing example, imagine applying a method that pharmaceutical companies would already be very familiar with in the clinical testing of drugs. Suppose that nearly all of the major health products companies (this includes drugs, medical instruments, hospital supplies, etc.) are recruited for a major risk management experiment. Let's say, in total, that a hundred different product lines that will be outsourced to China are given one particular risk management method to use. Another hundred product lines, again from various companies, implement a different risk management method. For a period of five years, each product line uses its new method to assess risks of various outsourcing strategies. Over this period of time, the first group experiences a total of 12 events resulting in adverse health effects traced to problems related to the overseas source. During the same period, the second group has only 4 such events without showing a substantial increase in manufacturing costs.

In this case, the results would be fairly good evidence that one risk management method was much better than the other. If we did the math (which I show on the website www.howtofixriskmgt.com), we would find that it would be unlikely for this result to be pure chance if, in fact, the probability of the events were not different. In both groups, there were companies that experienced unfortunate events and those that did not, so we can infer something about the performance of the methods only by looking at the aggregation of all their experiences.

A smaller sample might not tell us much at all. If we had only 20 separate product lines from different companies in each group and the results were two events in the first group compared to one in the second group, we could not be very confident that one method was any better than the other. To take it further, if our sample size was just one or two (as in the anecdote-driven approach), then we would know virtually nothing about the risk management effectiveness regardless of whether we experienced adverse events. Again, if the adverse events are so infrequent, we would usually need a large sample just to see enough adverse events to draw some conclusions. Fortunately, there are some mathematical methods that allow inferences even from extremely rare events (although they are virtually unheard of among risk managers). More about this in Part Three of this book.

Direct Evidence of Cause and Effect

Of course, a giant experiment is not usually very practical. Fortunately, we have some other ways to answer this question without necessarily conducting our own massive controlled experiments. There are some situations where the risk management method caught what obviously would have been a disaster, such as detecting a bomb in a suitcase only because of the implementation of a new plastic explosives sniffing device. Another example would be where an IT security audit uncovered an elaborate embezzling scheme. In those cases, we know it would have been extremely unlikely to have discovered—and addressed—the risk without that particular tool or procedure. Likewise, there are examples of disastrous events that obviously would have been avoidable if some prudent amount of risk management had been taken. For example, if a bank was overexposed on bad debts and reasonable procedures would never have allowed such an overexposure, then we can confidently blame the risk management procedures (or lack thereof) for the problem.

But direct evidence of cause and effect is not as straightforward as it might at first seem. There are times when it appears that a risk management effort averted one risk but exacerbated another that was harder to detect. For example, the FAA currently allows parents traveling with a child under the age of two to purchase only one ticket for the adult and hold the child in their lap. Suppose the FAA is considering requiring parents to purchase seats for each child, regardless of age. If we looked at a crash where every separately seated toddler survived, is that evidence that the new policy reduced risk? Actually, no—even if we assume it is clear that *particular* children are alive because of the new rule. A study already completed by the FAA found that changing the "lap-children fly free" rule would increase total fares for the traveling families by an average of $185, causing one-fifth of them to drive instead of fly. When the higher travel fatalities of driving are considered, it turns out that changing the rule would cost more lives than it saves. It appears we still need to check even the apparently obvious instances of cause and effect against some other independent measure of overall risk.

Component Testing of Risk Management

Lacking large controlled experiments, or obvious instances of cause and effect, we still have ways of evaluating the validity of a risk management method. The *component testing* approach looks at the *gears* of risk management instead of the entire *machine*. If the entire method has not been scientifically tested, we can at least look at how specific components of the method have fared under controlled experiments. Even if the data is from different industries or laboratory settings, consistent findings from several sources should give us some information about the problem.

As a matter of fact, quite a lot of individual components of larger risk management methods have been tested exhaustively. In some cases, it can be conclusively shown that a component adds error to the risk assessment or at least doesn't improve anything. In other cases, we can show that alternatives to those components have strong theoretical backing and have been tested repeatedly with objective, scientific measures. Here are a few examples:

- If we rely on expert opinion to evaluate the likelihood of an event, we might be interested in reviewing the research on how well experts do at assessing the likelihood of events. The research shows that human experts make particular errors consistently but that a combination of training, incentive systems, and mathematical adjustments will correct these.
- If we rely on various scoring or classification methods (e.g., a scale of 1 to 5 or high/medium/low), we should consider the results of research on how these methods are used and even misused by well-meaning analysts.
- If we are using more quantitative models and computer simulations, we should be aware of the most common known errors in such models. We also need to check to see whether the sources of the data in the model are based on methods that have proven track records of making realistic forecasts.

- If we are using models like AHP, MAUT, or similar systems of decision analysis for the assessments of risk, they should meet the same standard of a measurable track record of reliable predictions. We should also be aware of some of the known mathematical flaws introduced by some methods that periodically cause nonsensical results.

Check of Completeness

The final point I will make about evaluating risk management is not really about a measure of the validity of a particular method, but whether the method is applied to a reasonably complete list of risks. If a firm thinks of risk management as "enterprise risk management," then it ought to be considering *all* the major risks of the enterprise—not just legal, not just investment portfolio, not just product liability, not just worker safety, and not just security. This criterion is not, however, the same as saying that risk management can succeed only if all possible risks are identified. Even the most prudent organization will exclude risks that nobody could conceivably have considered.

But there are widely known risks that are excluded from some risk management for no other reason than an accident of organizational scope or background of the risk manager. If the scope of risk management in the firm has evolved in such a way that it considers risk only from a legal or a security point of view, then it is systematically ignoring many significant risks. A risk that is not even on the radar can't be managed at all.

The surveys previously mentioned and many "formal methodologies" developed detailed taxonomies of risks to consider and each taxonomy is different from the others. But completeness in risk management is a matter of degree. The use of a detailed taxonomy is helpful but it is no guarantee that relevant risks will be identified.

A risk manager should always assume the list of considered risks, no matter how extensive, is incomplete. All we can do is increase completeness by continual assessment of risks from several angles. Below I'm providing not an actual taxonomy, but four angles to consider when developing a taxonomy. (See www.howtofixriskmgt.com for an evolving taxonomy of major risks.)

Four Perspectives of Completeness in Risk Assessment

1. *Internal (Functional) completeness:* All parts of the organization should be in included in the identification of risks and even persons from various levels within each part of the organization. And don't let one arbitrary subset of the organization run the risk assessment, or the risks will be slanted in that direction to the exclusion of other risks. Industrial engineers may focus on risks related to industrial accidents, legal counsel may focus on litigation risks, IT may focus on IT risks, and so on.
2. *External Completeness:* Vendors and customers have a special place in risk analysis as do utilities, municipal, state, and federal agencies. Each thinks of different events when they think of disasters and your organization depends on them in different ways. Even studying events in organizations that have little to do with you can be enlightening. If you do an internet search on news articles related to "disaster," for example, you will find that many events that occurred in other organizations are the types that could have occurred in your firm. In a similar fashion, although I've never had cancer, my insurance company looks at a larger group of individuals to determine that it is still possible for me.
3. *Historical completeness:* The "worst case scenario" you thought of is rarely such. Events that have not happened in the past decade or two are seen as effectively impossible by many managers. Think about major catastrophes in the last century and whether anyone would have thought them to be possible just a few years before. Plagues, tsunamis, major industrial accidents, economic depressions, and multi-day power outages in major metropolitan areas have happened before. There is no reason to believe they can't happen again (some risks, such as plagues, may actually have grown due to increased international travel and drug resistant pathogens.)
4. *Combinatorial Completeness:* This kind of completeness is increased as a risk manager begins to consider combinations of events from the previously listed sources. Considering all combinations would usually be infeasible, but even combinations of the more likely events could lead to other risks. Ask how the occurrence of one event increases the probability or impact of another event. The common

mode failures of the sort that happened on Flight 232 or the cascade failures (a domino-effect) of major banks in 2008 could be revealed only by this kind of analysis.

What We May Find

Even if risk managers use only component testing in their risk management process, they are likely to find serious shortcomings in their current approach. Many of the components of popular risk management methods have no evidence of whether they work and some components have shown clear evidence of adding error. Still other components, though not widely used, can be shown to be convincing improvements compared to the alternatives.

Lacking real evidence of effectiveness, firms may use one of the claims of the "defenses" listed previously. But these could have been used to make the case for the "validity" of astrology, numerology, or crystal healing. When managers can begin to differentiate the astrology from the astronomy, then they can begin to adopt methods that work. But to do that they will have to adopt some of the language and concepts used by statisticians and actuaries.

Many organizations will also find that when they assess the completeness of their risk assessments, the risks assessed are from a far-too-limited list. Risk is generally thought of in highly partitioned subjects with very little awareness of the larger picture of risk management. For example, a search on the Internet will identify many organizations with a generic risk management name like "______ Risk Management, Inc." (e.g., National Risk Management, ABC Risk Management, etc.). But an organization looking for a vendor to support risk management will be disappointed to find out that the vendor was just a security guard service, a brokerage for fire insurance, a consulting firm that does environmental compliance audits, or a software company that sells PC network audit tools. And this overreach of terminology is not limited to vendors. I even notice this curious naming convention inside organizations when I find that a "risk analyst" is really just an auditor or an IT security specialist. Even many well-intentioned efforts to consider a holistic approach to risk fall short.

In an apparent recognition of the need for some kind of broader solution to risk management, certain organizational changes have become more popular. As the surveys have shown, some organizations are adopting the use of enterprise risk management (ERM). The approaches to ERM vary widely from the very soft and informal to the elaborately quantitative. Companies have also begun to adopt the idea of appointing a chief risk officer (CRO) as a kind of "risk czar."

A firm that conducts an honest evaluation of itself using the prescribed methods will find it falls somewhere along a spectrum of success and failure. Based on the standards I've described for the success of risk management, the reader has probably already figured out that I believe the solution to be based on the more sophisticated, quantitative methods. You may not yet be convinced that such methods are best or that they are even practical. We'll get to that later. For now, let's look at the proposed success/failure spectrum. (See Risk Management Success/Failure Spectrum box).

RISK MANAGEMENT SUCCESS/FAILURE SPECTRUM

1. *Best.* The firm builds quantitative models to run simulations; all inputs are validated with proven statistical methods, additional empirical measurements are used where optimal, and portfolio analysis of risk and return is used. Always skeptical of any model, the modelers check against reality, and continue to improve the risk models with objective measures of risks. Efforts are made to systematically identify all risks in the firm.
2. *Better.* Quantitative models are built using at least some proven components; the scope of risk management expands to include more of the risks.
3. *Baseline.* Intuition of management drives the assessment and mitigation strategies. No formal risk management is attempted.
4. *Worse* (the "merely useless"). Detailed "soft" or "scoring" methods are used, or perhaps misapplied quantitative methods are used, but at least they are not counted on by management. This may be no worse than #3, except that they did waste time and money on it.

5. *Worst* (the "worse than useless"). Ineffective methods are used with great confidence even though they add error to the evaluation. Perhaps much effort is spent on seemingly sophisticated methods, but there is still no objective, measurable evidence they improve on intuition. These "sophisticated" methods are far worse than doing nothing or simply wasting money on ineffectual methods. They cause erroneous decisions to be taken that would not otherwise have been made.

Note that, in this spectrum, doing nothing about risk management is not actually the worst case. It is in the *middle* of the list. Those firms invoking the infamous "at least I am doing something" defense of their risk management process are likely to fare worse. Doing nothing is not as bad as things can get for risk management. The worst thing to do is to adopt a soft scoring method or an unproven but seemingly sophisticated method (what some have called "crackpot rigor") and act on it with high confidence.

NOTES

1. N. Nohria, W. Joyce, and B. Roberson, "What Really Works," *Harvard Business Review,* July 2003.
2. "It's Academic," *Stanford GSB Reporter,* April 24, 2000, pp. 14–15.
3. E. Zuckerman and J. Jost, "What Makes You Think You're So Popular? Self-Evaluation Maintenance and the Subjective Side of the 'Friendship Paradox,'" *Social Psychology Quarterly* 64(3), 2001, 207–223.
4. D.M. Messick, S. Bloom, J.P. Boldizar, and C.D. Samuelson, "Why We Are Fairer Than Others," *Journal of Experimental Social Psychology* 21, 1985, 480–500.
5. N.D. Weinstein, "Unrealistic Optimism About Future Life Events," *Journal of Personality and Social Psychology* 39, 1980, 806–820.
6. O. Svenson, "Are We All Less Risky and More Skillful Than Our Fellow Drivers?," *Acta Psychologica* 47, 1981, 143–148.

PART TWO

Why It's Broken

CHAPTER 4

The "Four Horsemen" of Risk Management: Some (Mostly) Sincere Attempts to Prevent an Apocalypse

History is a race between education and catastrophe.

—H. G. WELLS

The market turmoil that started in 2008 and every other major disaster generates a search for cause and, in response to that demand, experts will provide a wide variety of theories. Most of these theories are judgment-laden. Explanations involving conspiracy, greed, and even stupidity are easier to generate and accept than more complex explanations that may be closer to the truth.

A bit of wisdom called Hanlon's Razor advises us, "Never attribute to malice that which can be adequately explained by stupidity."[1] I would add a clumsier but more accurate corollary to this: "Never attribute to malice or stupidity that which can be explained by moderately rational individuals following incentives in a complex system of interactions." People behaving with no central coordination and acting in their own best interest can still create results that appear to some to be clear proof of conspiracy or a plague of ignorance.

With that in mind, we need to understand how very different forces have evolved to create the state of risk management methods as we see them today. Like most systems, cultures, and habits, the current state of risk management is a result of gradual pressures and sudden events that happened along the way. Influential individuals with great ideas appear where and when they do more or less randomly. Wartime necessities and new technologies drove other developments that affect risk management today. Institutions with their own motivations arose and would create momentum for certain methods. Different research objectives and methods created academics with very different perspectives on the same problem. Those that would apply these methods were influenced by associations that were accidental at least as often as designed.

To map out the current state of affairs, I've divided risk management into four general groups according to the types of problems they focus on and the methods they use. There is a lot of overlap in these sets, and I'm sure others could come up with different and equally valid taxonomies. But I think that individuals who think of themselves as risk managers will tend to associate with one of these groups or the methods developed by that group.

The "Four Horsemen" of Risk Management

1. *Actuaries.* These original professional risk managers use a variety of scientific and mathematical methods but focus on assessing and managing the risks in insurance and pensions.
2. *War Quants.* Engineers and scientists during World War II used simulations and set up most decisions as a particular type of mathematical game. Today, their descendents are users of "probabilistic risk analysis," "decision analysis," and "operations research."
3. *Economists.* After World War II, a new set of financial analysis tools were developed to assess and manage risk and return of various instruments and portfolios. Today, financial analysts of various stripes are the primary users of these methods.
4. *Management consultants.* Most managers and their advisors use more intuitive approaches to risk management that rely heavily on

individual experience. They have also developed detailed "methodologies" for these softer methods, especially after the rising influence of managers addressing information technology. Users and developers of these methods are often business managers themselves or nontechnical business analysts.

Which of these groups are you in? Someone with a management consulting orientation may not have heard of some of the methods used by engineers or actuaries or, if they have, are probably thinking that such methods are impractical. An engineer reading this book may already know that the methods I'm going to discuss are entirely practical but may be unaware that their methods contain systematic errors. A financial analyst or economist may be vaguely aware of some of these solutions from other fields but probably not all of them. Academic researchers (who could have a research focus on any combination of these methods) might not necessarily be following how well methods they research are used in the real world. No matter who you are, there is also a good chance that we will discuss at least some issues outside of your area of focus.

Actuaries

Certainly the oldest profession (in risk management) is practiced in the insurance industry by actuaries. The insurance industry is now often an example of fairly quantitative risk analysis, but there was a period of time—a long one—when insurance existed without what we know today as actuaries.

Prior to the mid-1800s, having an ownership stake in an insurance company was more like gambling than investing (although shareholders in AIG in 2008 would probably claim this hasn't changed much). And buying an insurance policy was no guarantee that the insurer would be financially able to cover your losses in a legitimate claim. In the days before the general acceptance of (and legal requirement for) actuaries in insurance, using quantitative methods of assessing risk was a kind of competitive advantage and those who did not use statistical methods paid the price for it. For example, in the United Kingdom between 1844 and 1853, 149 insurance companies were formed. By the end of this period, just 59 survived.[2] This is far worse than the failure rate of insurers in modern times, even in 2008.

Those that failed tended to be those that did not use mathematically valid premium calculations. According to the International Actuarial Association, one particular insurer—Equitable—survived this period "in good shape and flourished because of the scientific methods it employed."[3]

While some statistical methods were used in insurance as early as the 17th century, actuarial practice was not a profession until the 19th century. In 1848, the Institute of Actuaries in London was formed as a society for the actuarial profession and actuarial societies in other countries soon followed. Today, when it comes to the question of whether more quantitative methods add value, there is not much of a debate in the insurance industry. It is generally understood that it would be foolish to attempt to compete in the insurance industry without sound actuarial methods (even if going without actuarial methods were legal, which it isn't). For example, insurance companies have to estimate contingent losses and make sure they have enough reserves on hand to pay out claims if and when they come. The companies that did not calculate this correctly eventually would not be able to pay claims when a disaster occurred or, on the other extreme, would keep far too much in reserve at the expense of paying too few dividends to investors (although anxious investors would ensure the latter was almost never the case).

But, after events like the financial crisis of 2008/9, some might wonder whether actuaries really had any more answers than anyone else. If actuarial science were effective, would the U.S. government have had to take over the insurance giant AIG when it was in danger of becoming insolvent? This is another example where anecdotes are not that helpful when evaluating risk management approaches, especially when the facts are misunderstood. AIG had taken a large position on instruments called *credit default swaps (CDSs).* A CDS is purchased by mortgage banks to offset the risk of borrowers defaulting on loans. It is called a *swap* in the financial world because the parties both exchange cash but with different conditions and payment schedules. In the case of a CDS, one party pays cash up front to the other in exchange for a future cash payment on the condition that a borrower defaults on a loan. To most people, this sounds a lot like insurance. The lender is buying a type of insurance in case the borrower doesn't pay up.

This looks like insurance, sounds like insurance, feels like insurance—but, legally, it's not regulated like insurance. The actuaries of AIG, as with any other insurance company, would have to validate the reserves of the firm to ensure it can meet its responsibility to pay claims. But since a CDS is not legally insurance, actuaries are not responsible to review this risk. The part of AIG's business that actuaries did review was not the part that brought down the company. The actuarial profession, unfortunately, is one of a narrow focus. No certified, regulated *profession* like the actuarial practice exists outside of what is strictly considered *insurance*.

The basic idea of the actuarial profession is sound. They are professional risk managers utilizing scientifically and mathematically sound methods and they are held to high standards of conduct. When an actuary signs a statement claiming that an insurance company can meet its contingent liabilities and is in a position to weather all but the rarest catastrophes, he or she puts his or her license to practice on the line. As with engineers, doctors, or auditors, actuaries are duty-bound to report their best judgment about truth and, if necessary, resign if pressured to do otherwise.

Like most venerable institutions, actuarial societies were not always known for keeping up with the latest developments in related fields. The name *actuarial science* aside, actuaries are not primarily trained to be scientists. While some actuaries may get involved in original research, most are more like engineers and accountants applying already-established methods. As they are a necessarily conservative lot, it's understandable that actuaries would be cautious about adopting new ideas. Even a slew of new developments coming out of World War II would take some time to be adopted by actuaries. But now the new and powerful methods developed by wartime necessity are considered standard risk analysis by actuarial science.

War Quants: How World War II Changed Risk Analysis Forever

When Churchill said "Never have so many owed so much to so few," he was talking about the pilots of the Royal Air Force (RAF) defending the citizens of Britain from German bombers. Of course, the RAF deserved every bit of this recognition, but Churchill might as well have been talking about an even smaller group of mathematicians, statisticians, economists, and scientists solving critical problems in the war effort. Mathematicians and scientists have had some influence on business and government operations for centuries, but World War II arguably offered a unique showcase for the power and practicality of such methods. During the war, such thinkers would develop several interesting approaches to problem solving that would affect business and government operations for decades to come, including the analysis of risk.

One of these groups of wartime mathematicians was the Statistical Research Group (SRG) at Columbia University. The SRG and similar groups among the Allies had been working on complicated problems like estimating the effectiveness of offensive operations and developing tactics that improved antisubmarine operations.[4] In military intelligence, such statistical analyses were consistently better than spies at estimating monthly German tank production.[5] This diverse group of problems and methods was the origin of the field of *operations research (OR)*.

Later in the war, a group of physicists who had worked on the Manhattan Project were running into a particularly difficult problem that required a truly revolutionary solution. The problem was how to model fission reactions. Radioactive materials such as uranium or plutonium gradually decay to produce lighter elements and neutrons. When one atom of a heavy element like uranium splits (i.e., undergoes *fission*), it releases energy and more neutrons. Those neutrons cause other atoms to split. If this process occurs at a certain sustained, steady rate, it is called *critical* and the heat it generates can be harnessed to create electricity for consumption. If the chain reaction rapidly accelerates, it creates a runaway effect called *supercriticality*. The heat suddenly released from this process creates a rather powerful explosion or at least a meltdown. As you might guess, getting this distinction right is important.

The problem is that lots of factors affect the rate of reaction. How much fissile material there is in a given volume is one factor. Another factor is that the container housing this reaction might be made of material that absorbs neutrons or reflects neutrons, which decelerates or accelerates the reaction. And the shape of the fuel and the container affects the rate of reaction. Even under ideal conditions, physicists could not calculate exact trajectories of neutrons—they could merely model them as probabilities. Modeling the behavior of this system proved to be impossible with conventional mathematical methods. As a solution, some of the physicists, notably Stanislaw Ulam and Nicholas Metropolis (and separately, Enrico Fermi), worked on the idea of modeling randomly generated neutrons using the powerful new computers developed by John Von Neumann. They called this a *Monte Carlo* simulation, referring to a casino in Monaco frequented by Metropolis's uncle, an inveterate gambler.

After the war, the Monte Carlo simulation would find other applications in related fields. Norman C. Rasmussen of MIT developed *probabilistic risk analysis (PRA)* as a basis for managing risks in nuclear power safety. PRA initially used Monte Carlo models to a limited extent[6] to simulate detailed components of nuclear reactors and the interactions among them. The idea is that if the probability of failures of each of the components of a complex system could be described, the risk of failure of the entire system (e.g., a release of radioactive coolant, a meltdown, etc.) could be computed. This should apply even if that event had never occurred before or even if that particular reactor had not yet been built. PRA using Monte Carlo simulations continued to grow in scope, complexity, and influence in risk management in nuclear safety. It is now considered an indispensible part of the field.

While Von Neumann was helping to develop and promote the idea of Monte Carlo simulations, he was, nearly in parallel, developing what he called *game theory*, the mathematical description of games of all sorts. One of Von Neumann's fans was the young Abraham Wald, a member of the SRG. It was Wald and some of his peers who developed the theory around a special kind of game they called a "one-person game against nature."

In this type of game, the player had no competitor, but did have to make a decision under uncertainty—in a way, nature was the other player. Unlike competitive games, we don't expect nature to act rationally—just unpredictably. One such decision that can be modeled this way might be whether to invest in a new technology. If a manager invests, and the investment succeeds, then the manager gains some specified reward. But the investment could also be lost with nothing to show for it. However, if the manager rejects the opportunity, the investment itself can't be lost but a big opportunity might be missed, instead.

It turns out that quite a few decisions in both business and government can be described as types of one-person games against nature. This evolved into *decision-theory*. After the war, the ideas behind decision theory were being turned into practical tools for business and government. The RAND Corporation, founded just after the war, began applying the theories, Monte Carlo simulations, and a variety of other methods to everything from social welfare policy analysis to cold-war nuclear strategies. It also attracted a variety of thinkers who would influence the field of decision making and risk assessment for the rest of the 20th century.

In 1968, the term *decision analysis (DA)* was coined by Ron Howard at Stanford University to refer to practical applications of these tools to real-world problems. As was the focus of game theory and decision theory, Howard's original use of the term *decision analysis* was prescriptive.[7] That is, it was meant to specify what the decision maker *should* do, not necessarily describe what they will do. (To some, the term has since expanded to include both.)

The introduction of personal computers (PCs) greatly facilitated the practicality of the Monte Carlo method. In the 1990s, companies such as Decisioneering (now owned by Oracle) and Palisade developed software tools that allowed users to run Monte Carlo simulations on PCs. The intellectual descendents of the World War II team continue to promote these tools as both a practical and theoretically sound way to model risks.

One such person, Professor Sam Savage of Stanford University, is an *actual* descendent of one of the members of the World War II team. Leonard "Jimmie" Savage, his father, was part of the SRG and also the chief statistical consultant to John Von Neumann (this alone is just about the most impressive thing I've ever heard of any statistician). Jimmie Savage went on to author *The Foundations of Statistics*, which included practical applications of game theory and probabilistic reasoning in general. Savage the son is the author of his own Monte Carlo tools and an innovator of modeling methods in his own right.

This is the culture of risk management for many engineers, scientists, some financial analysts, and others who might have a quantitative background. Risk is something that is modeled quantitatively, often using simulations of systems. Actuaries, too, have adopted Monte Carlo simulations as a standard tool of risk analysis.

This group is generally the most surprised to learn what passes as "risk management" as practiced by other people. They are steeped in quantitative methods on a daily basis, they are often subjected to peer reviews by other mathematically oriented people, and their emphasis is on improving their own quantitative models more than studying the nonquantitative methods used by some people. When I describe softer methods to them, they shake their heads and wonder how anyone could believe an approach like that could work. When exposed to some of the more popular methods in risk analysis, they react in a way that I suspect is something like how an astrophysicist would react to theories proposed by a crackpot astrologer.

I also tend to see the quantitative risk analysts react positively to the question, "How do you know decisions are any better with your modeling approach?" So far, I see much more of a genuine interest in the question and less of a reaction of defensiveness. While most have not been collecting the data to validate their models, they agree that answering such a question is critical and have generally been helpful in efforts to gather data to answer this question. When I point out known problems with common methods used in Monte Carlo simulations, they seem eager to adopt the improvements. As a group with a scientific orientation, they seem ever wary of the weaknesses of any model and are open to scrutinizing even the most basic assumptions. I believe that it is from this school of thought we will find the best opportunity for improving risk management.

Economists

Prior to the 1990s, Nobel Prizes in Economics were generally awarded for explanations of macroeconomic phenomenon like inflation, production levels, unemployment, money supply, and so on. For most of the history of economics, risk and probabilistic methods were treated superficially. Prior to World War II, arguably the key academic accomplishment on that topic in economics was Frank Knight's *Risk, Uncertainty and Profit*[8]—a book that never once resorts to using a single equation or calculation about risk, uncertainty, profit, or anything else. Economist John Maynard Keynes's 1921 book, *Treatise on Probability*, did invoke equations, but it was more about philosophy and pure mathematics than risk in decision making.

Nor was there much attention paid to "optimization" problems for individuals—that is, how a person should ideally behave in a given situation—such as Wald's one-person games against nature. It wasn't until just after World War II, with at least indirect influence from the War Quants, that economists started to consider the problems of risk, mathematically. It was then that economists began to accept solutions to certain "one-person games against nature" as part of economics. And it was not until very recently that economics considered the issues of actually measuring human behavior regarding decisions under uncertainty in a manner more like a science.

Investors have always had to make decisions under uncertainty. Uncertainty about future returns affects how much they value a stock, how they hedge against losses, and how they select investments for a portfolio. But, as incredible as it seems today, the literature on the economic theory of investments was almost silent on the issue of risk until the 1950s. In 1952, 25-year-old Harry Markowitz, a former student of L.J. Savage and new employee of RAND Corporation, noticed this absence of risk in investment theory.

At RAND, Markowitz would meet George Dantzig, who, like Savage, earned his stripes as a War Quant (Dantzig was with the U.S. Air Force Office of Statistical Control). The older Dantzig would introduce Markowitz to some powerful OR optimization methods. Dantzig developed a method called *linear programming*, which would be influential for decades in OR and which gave Markowitz an idea about how to approach portfolio diversification mathematically. The same year that Markowitz started at RAND, his ideas were published in the *Journal of Finance*.[9]

Markowitz explained in his new theory that a portfolio of investments, like the investments that comprise it, has its own variance and return. By changing the proportion of various investments in a portfolio, it is possible to generate a wide variety of possible combinations of returns and volatility of returns. Furthermore, since some investments vary somewhat independently of each other, the variability of the portfolio could, in principle, be less than the variability of any single investment. By analogy, you are uncertain about the role of one die but you would be far less uncertain about the average of 100 rolls of dice. The effect of diversification together with the flexibility of setting the proportion of each investment in the portfolio allows the investor to optimize the portfolio for a given set of preferences for risk versus return. Markowitz's approach was to use Dantzig's linear programming method to find the optimal combination of investments depending on how much risk the investor was willing to accept for a given return.

When Markowitz presented this solution for his PhD dissertation in 1955, Milton Friedman (who would win the Economics Nobel in 1976) was on his review board. According to Markowitz, Friedman initially argued that Markowitz's *Modern Portfolio Theory (MPT)* was not part of economics.[9] Friedman might not have been all that serious, since Markowitz did successfully pass his orals—but it is hard to tell. The issue of optimizing the choice of an individual making decisions with risk was not previously part of economics. Friedman himself developed mathematical models about several economic topics as if the calculations were all deterministic. Clearly, discussing risk in a quantitative sense was a new idea to many economists.

This began a trend in economics to address risk in probabilistic terms and as a problem for individual decision makers, not just some vague macroeconomic force. Exhibit 4.1 shows the results of my historical research on the use of *risk* and *probability* in economic literature through the 20th century. Using the academic research database called *JSTOR*, I looked for how often the word *risk* appeared in economic literature. Of course, this includes a lot of nonquantitative uses of the term. To clarify the search further, I searched on *risk* and *probability* together—my theory being that when the two words are used together in the same article it usually has some

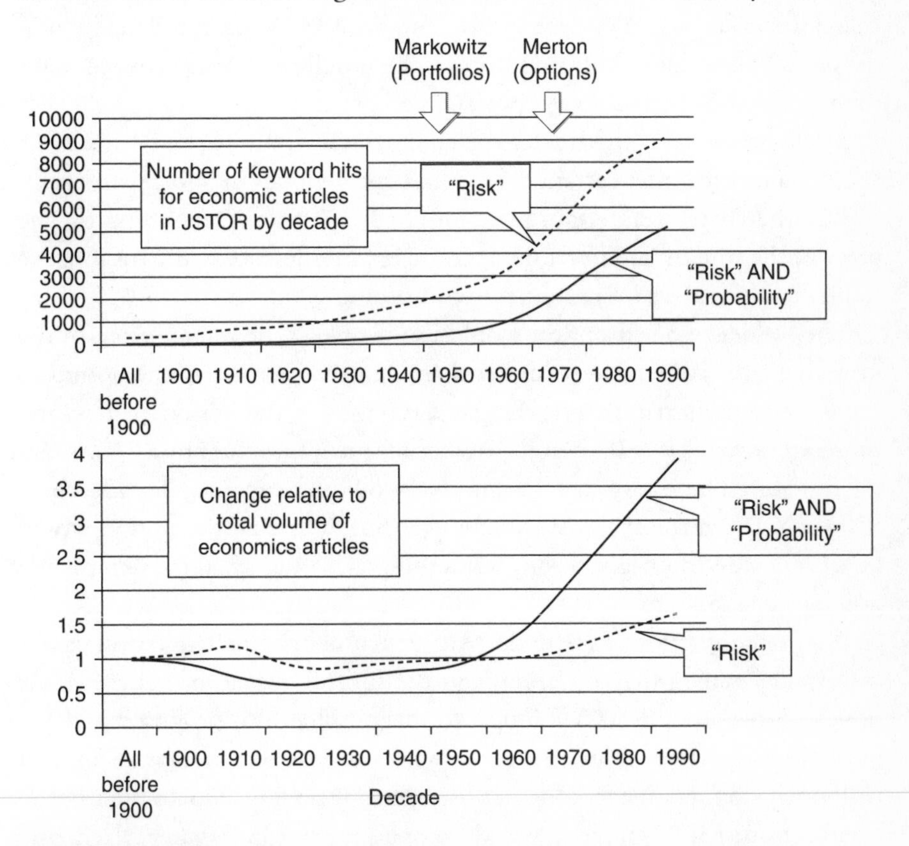

EXHIBIT 4.1 ***Risk* and *Probability* in Economic Literature**

quantitative slant on the topic. The top chart shows the actual number of hits in the search and the bottom chart shows relative frequency compared to all articles before 1900 and adjusted for the volume of economics literature (the overall volume of economics articles increased substantially in the 20th century). Clearly, risk was more likely to be treated as a *quantity* after the 1950s.

About two decades after Markowitz would first publish MPT, another influential theory would be proposed for using the risk of an investment to price an option. *Options* are types of derivatives that give the holder the right, but not the obligation, to buy or sell (depending on the type of option) another financial instrument at a fixed price at some future point. The instrument being bought or sold with the option is called the *underlying asset* and it could be a stock, bond, or commodity. This future point is called the *expiration date* of the option and the fixed price is called the *exercise price*. This is different from futures, which obligate both parties to make the trade at the future date at a prearranged price.

A *put* option gives the holder the right to sell, say, a share of some stock at a certain price on a certain date. A *call* option gives the holder the right to buy the share at a certain price on a certain date. Depending on the price of the underlying instrument at the expiration date of the option, the holder could make a lot of money—or nothing.

The holder of a call option would use it only if the selling price of the underlying instrument were higher than the exercise price of the option. If the underlying instrument is selling at $100 the day the option expires, and the exercise price is $80, then the owner of the option can buy a $100 share for just $80. The option has a value that would be equal to the difference: $20 each. But if the shares were selling at just $60, then the option would be of no value (the right to buy something at $80 is worth nothing if the going price is $60).

But since the price of the underlying instrument at the expiration date is uncertain—which may be months in the future—it was not always clear how to price an option. A solution to this problem was proposed in 1973 by Robert C. Merton, an economist who first was educated as an applied mathematician, engineer, and scientist before receiving a doctorate in economics from MIT. The idea was developed further by Fischer Black, another applied mathematician, and Myron Scholes (the only one in the group with degrees solely in economics). Merton and Scholes would receive the Nobel Prize in Economics in 1997 for the development of options theory (Black would probably have shared the prize but he died two years before and it is not awarded posthumously). The model is now known as the Black-Scholes equation for pricing options.

The next major development in economics introduced the idea of *empirical observation*. Some would say it would be the first time economics could even legitimately be called a science. MPT and Options Theory (OT) were about what people should do in ideal situations. Earlier economics simply assumed that market participants *did* act rationally and attempted to use that assumption to explain forces in the market. This was called *Homo economus*—the economically rational human. But around the 1970s, a group of researchers started to ask how people actually *do* behave in these situations. These researchers were not economists at all and, for a long time, had no impact on the momentum in the field of economics. However, by the 1990s, the idea of *behavioral economics* was starting to have an influence on economic thought. The tools developed in this field were even adopted by the most advanced users of PRA (more on that to come).

OT and MPT have at least one important conceptual difference from the PRA done by nuclear power. A PRA is what economists would call a *structural model*. The components of a system and their relationships are modeled in Monte Carlo simulations. If valve X fails, it causes a loss of backpressure on pump Y, causing a drop in flow to vessel Z, and so on.

But in the Black-Scholes equation and MPT, there is no attempt to explain an underlying structure to price changes. Various outcomes are simply given probabilities. And, unlike the PRA, if there is no history of a particular system-level event like a liquidity crisis, there is no way to compute the odds of it. If nuclear engineers ran risk management this way, they would never be able to compute the odds of a meltdown at a particular plant until several similar events occurred in the same reactor design.

Of course, there is some attempt in finance to find correlations among various factors such as the price of a given stock and how it has historically moved with oil prices or the price of another stock. But even correlations are simple linear interpretations of historical movements without the attempt to understand much about the underlying mechanisms. It's like the difference between meteorology and seismology—both systems are extremely complex but at least the former gets to directly observe and model major mechanisms (e.g., storm fronts). Often, the seismologist can merely describe the statistical distribution of earthquakes and can't say much about what goes on deep in the Earth at a given moment. A PRA is more like the former and MPT and OT are more like the latter.

Other methods have evolved from OT and MPT, although none are especially novel improvements on these earlier ideas. *Value at risk (VaR),* for example, is widely used by many financial institutions as a basis of quantifying risk. VaR is a worst-case scenario of a capital loss at a given probability (e.g., 1% confidence VaR is the estimated worst case out of 100 scenarios). VaR is more a method of expressing risk than a way of computing it since it can be computed with a variety of methods, including some similar to a PRA. Numerous other esoteric methods that I won't bother to list in detail have also grown out of these tools. But if the foundation of the house needs fixing, I'm not going to worry about the curtains just yet.

Even though OT, MPT, and VaR are widely used, they were the target of criticism well before the 2008/9 financial crisis (but much more so afterward). As this book will explain in more detail later, these models make assumptions that do not match observed reality. Major losses are far more common than these models predict. And since they don't attempt to model components of financial markets (e.g., individual banks, periodic major bankruptcies, etc.) the way that a PRA might, these models may fail to account for known interactions that produce common mode failures.

The 2008/9 financial crisis will cause many to think of these financial tools as being the risk management techniques most in need of repair. Certainly, there is plenty of room for improvement. But simply reacting to the most recent event is counter to good risk management. Risk management is about the *next* crisis. Calls are already being heard for improvements in popular financial tools. The really big problem may be in a far more popular approach to risk management promoted by the best salesmen among the "Four Horsemen": management consultants.

Management Consulting: How a Power Tie and a Good Pitch Changed Risk Management

In the late 1980s, I started what I considered a "dream job" for a brand-new MBA, especially one from a small Midwestern university. It was the era of the "Big 8" accounting firms, when, long before the demise of

Enron and Arthur Andersen, all the major accounting firms had management consulting divisions under the same roof. I was hired to join the management consulting services (MCS) of Coopers & Lybrand and, being in the relatively small Omaha office, we had no specialists. I was able to work on a variety of different problems in lots of organizations.

I tended to define problems we were working on as fundamentally quantitative ones, which also emphasized my key interests and talents. But that was not the modus operandi for most management consultants I saw. For some of my superiors, I noticed a tendency to see value in what I might now call "PowerPoint thinking." They thought of the graphics they made as poetry even if they were a little light on content. Since these graphics would get tweaked in committee, whatever meaning the chart first had would sometimes get diluted even further. For many management consulting engagements, even some of significant size and scope, the PowerPoint slides together with an oral presentation was the *only* deliverable.

The other junior-level consultants and I joked about the process as the *random deliverable generator (RDG)*, as if the actual content of the presentation didn't matter as much as the right combination of sexy graphics and buzzwords. Fortunately, Coopers also had pragmatic managers and partners that would keep the RDG from running completely unchecked. But what surprised me the most was how often the RDG actually seemed to generate deliverables (was *deliverable* even a word before the 1980s?) that satisfied the customers. Possibly, the credibility of the Big-8 name made some clients a little less critical than they otherwise would be.

I suppose some would expect me to be writing about the influence of Peter Drucker or W.E. Deming on management consulting if I claim to have a reasonably complete explanation of the field. But from where I sat, I saw another important trend more influenced by names like Tom Peters, Mike Hammer, and software engineer James Martin, all of whom had a much flashier pitch. Traditionally, management consultants were experienced managers themselves with a cadre of MBAs, typically from the best schools in the country. But a new kind of management consulting related to information technology was changing the industry. Now, it was more common for management consultants not to actually be consulting managers at all. Sometimes they would be software developers and project managers trying (with varying degrees of success) to solve the clients' problems with information technology.

When I started at Coopers & Lybrand, the IBM PC was only a few years old and still not taken seriously by many big organizations. Most critical software applications were mainframe and COBOL with relational databases. The Big 8 and others in the software development industry were providing services to help organize disparate development efforts in a way that, in theory, would put business needs first. This is where James Martin, a former IBM executive who evangelized developing systems based on a systematic way of documenting business needs, had a major impact.

But innovators like James Martin gave the Big 8 an even more important idea. Developing software for a client could be risky. If something went wrong, operations could be delayed, the wrong data would be generated, and the client could be seriously injured. Consultants found a way to get the same lucrative business of IT consulting—lots of staff billed at good rates for long periods—without any of the risks and liabilities of software. They could, instead, develop *methodologies.* Instead of spending that effort developing software, they could spend time developing nearly equally detailed written procedures for some management practice such as, say, running big software projects. The methodology could be licensed and, of course, would often require extensive training and support from the firm that sold it. James Martin had been licensing and supporting his "information engineering" methodology in the same way.

Methodologies like this were something the Big 8 knew they could sell. If you can't replicate a few superstar consultants, document some "structured methodology" and have an army of average management consultants implement it. The ideal situation for a consulting firm is a client where you can park dozens of junior associates for long periods of time and bill them out at a handsome daily rate befitting the Big 8 name. The business of getting "alignment" between business and computers was just the ticket.

Management consultants are, hands down, the most effective sales reps among the "Four Horsemen" and the best overall at making money in the business of advising others. The obvious motivation is billable hours and hourly rates of individual consultants. But making money also means being able to produce consulting on a large scale with a large number of consultants who have more modest resumes. It also means keeping other expenses low. As a result, a set of strategies has naturally evolved for most successful management consultants in the area of risk management or any other area see (How to Sell Snake Oil).

How to Sell Snake Oil

1. *Sell the FUD.* Fear, uncertainty, and doubt (FUD) help sell just about anything, but especially risk management services. All sales representatives repeat the mantra that buying is ultimately emotional and nothing evokes emotion like FUD. A key technique is being able to discuss the details of the most disastrous events in history. The audience will think they learned something even though they didn't.
2. *Sell "structured" approaches.* Selling a consulting gig that takes a week or two sometimes takes as much effort as one that goes on for a year or more, so if you are going to sell consulting, sell something that takes a lot of time but still justifies a high rate. One way to do that is to say that you follow a structured approach that has a lot of detailed deliverables. These have their own perceived value regardless of whether the method is proven in any scientific way. Most management consulting is in danger of being perceived by prospective customers as insubstantial. They don't know exactly what they are going to get. Having a structured approach tells clients that they will at least get some defined deliverables. It also conveys the sense that it's been done before. The structured approach is, in practice, as authoritative as the experience of individual experts on the team. It is also a differentiator, especially for major consulting firms, since usually only they have the resources to develop detailed methods.
3. *Sell intuitive approaches—don't worry whether they work.* To sell it, management has to understand it. Be dismissive of anything more scientific. Consultants, like everyone else, build self-reinforcing belief systems to defend against attack and reward acceptance of dogma. More sophisticated quantitative methods, regardless of how appropriate they might be, are often disregarded as impractically complex or too theoretical. More scientifically well-founded methods would also be more costly to develop procedures for and would require consultants with more specialized skills (a much smaller group).
4. *Sell what feels right.* Clients will not be able to differentiate a placebo effect from real value in most risk management methods. The following tricks seem to work to produce the sense of value:

- Convert everything to a number, no matter how arbitrary. Numbers sound better to management. If you call it a *score*, it will sound more like golf, and it will be more fun for them.
- As long as you have at least one testimonial from one person, you are free to use the word *proven* as much as you like.
- Use lots of "facilitated workshops" to "build consensus."
- Build a giant matrix to "map" your procedure to other processes and standards. It doesn't really matter what the map is for. The effort will be noticed.
- *Optional:* Develop a software application for it. If you can carry on some calculation behind the scenes that they don't quite understand, it will seem much more like magic and, therefore, more legitimate.
- *Optional:* If you go the software route, generate a "spider diagram" or "bubble chart." It will seem more like serious analysis.

The net result of this has been that the most popular risk management methodologies today are developed in complete isolation from more sophisticated risk management methods known to actuaries, engineers, and financial analysts. Whatever the flaws of some of these quantitative methods, the methods developed by the management consultants are the least supported by any theoretical or empirical analysis. The structured risk management methods that management consultants have developed are much more likely, no matter how elaborate and detailed the methodology, to be based on simple scoring schemes. Some smaller consulting organizations have developed half-baked variations on simple spreadsheet calculations that in most fields would be considered crackpot solutions. But they still make a good business selling them.

There is also a trend to see risk management solutions as a problem to be managed by the right enterprise software, especially enterprise risk management (ERM). The specific methods employed in ERM, regardless of whether software is used, don't have much to do with the actuarial, War Quant, and financial analysis tools discussed before. The methods employed are influenced much more by management consulting and sometimes IT consulting. When ERM software is used, ERM is seen as a matter of collecting all the data organizations already collect in databases and as just another major software tool. Quantitative methods used in other fields are almost never a consideration.

The influence of these softer methods cannot be understated. These methods are used for major decisions of all sorts. They have also worked their way into the "best practices" promoted by respected standards organizations and are quickly being adopted by organizations all over the world who want to be able to say they were at least following convention. Here are some examples that have much more in common with these consulting methods I have described than any of the previous quantitative methods:

- *Control Objectives for Information and Related Technology (CobIT).* This standard was developed by the Information Systems Audit and Control Association (ISACA) and the IT Governance Institute (ITGI). This includes a scoring method for IT risks.
- *The Project Management Body of Knowledge (PMBoK).* This standard was developed by the Project Management Institute (PMI). Like CobIT, it includes a scoring method for evaluating project risk.
- *The 800-30 Risk Management Guide for Information Technology Systems.* This was developed by the National Institute of Standards & Technology (NIST). It advocates another scoring method based on a high/medium/low evaluation of likelihood and impact.

All of these standards bodies have developed detailed methods based on scoring approaches. None indicate even an awareness of better methods that could be applied other than to presume that any method slightly more scientific would have to be impractical. A contributor to the CobIT approach told me that only the scoring method is feasible because "a real number would be impossible to get." I have a hard time believing that some of these organizations even represent the best practices in their own field, much less the separate specialty of risk management. PMI's own *Organizational Project Management Maturity Model (OPM3)* manual says the manual was three years overdue in the making. Presumably, PMI is the premier project management authority for how to get things done on time.

Other standards organizations do not recommend specific methods but explicitly condone softer scoring methods as an adequate solution. The International Standards Organization (ISO) 31000 standard stipulates only that "Analysis can be qualitative, semi-quantitative or quantitative, or a combination of these, depending on the circumstances."[10] It does add, "When possible and appropriate, one should undertake more specific and quantitative analysis of the risks as a following step," but does not indicate what constitutes "quantitative." This gives the adopter of this standard plenty of room for interpretation. Since the scoring methods are easier to implement, this virtually assures that such methods will be the predominant approach taken to comply with the standard.

As the third point in the "How to Sell Snake Oil" list indicates, when management consultants are confronted with more sophisticated methods, their natural reaction is to dismiss it as impractical even though they are likely not to have any actual experience with the method. I was once explaining the quantitative methods I use, including Monte Carlo simulations to compute risk, to a group of government contractors. One consultant, who had co-authored a book on managing IT investments, dismissed the idea and said he had never seen Monte Carlo simulations successfully used on an IT project. I pointed out that I run Monte Carlo simulations on most IT investments I've analyzed, which, by that time, added up to more than 50 risk/return analyses in the previous 12 years. He was embarrassed and silent for the rest of the meeting. How long had he been telling people that a method with which he had no experience was not practical? Quite a while, according to co-workers. This is not at all uncommon in consulting. It makes sense to classify any method that seems more complex than your own as "impractical" if you are unfamiliar with it—unless someone calls your bluff.

Much of this book is an argument for why the most sophisticated methods are, in fact, entirely practical and justified for most major decisions once a few improvements are made. At the same time, I'll be arguing for the discontinuation of popular but ineffectual scoring methods regardless of how practical they seem to be.

Comparing the Horsemen

The "Four Horsemen" represent four different, although sometimes related, lineages of risk management methods. They all have different challenges, although some have more than others. Exhibit 4.2 sums up the issues.

Even though there are impressive individuals in other areas, actuarial practice is the only area wherein there are some formal, professional standards and ethics. Actuaries tend to eventually adopt the best quantitative methods

EXHIBIT 4.2 **SUMMARY OF THE "FOUR HORSEMEN"**

The Horsemen	Used by/for	Short Description	Challenges
Actuaries	Mostly insurance and pensions (some branching out into other areas)	Highly regulated and structured certification process. Build on established methods, conservative.	Tend to be late adopters; authority not wide enough to deal with other risks.
War Quants	Engineers, a small minority of business analysts and some financial analysts	Tend to see the risk analysis problem like an engineering problem—detailed systems of components and their interactions are modeled.	Where subjective inputs are required, known systemic errors are not adjusted for. Empirical analysis is rarely incorporated into modeling.
Economists	Financial analysts, some application to nonfinancial investments (projects, equipment investments, etc.)	Focus on statistical analysis of historical data instead of detailed structural models (although there are exceptions)	Still make assumptions known to be false regarding the frequency of extreme market changes. Tend to avoid structural models or see them as impossible.
Management Consultants	Almost everyone else not listed above	Mostly experience based. May have detailed, documented procedures for analysis. Use scoring schemes.	Methods are not validated. Errors are introduced by the subjective inputs and further magnified by the scoring method.

from other fields but, as AIG unfortunately proved, the biggest risks are often outside of the actuaries' legal and professional responsibility.

The nuclear engineers and others who use the PRA and other methods inherited from wartime quantitative analysts may have the best, most scientific approach. However, they are not immune to some errors and their powerful methods are still considered esoteric and too difficult to use.

Methods and tools exist that would overcome this objection, but most risk analysts are not aware of them.

Whereas some financial analysts are extraordinarily gifted mathematicians and scientists themselves, many of the basic assumptions of their financial models seem to go unquestioned. The kinds of common mode failures and cascade effects that caused the 2008/9 financial crisis perhaps could have been caught by the more detailed modeling approach of a PRA, if anyone had built them (or if they did, they apparently didn't influence management). Instead, the financial models use simple statistical descriptions of markets that ignore these sorts of system failures.

Finally, the management consultants have the softest sell, the easiest sell, and the most successful sell of all the major risk management schools of thought. Unfortunately, they are also the most removed from the science of risk management and may have done far more harm than good.

Major Risk Management Problems to Be Addressed

The remainder of this book is an attempt to analyze the problems faced by one or more of these schools of thought and propose methods to fix them. Seven of these challenges are summarized below. The first five points are addressed in the remainder of Part Two of this book (Why It's Broken). The last couple of points will be deferred until we get to the final part of this book, Part Three (How to Fix It).

Seven Challenges for Risk Management

1. *Confusion regarding the concept of risk.* Among different specialties in risk management, analysts and managers are using the word *risk* to mean some very different things. Since part of the solution is better collaboration, we need to get on the same sheet of music.
2. *Completely avoidable human errors in subjective judgments of risk.* Most of the methods of risk assessment must rely on at least some subjective inputs by human experts, but, without certain precautions, human experts make surprisingly consistent types of errors in judgment about uncertainty and risk. Although research shows that there are methods that can correct for certain systemic errors that people make, very few do so and the net result is an almost universal understatement of risk.

3. *Entirely ineffectual but popular subjective scoring methods.* The numerous arbitrary rules and values created in scoring methods not only fail to consider the problems with subjective risks (see previous point), they introduce errors of their own and may actually make decisions worse. There is no large, important decision that would not be better served with some other analysis approach.
4. *Misconceptions that block the use of better, existing methods.* Even some experienced risk analysts defend the use of ineffectual methods by arguing that better, more sophisticated methods will not work. But each of these arguments is based on fundamental fallacies about the nature of quantitative risk analysis.
5. *Recurring errors in even the most sophisticated models.* Most users of the more quantitative approaches do not attempt to measure the reliability of their models by checking against historical data. Quality control is mostly nonexistent in users of popular quantitative modeling tools and the use of real-world observations is too rare. These are all avoidable problems and should not be considered obstacles to the use of better risk analysis. Some analysts assume that their models take on a level of authority and "truth" that is never justified. Half-understood models are misapplied in a variety of situations.
6. *Institutional factors.* Unnecessary isolation of risk analysts from each other—both within the same organization and among organizations—means that important shared risks and relationships will be ignored in overspecialized models.
7. *Unproductive incentive structures.* The methods will not matter much if the incentives to make better decisions and manage risks are not improved. Minimizing risk is not a factor in most executive bonus calculations. Human experts are not incentivized to give reliable forecasts and there is little incentive to verify old forecasts against observations. As the surveys in Chapter 2 described, a key motivator is compliance and use of so-called best practices. If a ship is sinking, at least the captain can point out that he followed established procedures. This is not an irrational motivation from the point of view of the captain (we all seek to reduce the risk of blame), but it may be inadequate in the eyes of the passengers.

NOTES

1. Attributed to a "Robert Hanlon" by Arthur Bloch in *Murphy's Law Book Two: More Reasons Why Things Go Wrong,* (Leisure Arts, 1981), but a similar quote was also used by Robert Heinlein in his short story "Logic of Empire," in an anthology by (Baen Books, 1951).
2. H. Bühlmann, "The Actuary: The Role and Limitations of the Profession since the Mid-19th Century," *ASTIN Bulletin* 27(2), November 1997, 165–171.
3. Ibid.
4. D. Christopherson and E.C. Baughan, "Reminiscences of Operational Research in World War II by Some of Its Practitioners: II," *Journal of the Operational Research Society* 43(6), June 1992, 569–577.
5. R. Ruggles and H. Brodie, "An Empirical Approach to Economics Intelligence in World War II," *Journal of the American Statistical Association* 42(237), March 1947, 72–91.
6. R. A. Knief, *Nuclear Engineering: Theory and Technology of Commercial Nuclear Power,* (Taylor & Francis, 1992), pg. 391.
7. R. Howard, "Decision Analysis: Applied Decision Theory" *Proceedings of the Fourth International Conference of Operations Research,* Boston, Mass., 1966.
8. F. Knight, *Risk, Uncertainty and Profit*, Kessinger Publishing, 1921.
9. H.M. Markowitz, "Portfolio Selection," *Journal of Finance* 7(1), March 1952, 77–91.
10. H.M. Markowitz, "Foundations of Portfolio Theory," *Journal of Finance* 46(2), June 1991, 469–477.
11. ISO/DIS 31000—*Risk Management: Principles and Guidelines on Implementation*, ISO 2008/9.

CHAPTER 5

An Ivory Tower of Babel: Fixing the Confusion about Risk

If you wish to converse with me, define your terms.

—VOLTAIRE

Concepts about risk and even the word *risk* are a source of considerable confusion even among those who specialize in the topic. There are a lot of well-entrenched and mutually exclusive ideas about risk and risk management and if we are going to make any progress, we have to work out these differences.

You might think that agreement on what the word *risk* means should be relatively simple and, for that matter, should have been resolved long ago. If only that were the case. Multiple definitions have evolved in multiple professions. Even worse, some will not even know they are using it differently from others and may incorrectly believe they are clearly communicating with other risk professionals.

We need our vocabulary and concepts on firm footing before we can begin any heavy lifting with risk management. First, let's clear up some confusion about how the word *risk* is used in different fields. I offered a clear definition of risk in Chapter 2, but it is worth restating here. While we're here, let's also clarify the related concept of *uncertainty* and distinguish between the *qualitative* and *quantitative* use of these terms. (Note that this is

UNCERTAINTY VERSUS RISK AND THE MEASUREMENTS OF EACH

- *Uncertainty.* The lack of complete certainty—that is, the existence of more than one possibility. The "true" outcome/state/result/value is not known.
  - *Measurement of uncertainty.* A set of probabilities assigned to a set of possibilities. For example, "There is a 60% chance it will rain tomorrow, and a 40% chance it won't."
- *Risk.* A state of uncertainty where some of the possibilities involve a loss, injury, catastrophe, or other undesirable outcome (i.e., something bad could happen).
  - *Measurement of risk.* A set of possibilities each with quantified probabilities and quantified losses. For example, "We believe there is a 40% chance the proposed oil well will be dry with a loss of $12 million in exploratory drilling costs."

the same distinction I make in my earlier book, *How to Measure Anything: Finding the Value of Intangibles in Business*.)

This specific distinction of the terms not only represents the de facto use of the terms in the insurance industry and certain other types of professions and areas of research, but is also closest to how the general public uses the term. And although risk professionals need to be a bit more precise in the use of these terms than the general public, these definitions are otherwise entirely consistent with the definitions offered in all of the major English dictionaries.

But a risk manager needs to know that this specific language is not universally adopted—not even by all risk professionals and academics. Some circles will use a language all their own and many of them will insist that their definition is the "formal" or the "accepted" definition among experts—unaware that other experts believe the same of other definitions. A risk manager needs to know these other definitions of risk, where they came from, and why we can't use them.

The Frank Knight Definition

Frank Knight was an influential economist of the early 20th century who wrote a text titled *Risk, Uncertainty and Profit* (1921). The book, which expanded on his 1917 doctoral dissertation, has become what many economists consider a classic. In it, Knight makes a distinction between uncertainty and risk that still influences a large circle of academics and professionals today:

> [To differentiate] the measurable uncertainty and an unmeasurable one we may use the term "risk" to designate the former and the term "uncertainty" for the latter.

According to Knight, we have uncertainty when we are unable to quantify the probabilities of various outcomes whereas risk applies to situations where the odds of various possible outcomes can be known. But Knight's definition was and is a significant deviation from both popular use and the practical use of these terms in insurance, statistics, engineering, public health, and virtually every other field that deals with risk.

First, Knight makes no mention of the possibility of loss as being part of the meaning of risk. It states that all we need for a state of risk is that we can quantify probabilities for outcomes—contrary to almost every other use of the term in any field. Whether any of those outcomes are undesirable in some way is irrelevant to Knight's definition. Second, Knight's definition of uncertainty seems to be routinely contradicted by researchers and professionals who speak of "quantifying uncertainty" by applying probabilities to various outcomes. In effect, Knight's definition of *risk* is what most others would call *uncertainty*.

Knight starts the preface of his book by stating, "There is little that is fundamentally new in this book." But his definitions of *uncertainty* and *risk* were quite new—in fact, previously unheard of. Even Knight must have felt that he was breaking new ground, since he apparently believed there were no adequate definitions to date that distinguished *risk* from *uncertainty*. He wrote in the same text, "Uncertainty must be taken in a sense radically distinct from the familiar notion of risk, from which it has never been properly separated."[1]

In reality, there was already an extremely consistent, and sometimes mathematically unambiguous, use of these terms in many fields. Even within economics, it was generally understood that uncertainty can be represented quantitatively by probabilities and that risk must include loss. Consider the following quotes from economics journals, one published just after Knight's text and one well before it:

- "Probability, then, is concerned with professedly *uncertain* [emphasis added] judgments."[2]
- "The word risk has acquired no technical meaning in economics, but signifies here *as elsewhere* [emphasis added] chance of damage or loss."[3]

The first speaks of *probabilities*—a term that is widely understood in economics, math, and statistics to be a quantity—as something that applies to uncertainty in judgments. The second quote acknowledges that risk as a chance of loss is generally understood.

The definitions I previously presented for *risk* and *uncertainty* were also used consistently in mathematics, especially in regard to games of chance, long before Knight wrote his book. Prior to 1900, many famous mathematicians such as Bayes, Poisson, and Bernoulli discussed uncertainty as being expressed by quantified probabilities. This directly contradicts Knight's use of the word *uncertainty* as something immeasurable. And there was so much of this work that I could have written an entire book just about the measurement of uncertainty before 1900. Fortunately, I didn't need to, because one was already written (Stephen Stigler, *The History of Statistics: The Measurement of Uncertainty before 1900*, Harvard University Press,1986).

One intriguingly short definition of *uncertainty* that I came across was in the field of the psychology of gambling (where, again, uncertainties are quantified) in the early 1900s. Clemens J. France defined uncertainty as "a state of suspense" in his article, "The Gambling Impulse," in the *American Journal of Psychology* in 1902. In 1903, this use of the concept of uncertainty within gambling was common enough that it shows up in the *International Journal of Ethics*: "Some degree of uncertainty, therefore, and willingness to take the risk are essential for a bet."[4]

Even shortly after Knight proposed his definitions, other fields carried on quantifying uncertainty and treating risk as the chance of a loss or injury. In 1925, the physicist Werner Heisenberg developed his famous *uncertainty principle*, which quantified minimum uncertainty of the position and velocity of a particle. The mathematicians who dealt with decisions under uncertainty continued to define *uncertainty* and *risk* as we have. And the entire insurance industry carried on doing business as usual apparently without any regard for Knight's proposed alternative definition.

A simple test will demonstrate that Knight's use of the term *uncertainty* is not the way common sense would tell us to use it. Ask people around you the following three questions:

1. "If I were to flip a coin, would you be *uncertain* of the outcome before I flipped it?"
2. "What is the chance that the outcome will be tails?"
3. "Assume you are not betting anything on the flip or depending on the flip in any other way. Do you have risk in the coin flip?"

Almost anyone you asked would answer "yes, 50%, and no." Knight's definitions would have to answer "no, 50%, and yes" if he were serious about his definitions. Since our answer to question #2 indicates the odds are quantifiable, Knight would have to say a coin flip is not uncertain (he says uncertainty is immeasurable) even though almost anyone would say it is. Also, since the coin flip meets his only criterion for risk (that the odds are quantifiable) then he has to answer "yes" to #3, even though the lack of having any stake in the outcome would cause most of the rest of us to say there is no risk.

While Knight's definitions are quite different from many risk management professionals', his definitions influence the topic even today. I was corresponding with a newly minted PhD who had conducted what she called a "prequantitative" risk analysis of a major government program. While discussing risk, it became clear that we had a different vocabulary. She was using the term *uncertainty* as *unquantifiable randomness*, just as Knight did. She didn't mention Knight specifically but pointed out that, even though it was not the common use, this is how the term is "defined in the literature." For evidence of this, she cited a definition proposed by the editors of a fairly important anthology of decision science, *Judgment and Decision Making: An Interdisciplinary Reader*, which defined the terms as Knight did.[5] I happened to have a copy of this book and in less than five minutes found another article in the same text that discusses how uncertainty is "expressed in terms of probabilities" (Fischhoff, p. 362)—which is consistent with nearly every other source I find.

Knight himself recognized that this was not the common use of these terms. But, for some reason, despite the volume of prior work that quantified both risk and uncertainty, he felt that he needed to define risk *proper*. Unfortunately, Knight's views held a lot of sway with many economists and non-economists alike and it still contributes to confusion in the advancement of risk management. Let's just call it what it is—a blunder. This will brand me a heretic with fans of legendary economists (and there is more of that to come), but it was ill-conceived and didn't clarify anything.

Risk as Volatility

In the world of finance, *volatility*, *variance*, and *risk* are used virtually synonymously. If a stock price tends to change drastically and frequently, it is considered to be volatile and, therefore, it is risky. This is sometimes associated with Harry Markowitz, the economist who won the Nobel Prize in Economics for Modern Portfolio Theory (MPT). As briefly mentioned in Chapter 4, MPT attempts to define how a rational investor would select investments in a portfolio in a way that makes the best overall risk and return for the portfolio.

Actually, Markowitz never explicitly promotes such a definition. He merely states that, in most financial articles in general, "if . . . 'risk' [were replaced] by 'variance of return,' then little change of apparent meaning would result." He treats volatility, like risk, as something that is acceptable if the return is high enough. In practice, though, analysts who use MPT often equate *historical* volatility of return to risk.

While it is true that a stock with historically high volatility of returns is probably also a risky stock, we have to be careful about how this is different from the definitions I proposed earlier. First—and this may seem so obvious that it's hardly worth mentioning—volatility of a stock is risky for you only if you own a position on that stock. I usually have a lot of uncertainty about the outcome of the Super Bowl (especially because I don't follow it closely), but unless I were to bet money on it, I have no risk.

Second, even if I have something at stake, volatility doesn't necessarily equate to risk. For example, suppose we played a game where I roll a six-sided die and whatever comes up on the roll I multiply by $100 and pay you that amount. You can, therefore, win anywhere from $100 to $600 on a roll. You only have to pay me $100 to play. Is there uncertainty (i.e., variance or volatility) in the outcome of the roll? Yes; you could net nothing from the game or you could net as much as $500. Do you have risk? No; there is no possible result that ends up as a loss for you.

Of course, games like that don't usually exist in the market, and that's why it is understandable how *volatility* might be used as a sort of synonym for *risk*. In an actively traded market, the price of such a game would be "bid up" until there was at least some chance of a loss. Imagine if I took the same game and, instead of offering it only to you, I offered it to whoever in your office would give me the highest bid for it. It is very likely that someone out of a group of several people would be willing to pay more than $100 for one roll of the die, in which case that person would be accepting a chance of a loss. The market would make any investment with a highly uncertain outcome cost enough that there is a chance of a loss—and therefore a risk for anyone who invests in it.

But what works in the financial markets is not always relevant to managers dealing with investments in the operation of a firm. If you have the opportunity to invest in, say, better insulated windows for your office building, you may easily save substantially more than the investment. Even though energy costs are uncertain, you might determine that, in order for the new windows not to be cost effective, energy costs would have to be a small fraction of what they are now. The difference between this and a stock is that there is no wider market that has the opportunity to compete with you for this investment. You have an exclusive opportunity to make this investment and other investors cannot just bid up the price (although, eventually, the price of the windows may go up with demand).

It is also possible for operational investments with very little variance to be risky where the expected return is so small that even a slight variance would make it undesirable. You would probably reject such an investment, but in the market the investment would be priced down until it was attractive to someone.

In summary, volatility implies risk only if some of the outcomes involve losses. Our definition of *risk* applies equally well regardless of whether the investment is traded on the market or is an operational investment exclusive to the management of a business.

A Construction Engineering Definition

I came across another use of the term *risk* when I was consulting on risk analysis in the engineering construction industry. It was common for engineers to put ranges on the costs of an engineering project and they would refer to this as the *variance model.* The price of steel might vary during the course of construction, so they would have to put a range on this value. This was likewise done for the hourly rates of various labor categories or the amount of effort required for each category. The uncertainty about these items would be captured as ranges such as "The hourly cost of this labor next year will be $40 to $60 per hour" or "This structure will take 75 to 95 days to finish."

Fair enough; but they didn't consider this a risk of the project. The separate "risk model" was a list of specific events that may or may not happen, such as "There is a 10% chance of an onsite accident that would cause a work stoppage" or "There is a 20% chance of a strike among the electricians." This use of the word *risk* makes an arbitrary distinction about risk based on whether the source of the uncertainty is a range value or a discrete event.

In the definition I propose for *risk*, the price of steel and labor, which could be much higher than they expected, would be a legitimate source of risk. The construction project had some expected benefit and it is quite possible for increasing costs and delayed schedules to wipe out that benefit and even cause a net loss for the project. Some uncertain outcomes result in a loss and that is all we need to call it a risk. Risk should have nothing to do with whether the uncertainty is a discrete event or a range of values.

Risk as Expected Loss

I sometimes come across *risk* defined as "the chance of an unfortunate event times the cost if such an event occurred." I've encountered this use of the term in nuclear power, many government agencies, and sometimes IT projects. The product of the probability of some event and the loss of the event is called the *expected loss* of the event.

Any reader new to the decision sciences should note that when risk analysts or decision scientists use the word *expected* they mean "probability weighted average." An expected loss is the chance of each possible loss times the size of the loss totaled for all losses (this value can be very different from the loss that is the most likely).

This definition was going down the right path before it took an unnecessary turn. It acknowledges the need for measurable uncertainty and loss. But this definition requires an unnecessary assumption about the decision maker. This definition assumes the decision maker is "risk neutral" instead of being "risk averse," as most people are. A risk-neutral person always puts a value on anything that is equal to its expected value, that is, the probability weighted average of all the outcomes. For example, consider which of the following you would prefer:

- A coin flip that pays you $20,000 on heads and costs you $10,000 on tails.
- A certain payment to you of $5,000.

To a risk-neutral person, these are identical, since they both have the same expected value: $(\$20,000 \times .5) + (-\$10,000 \times .5) = \$5,000$. However, since most people are not risk neutral, it's too presumptuous to just compute the expected loss and equate that to their risk preference.

But why do we have to reduce risk to a single value just yet? How much the manager values a given risk (that is, how much she is willing to pay to avoid it) depends on her risk aversion and this cannot be determined from simply knowing the odds and the losses involved. Some people might consider the two options above equivalent if the certain payment were $2,000. Some might even be willing to pay not to have to flip the coin to avoid the chance of a $10,000 loss. But we will get to quantifying risk aversion later.

We can, instead, just leave the risk in its separate components until we apply it to a given risk-averse decision maker. This treats risk as a sort of *vector quantity*. Vector quantities are quantities that can be described only in two or more dimensions and they are common in physics. Quantities that are a single dimension, like mass or charge, are expressed with one number, such as "mass of 11.3 kilograms" or "charge of .005 coulombs." But vector quantities, such as velocity or angular momentum, require both a magnitude and a direction to fully describe them.

As with vector quantities in physics, we don't have to collapse the magnitude of the losses and the chance of loss into one number. We can even have a large number of possible outcomes, each with its own probability and loss. If there are many negative outcomes and they each have a

EXHIBIT 5.1 **EXAMPLE OF THE RISK OF A PROJECT FAILURE EXPRESSED AS A VECTOR QUANTITY**

(The whole table is the risk vector—it is not collapsed to one risk number.)

Event	**Probability**	**Loss**
Total project failure—loss of capital investment	4%	$5–12 million
Partial failure—incomplete adoption	7%	$1–4 million

probability and a magnitude of loss, then that entire table of data is the risk. (See Exhibit 5.1.) Of course, losses and their probabilities often have a continuum of values. If a fire occurs at a major facility, there is a range of possible loss and each point on that range has an associated probability.

Any of the definitions you might find for risk that state that risk is "the probability/chance and magnitude/amount/severity of a danger/harm/loss/injury" implicitly treat risk as a vector (an Internet search will reveal quite a few such definitions, including those from scientific literature). The definition simply states that risk is *both* the probability and the consequence and doesn't say that they should necessarily be multiplied together.

Risk as a Good Thing

It's clear that most people use the word *risk* to refer to the possibility of some negative outcome. But can risk mean the chance of a good thing happening? Oddly enough, it does mean that to some in the emerging profession of project management.

The *Guide to the "Project Management Body of Knowledge" (PMBoK)*, 2000 edition, published by the Project Management Institute (PMI), defines *project risk* as "an uncertain event or condition that, if it occurs, has a *positive or negative* [emphasis added] effect on a project objective."

This definition is acknowledged by a large number of people in project management. The PMI began in 1969 and by 2008 had over 265,000 members worldwide. In addition to publishing the *PMBoK*, it certifies individuals as Project Management Professionals (PMPs). Although PMI attempts to cover projects of all sorts in all fields, there is a large presence of information technology (IT) project managers in its membership.

There are also UK-based organizations that define risk in this way. The *Project Risk Analysis & Management Guide* (*PRAM Guide*, 1997) of the UK

Association for Project Management (APM) defines *risk* as "an uncertain event or set of circumstances which, should it occur, will have an effect on achievement of objectives," and further notes that "consequences can range from positive to negative." And the British Standards BS6079-1: 2002 Guide to Project Management and BS6079-2: Project Management Vocabulary define *risk* as a "combination of the probability or frequency of occurrence of a defined threat *or opportunity* [emphasis added] and the magnitude of the consequences of the occurrence."

I was discussing this definition of *risk* with a PMI-certified PMP and I pointed out that including positive outcomes as part of risk is a significant departure from how the term is used in the decision sciences, insurance, probabilistic risk analysis in engineering, and most other professions that had been dealing with risks for decades. He asked why we wouldn't want to include all possible outcomes as part of risk and not just negative outcomes. I said, "Because there is already a word for that—*uncertainty*."

I had another project manager tell me that risk can be a good thing because "sometimes you have to take risk to gain something." It is true that you often have to accept a risk in order to gain some reward. But, if you could gain the same reward for less risk, you would. This is like saying that expenses—by themselves—are a good thing because you need them for business operations. But, again, if you could maintain or improve operations while reducing spending, you would certainly try. The fact that rewards often require other sacrifices is not the same thing as saying that those sacrifices are themselves desirable. That's why they are called *sacrifices*—you are willing to endure them to get something *else* that you want. If it were a good thing, you would want more of it even if all other things were held constant. You accept more costs or more risks, however, only if you think you are getting more of something else.

Perhaps this definition is somehow connected to Knight's use of the term, since Knight also made no distinction about loss (he merely required measurable probabilities of outcomes). This may also be influenced by the use of *risk* as meaning simply *volatility* even if the uncertainties contain no negative outcomes. But even some of the editors of the *PMBoK* don't seem to be aware of Knight's use of the word. They apparently made this up on their own.

The fact is that every English dictionary definition you can find—including *Merriam-Webster, American Heritage, Oxford English,* or even Dictionary.com—

defines *risk* in terms of peril, danger, chance of loss, injury, or harm. Not one mentions risk as including the possibility of a positive outcome alone. Risk as "opportunity," in and of itself (as opposed to something one is willing to accept in exchange for opportunity), also contradicts the most established use of the word in the practical world of insurance as well as the theoretical world of decision theory.

Such an odd deviation from the general use of a common word can happen only in an insular group that feels it has to reinvent such concepts. And being confused about the meaning of the word *risk* isn't the only problem with PMI's approach to risk management. I will be discussing PMI again when I talk about problems with their risk assessment approach. But the vocabulary would not be such a problem if we familiarized ourselves with the other work on the topic before creating a "new" risk management approach.

The problem with PMI, as with many other home-brewed versions of risk and risk management, is that risk was added almost as an afterthought. I can tell by looking at the content that they had nobody on their committee with a background in decision science, actuarial science, or probabilistic risk analysis. To their credit, somebody realized that part of project management must be risk management. But, apparently, they sat down and made up risk management (and the new definitions) with no input from existing literature on the topic.

Risk Analysis and Risk Management versus Decision Analysis

Part of the desire to include opportunities and benefits in risk analysis and risk management can be traced to lack of familiarity with the field that already includes those things. *Decision analysis (DA)*, introduced in Chapter 4, is a large body of theoretical and applied work that deals with making decisions under a state of uncertainty. It addresses decisions where tradeoffs have to be made between uncertain costs, uncertain benefits, and other risks.

Part of the problem with risk management, at least in some organizations, has been its rapid growth—mostly in isolation—from already well-developed quantitative methods such as those found in decision analysis. But now the additional implications of the term *risk management* need to be considered. Management itself denotes that decision making and risk management must include analysis of decisions. Clearly, nearly all management decisions have risks. Is risk management now the home of all decision analysis in the firm?

I propose a solution: Risk managers do deal with decisions as they are related to tracking and reducing risks inherent in the business. If a risk manager can find a cheaper way to mitigate a risk without interfering with other business operations and do so within his own budget, then he has the authority to do so. When it comes to assessing decisions with other business opportunities where risk is a factor, the risk professional simply provides the input for the risk assessment to be used in the decision analysis. I will write more later about how risk analysis, risk management, and decision analysis should come together.

Enriching the Lexicon

Let's summarize risk terminology and add a few more items to our lexicon. We just reviewed several definitions of *risk*. Many of these were mutually exclusive, contradicted commonsense uses of the language, and defied even the academic literature available at the time. A risk manager in a large organization with professionals in finance, IT, and perhaps engineering could have easily encountered more than one of these definitions just within his own firm. If a risk manager does run into these alternative uses of the word, we have to respond:

- Risk has to include some probability of a loss—this excludes Knight's definition.
- Risk involves only losses (not gains)—this excludes PMI's definition.
- Outside of finance, volatility may not necessarily entail risk—this excludes considering volatility alone as synonymous with risk.
- Risk is not just the product of probability and loss. Multiplying them together unnecessarily presumes that the decision maker is risk-neutral. Keep risk as a vector quantity where probability and magnitude of loss are separate until we compare it to the risk aversion of the decision maker.
- Risk can be made of discrete or continuous losses and associated probabilities. We do not need to make the distinctions sometimes made in construction engineering that risk is only discrete events.

One final note about this terminology is that it has to be considered part of a broader field of decision analysis. Just as risk management must be a subset of management in the organization, risk analysis must be a subset of decision analysis. Decisions cannot be based entirely on risk analysis alone but require an analysis of the potential benefits if managers decide to accept a risk. Later in the book we will get into the implications of this for various types of decisions in the firm, but, for now, let me introduce the idea along with some additional required terminology.

An enriched professional vocabulary doesn't mean shoe-horning disparate concepts into a single word (like PMI did with *risk*). We have different terms for different concepts and they seem to me to be less about hair-splitting semantics than about clear-cut night-and-day differences. Here are some clarifications and a couple of new terms that might have been useful to the authors of some of the definitions we just reviewed:

- *Uncertainty.* This includes all sorts of uncertainties, whether they are about negative or positive outcomes. This also includes discrete values (such as whether there will be a labor strike during the project) or continuous values (such as what the cost of the project could be if the project is between one and six months behind schedule). Uncertainty can be measured (contrary to Knight's use of the term) by the assignment of probabilities to various outcomes.
- *Strict uncertainty.* This is what many modern decision scientists would call Knight's version of uncertainty. Strict uncertainty is where the possible outcomes are identified but we have no probabilities for each. For reasons we will argue later, this should never have to be the case.
- *Risk/reward analysis.* This considers the uncertain downside as well as the uncertain upside of the investment. By explicitly acknowledging that this includes positive outcomes, we don't have to muddy the word *risk* by force-fitting it with positive outcomes. Part of risk/return analysis is also the consideration of the risk aversion of the decision maker, and we don't have to assume the decision maker is risk neutral (as we would when we assume that risk is loss times probability).

- *Ignorance*. This is worse than strict uncertainty since in the state of ignorance, we don't even know the possible outcomes, much less their probabilities. This is what former U.S. Secretory of Defense Donald Rumsfeld and others would have meant by the term "unknown unknowns." In effect, most real-world risk models must have some level of ignorance, but this is no showstopper toward better risk management.

NOTES

1. F. Knight, *Risk, Uncertainty and Profit,* (New York: Houghton-Mifflin, 1921), pp. 19–20.
2. A. Wolf, "Studies in Probability," *Economica* 4, January 1922, 87–97.
3. J. Haynes, "Risk as an Economic Factor," *Quarterly Journal of Economics* 9(4), July 1895, 409–449, MIT Press.
4. W.R. Sorley, "Betting and Gambling," *International Journal of Ethics*, July 1903.
5. T. Connolly, H.R. Arkes, and K.R. Hammond, *Judgment and Decision Making: An Interdisciplinary Reader* (2nd ed.), Cambridge Series on Judgment and Decision Making (New York: Cambridge University Press, 1999).

CHAPTER 6

The Limits of Expert Knowledge: Why We Don't Know What We Think We Know about Uncertainty

Experience is inevitable. Learning is not.

—Paul J.H. Schoemaker

We are riding the early waves of a 25-year run of a greatly expanding economy that will do much to solve seemingly intractable problems like poverty and to ease tensions throughout the world.

—*Wired* (July 1997)

Naturally, we value expertise whether it's in a business colleague, a politician, or an electrician. And the vast majority of attempts to assess risks will at some point rely on the subjective input of some kind of expert. The only possible exceptions to this are situations where great volumes of historical data are available, such as in the analysis of stocks or most forms of consumer insurance (we'll talk about those later). But for almost all operational and strategic risk assessments in business, someone who is deemed an expert in that issue is asked to assess a probability either directly or indirectly.

They may assess a probability quantitatively (e.g., "There is a 10% chance this project will fail") or they may be asked to provide this estimate in some verbal form (e.g., "It is unlikely this project will fail"). They are sometimes even asked to express this likelihood on some sort of scale other than explicit probabilities (e.g., "On a scale of 1 to 5, the likelihood of this project failing is a 2"). Even in some of the most quantitative analysis of risks, human beings must use their judgment to identify possible risks before they can be included in an equation.

But if we are going to rely on human experts, shouldn't we know something about the performance of human experts at assessing the probability or impact of potential risks? How about their ability to even identify the risks in the first place? Technicians, scientists, or engineers, for example, using an instrument to measure weight wouldn't want to use the instrument if they didn't know it was calibrated. If they knew a scale was always overstating weight by 5%, they would adjust the readings accordingly. For managers and analysts, too, we should apply a measure of some kind to their past performance at estimating risks. We should know whether these "instruments" consistently overestimate or underestimate risks. We should know whether they are so inconsistent that they give completely different answers even for the identical scenario presented at different times.

Fortunately, this has been extensively researched. We know there are limits to the value of experience for several reasons. In the case of risk management, I believe experience has certain features we should always keep in mind:

- Experience is a nonrandom, nonscientific sample of events throughout our lifetime.
- Experience is memory-based, and we are very selective regarding what we choose to remember.
- What we conclude from our experience (or at least that part we choose to remember of it) can be full of logical errors.
- Unless we get reliable feedback on past decisions, there is no reason to believe our experience will tell us much.
- No matter how much experience we accumulate, we seem to be very inconsistent in its application.

As a result, it turns out that all people, including experts and managers, are very bad at assessing the probabilities of events—a skill we should expect to be critical to proper assessments of risks. The good news is that, even though research shows some profound systemic errors in the subjective assessment of risks, relatively simple techniques have been developed that make managers fairly reliable estimators of risks. The bad news is that almost none of these methods are widely adopted by risk managers in organizations.

The Right Stuff: How a Group of Psychologists Saved Risk Analysis

In the 1970s, one of the most productive collaborations of any science was in the field of *judgment and decision making (JDM)* psychology. The team of Daniel ("Danny") Kahneman and Amos Tversky would conduct research that would turn out to be important well beyond the tight circle of their colleagues in JDM. Some of the research in this area would have such an impact in economics that, in 2002, Kahneman would become the first psychologist to win the Nobel Prize in Economics—an honor Tversky would certainly have received as well if he had lived long enough to see how far their influence spread.

Kahneman and Tversky were interested in how the human mind deals with uncertainty, risks, and decisions. Their research touched virtually every major topic in this field and it is difficult to find a research paper in JDM that does not cite them. At one level, the work of Kahneman and Tversky could be described as a catalogue of quirks and flaws in human judgment. At another level, it is powerful insight into what drives human behavior that should have implications for all managers. Kahneman describes his interests as being related to the "quality control of decisions" and it is clear to him that the research shows what doesn't work and what does.

The human mind, obviously, is not a computer. We don't recall events with 100% accuracy as if we were accessing a hard drive. And except for a few savants, once we recall those events we don't do statistical calculations in our heads to determine what those events really mean. Instead, we resort to a set of heuristics. A *heuristic* is a sort of mental shortcut that in our simpler, hunter-gatherer days probably sufficed for a variety of situations and still does today. A related concept is *bias*—a tendency to think and behave in a way that interferes with rationality and impartiality. A heuristic, in some cases, may actually be productive, but a bias is generally thought of as undesirable. These heuristics and biases affect both what we manage to recall and how we interpret what we recall.

Some would call a heuristic a kind of rule of thumb, but there is an important difference. Usually, we think of a rule of thumb as a simple rule we consciously apply, such as "Your mortgage on a new home should not be more than three times your annual income" (a rule that was not followed by a lot of people prior to the mortgage crisis of 2008). But, biases and heuristics that have been discovered regarding how people assess risk are generally not consciously applied. Because people are not aware of these heuristics and biases, they can be inferred only by observing how individuals respond in a variety of situations.

Unlike some areas of science, JDM research is not terribly expensive to produce. It usually involves giving large numbers of individuals a variety of problems to solve and evaluating their answers. Often, researchers ask subjects questions where a rational answer is known and the subjects' responses can be compared with rational responses. Other times, there may not be a single, rational response, but researchers are interested in what conditions affect the subjects responses and how they make decisions.

Other influential researchers included Paul Slovic, who, sometimes with Kahneman, did important work on how we perceive risks. Sarah Lichtenstein and Baruch Fischhoff conducted a variety of experiments in how we assess our own uncertainty. Robyn Dawes did important work in how some simple systems outperformed human judgment in a variety of tasks. Richard Thaler was an economist who was central to introducing much of Kahneman's work to other economists. It is my belief that nobody who wants to be a "risk analyst" or "risk manager" can claim to know much about that topic without knowing something about the work of these thinkers.

Some of this will be unavoidably redundant with my first book, *How to Measure Anything: Finding the Value of Intangibles in Business*. There I spoke of methods that researchers have found for assessing risk using subjective inputs and how often subjective estimates of probabilities are far off the mark. But, as I also mention in the previous book, research tells us that there are solutions to this problem.

MENTAL MATH: WHY WE SHOULDN'T TRUST THE NUMBERS IN OUR HEADS

When a contractor estimates the cost of building a house, he will often make a detailed list of materials requirements for each wall, kitchen cabinet, plumbing fixture, and so forth along with the estimated labor of each. Understandably, this would provide an estimate one can have a lot more confidence in than one made without specifying these details.

But, when it comes to risks, managers and experts will routinely assess one risk as "very high" and another as "very low" without doing any kind of math. The math regarding probabilities is less intuitive to most people than adding up the cost of a house or the items in a grocery bag. And without deliberate calculations, most people will commit a variety of errors when assessing risks.

First, we have limited ability to recall the relevant experiences we would use to assess a risk. A heuristic that appears to influence our recall of facts is one that Daniel Kahneman named the *peak end rule*: We tend to remember extremes in our experience and not the mundane. As you can imagine, this will have an effect on how we are assessing the odds of various events. When we believe that weather forecasters are bad at assessing the chance of rain tomorrow, is it because we are actually recalling all the times they said there was only a 5% chance of rain and comparing this to the actual number of times it rained on the following day? No, we remember the one time we planned a family reunion at the park when the forecaster said there was only a 5% chance of rain, and it rained. Studies show that when a weather forecaster says there is a 5% chance of rain, it rains only about 5% of the time.[1] But, we remember the exceptions instead of computing the actual averages and this throws off our entire "experience" with the problem.

Even if we don't have to rely on our faulty memory of events, our heuristics seem to cause us to make logical errors in the assessments of probabilities. Here are just a few of the myriad items discovered by Kahneman, Tversky, and others:

- *Misconceptions of chance.* If you flip a coin six times, which result is more likely (H = heads, T = Tails): HHHTTT or HTHTTH? Actually, they are equally likely. But researchers found that most people assume that since the first series looks "less random" than the second, it must be less likely.[2] Kahneman and Tversky cite this as an example of what they call a *representativeness bias*.[3] We appear to judge odds based on what we assume to be representative scenarios. The same research shows that when people are asked to simulate random coin flips, they tend to generate far too many short runs of the same result (e.g., two or three heads in a row) and far too few longer runs (four or more heads in a row). We simply tend to confuse patterns and randomness. In World War II, during the blitz on London, it was believed that bombing patterns were not random because some neighborhoods were hit more often than others. Analysis showed that the distribution of multiple hits in areas of a given size was exactly what we would expect a random bombing pattern to generate.[4]

- *The conjunction fallacy*. When people are offered the opportunity to buy air travel insurance just prior to taking a flight, they are apparently willing to pay more for insurance that covers terrorism than insurance that covers any cause of death due to air travel—including terrorism.[5] Clearly, insurance that covers only terrorism should be worth less than insurance that covers terrorism in addition to several other risks. Perhaps because we can imagine them more clearly, we often see specific events as more likely than broader categories of events.
- *Belief in the "Law of Small Numbers."* Suppose a U.S. pharmaceutical company gets batches of ingredients from two suppliers in a country known to be notoriously underregulated. The U.S. company knows that if one particular batch processing method is used, only 30% of batches will be acceptable. If a more advanced method is used, then 70% should be acceptable. For one supplier, we already had 12 batches, of which 4 were unacceptable. For the newer supplier, we had just 4 batches but all were acceptable. In which supplier should you be more confident that they are using the modern processing method? When we do the math, both have exactly the same probability of using the newer process. But most people will apparently believe they should be more confident in the newer supplier. We will discuss some of this math a little later, but you can find a spreadsheet calculation of this outcome under "reader downloads" at www.howtofixriskmgt.com.

- *Disregarding variance in small samples.* The fact that small samples will have more random variance than large samples tends to be considered less than it should be. Kahneman and Tversky discovered that when subjects are asked to estimate the probability that a randomly selected group of men will have an average height of greater than six feet, subjects gave essentially the same probability whether the group was 1,000 men or 10 men.[6] But a little math shows that the average of the group of 1,000 randomly selected men should fall within a very narrow range compared to the averages of just 10 randomly selected men. In other words, a very small group of men should have a much higher chance of producing a very tall group average or a very short group average.
- *Insensitivity to prior probabilities.* If the doctor told you that a "very reliable" test gave you a positive result for a very rare medical condition, how worried should you be? It depends on how reliable the test is and how rare the condition is. But Kahneman and Tversky found that when people are given specific scenarios, they tend to ignore how rare the condition is in the first place and focus much more on the new information.[7] Suppose, if a person is known to have the condition, the test will return a positive result 99% of the time. Now, suppose the test also gives a negative result 99% of the time when we apply it to a person we know does not have the condition. We also know that only one person in 10,000 has this condition. In this case, the vast majority of positive results would be "false positives." If 10,000 people were tested at random, there would be about 100 false positives while there should be only about one person with the condition.

These miscalculations and our limited ability to recall the relevant data can affect our estimate of risks every time someone asks, "Which of these events is more likely?" If you are giving a subjective judgment of a risk, you should assume your answer is influenced by one or more of the effects listed above. Kahneman and Tversky even showed that otherwise statistically sophisticated experts can make the same errors when asked to provide a subjective estimate.[8] That's the problem with unconscious heuristics and biases in general—if you are not aware of this influence on your thinking, you can't do much about it regardless of your experience and knowledge of statistics in general.

"Catastrophic" Overconfidence

Perhaps one of the most pervasive, exhaustively researched, and thoroughly confirmed phenomena discovered by JDM psychologists is that almost everyone is naturally overconfident in their predictions. For decades, Kahneman, Tversky, Lichtenstein, Fischhoff, and other researchers have been showing that if we ask people for the chance that some prediction they made will come true, they will systematically apply too high a probability of being correct. In short, they are not correct as often as they expect to be.

Of all of the phenomena uncovered by JDM researchers, Danny Kahneman believes overconfidence stands out. "They will underestimate real risk systematically," he told me in a phone call. "The work we did showed the direction of the bias but it is the degree of the bias that is really catastrophic." Danny Kahneman is not one to throw around a word like *catastrophic* casually, but it seems justified by the overwhelming results in every study done in this area.

Overconfidence can be measured using a very simple method. Researchers track how often someone is right about an estimate or forecast and compare that to how often they expected to be right. But one or two forecasts are not enough. If someone says she is 90% confident in a prediction, and she is wrong on the first try, was she overconfident? Not necessarily. That's why we have to ask a large number of questions to be sure.

After asking a subject a large number of questions, researchers compute what the "expected" number correct should be. As I mentioned in Chapter 5, in the world of decision analysis the word *expected* usually means "probability weighted average." If you make 50 predictions, where you are 70% confident in each one, then you are expecting to get 35 of the predictions right.

Try testing yourself. In Exhibit 6.1, state which of the questions are "true" or "false," and then circle the probability that reflects how confident you are in your answer. For example, if you are absolutely certain in your answer, you should say you have a 100% chance of getting the answer right. If you have no idea whatsoever, then your chance should be the same as a coin flip (50%). Otherwise it is one of the values in between 50% and 100%. This is a very small sample, of course. But if you perform like most people, you don't need many samples to see the effect of overconfidence.

Again, this is a very small sample of questions, but you get the idea. (You can check the answers at the end of the chapter.) If you were asked a large number of such questions, and if you are like most people, you wouldn't do

EXHIBIT 6.1 **SAMPLE CALIBRATION TEST WITH TRUE/FALSE TRIVIA QUESTIONS**

	Statement	Answer (True or False)	Confidence that You Are Correct (Circle One)
1	The ancient Romans were conquered by the ancient Greeks.		50% 60% 70% 80% 90% 100%
2	There is no species of three-humped camel.		50% 60% 70% 80% 90% 100%
3	A gallon of oil weighs less than a gallon of water.		50% 60% 70% 80% 90% 100%
4	Mars is always further away from Earth than Venus.		50% 60% 70% 80% 90% 100%
5	The Boston Red Sox won the first World Series.		50% 60% 70% 80% 90% 100%
6	Napoleon was born on the island of Corsica.		50% 60% 70% 80% 90% 100%
7	*M* is one of the three most commonly used letters.		50% 60% 70% 80% 90% 100%
8	In 2002, the price of the average new desktop computer purchased was under $1,500.		50% 60% 70% 80% 90% 100%
9	Lyndon B. Johnson was a governor before becoming vice president.		50% 60% 70% 80% 90% 100%
10	A kilogram is more than a pound.		50% 60% 70% 80% 90% 100%

very well. When most people say they have a given chance of being right about a forecast, they will be right much less often than that chance would indicate. For example, if a manager says there is a 90% chance that some prediction he makes will come true (e.g., "The project will not fail," "We will finish by January," or "Sales will increase next quarter"), and he has done so for each of a large number of predictions, we will find that he will be right much less often than 90% of the time.

The good news is that with practice and with some other relatively simple techniques (we'll discuss more later) a person can get fairly good at this. A person who is good at assessing subjective odds in this way is called *calibrated*. Most of the rest of the world is *uncalibrated*. In Exhibit 6.2, I combined the results of several published calibration studies along with my own client projects into one chart. The authors of the published studies

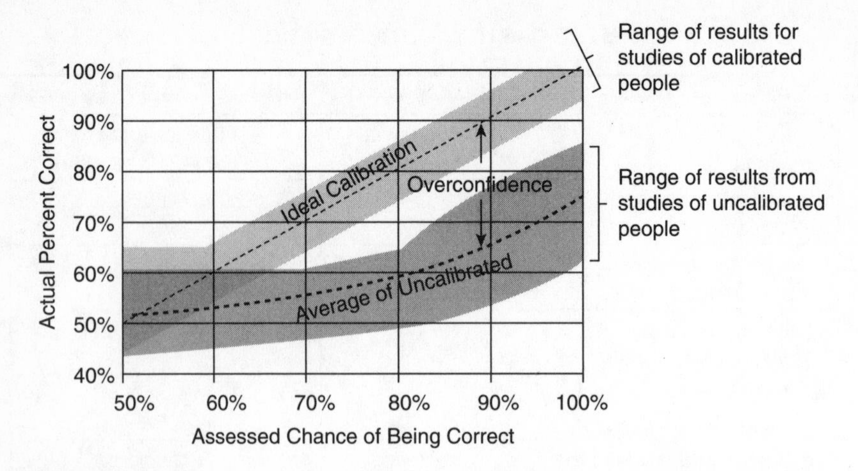

EXHIBIT 6.2 **Comparison of Uncalibrated and Calibrated Individuals**

included Sarah Lichtenstein and Baruch Fischhoff, as well as other researchers. Including my own client data, I show the results of 11 studies using uncalibrated groups of people and 5 studies using calibrated groups.

The results of all of these combined studies are striking. Here we see that when uncalibrated people say they are 90% confident in an answer they gave, the average of the studies show that they are closer to having a 66% chance of being right. When they say they are 95% sure, they have a 70% chance of being right. So, if a procurement officer says he or she is 95% confident that that the bankruptcy of a vendor won't cause a supply chain disruption, or if an IT security specialist says there is a 90% probability there will be no hacker attacks this year, overconfidence needs to be considered.

The other finding shown in the chart is encouraging. Calibration training seems to have a significant effect on the ability of individuals to subjectively assess odds. Unfortunately, the vast majority of risk assessment methods practiced make no use of this training.

Calibration may be especially important when dealing with rare, catastrophic risks. When managers say there is a 5% chance that an overseas client will default on the payment for a major order, they are saying there is a 95% probability that they won't default. Here, a difference of a few percentage points may be critical. A 1% chance of default may be acceptable and a 10% chance may be far too risky. How fine-tuned a manager's calibration is starts to make a big difference in these situations.

The overconfidence phenomenon also appears when we ask experts about range estimates. Suppose I asked you for an estimate of what the Dow Jones will be at close of business tomorrow. Of course, you don't know the actual number, but you can put a wide range on it. Let's say you make the range wide enough that you believe there is a 90% chance the actual index at the close of trading on the NYSE tomorrow will be within your upper and lower bounds. That means you give me two numbers: one that is so low that you think there is only a 5% chance the real number will be below it and another number that is so high that you think there is only a 5% chance the real number will be above it.

Try another calibration test to see how well you do with ranges. For Exhibit 6.3, provide both an upper bound and a lower bound. Remember that the range should be wide enough that you believe there is a 90% chance that the answer will be between your bounds. When you are finished, you can check your answers at the end of the chapter.

I have given tests such as this to hundreds of people over the years. Each time, I find that, instead of getting 90% of the answers between their upper and lower bounds, about 30% to 50% of the answers will be within their upper and lower bounds. Other studies consistently find that even when subjects are asked for *99%* confidence intervals, they get only about 60% of the answers between their upper and lower bounds. That means they were "surprised" about 40% of the time when they should have expected answers to be outside of their bounds only about 1% of the time.

Most people will do much worse on this test than the prior true/false test (by chance alone, you should have got about half right in the first test, but you can easily get all of the range questions wrong). My experience shows that calibration training for ranges is more challenging for most people, but, again, training is shown to make a significant improvement in the ability of experts to provide ranges.

As much as we need to rely on experts for knowledge in their particular field, chances are they are not experts in assessing likelihoods. Assessing probabilities—or getting other people to provide probabilities—turns out to be a special kind of expertise in itself.

Here is a key lesson so far: *The detection of overconfidence is only possible if probabilities are used and compared to real performance of correctly estimating outcomes.* How would we know whether someone is overconfident when he

EXHIBIT 6.3 SAMPLE CALIBRATION TEST WITH 90% CONFIDENCE INTERVAL* QUESTIONS

		90% Confidence Interval	
	Question	**Lower Bound**	**Upper Bound**
1	In 1938, a British steam locomotive set a new speed record by going how fast (mph)?		
2	In what year did Sir Isaac Newton publish the Universal Laws of Gravitation?		
3	How many inches long is a typical business card?		
4	The Internet (then called "Arpanet") was established as a military communications system in what year?		
5	What year was William Shakespeare born?		
6	What is the air distance between New York and Los Angeles in miles?		
7	What percentage of a square could be covered by a circle of the same width?		
8	How old was Charlie Chaplin when he died?		
9	How many days does it actually take the Moon to orbit Earth?		
10	The TV show *Gilligan's Island* first aired on what date?		

**Note on Confidence Intervals (CIs):* I am using the term *confidence interval* to mean a range with a stated probability of containing an answer. That is, a 90% CI has a 90% chance of containing the answer within its upper and lower bounds. *CI* is the same term used in statistics when computing errors around some estimate based on samples from a population. I use the same term for both. Some statisticians—not a clear majority—argue that the 90% CI doesn't really mean there is a 90% probability the answer is within the range. I will argue later that this is a flawed distinction.

tells us there is a "medium" likelihood of a particular event happening? If the event happens 50% of the time, is that right? If we look at all the times he said the risk of a project failure was a "2" and 12 out of 40 projects with the same risk score failed, was he right? Ambiguous terms like this can't be evaluated against real-world observations because, as measurements, they are meaningless. The good news is that experts *can* learn to adjust for effects like overconfidence. There is no reason to ever use anything else. If experts can be taught to assess probabilities quantitatively, then that's how we should ask for their input.

The Mind of "Aces": Possible Causes and Consequences of Overconfidence

Unless managers take steps to offset overconfidence in assessments of probabilities, they will consistently underestimate various risks (i.e., they will be more confident than they should be that some disaster won't occur). This may have had some bearing on very-high-profile disasters such as those of the Space Shuttle Orbiters *Challenger* and *Columbia*.

The Nobel Prize–winning physicist, Richard Feynman, was asked to participate in the investigation of the first Space Shuttle accident (involving *Challenger*). What he found was some risk assessments that seemed at first glance to be obviously optimistic. He noted the following in the *Rogers Commission Report on the Space Shuttle* Challenger *Accident*:

> It appears that there are enormous differences of opinion as to the probability of a failure with loss of vehicle and of human life. The estimates range from roughly 1 in 100 to 1 in 100,000. The higher figures [1 in 100] come from the working engineers, and the very low figures [1 in 100,000] from management. What are the causes and consequences of this lack of agreement? Since 1 part in 100,000 would imply that one could put a Shuttle up each day for 300 years expecting to lose only one, we could properly ask "What is the cause of management's fantastic faith in the machinery?"[9]

Feynman believed that if management decisions to launch were based on such an extraordinary confidence in the Shuttle, then these decisions were flawed. As was Feynman's frequent practice, he applied simple tests and reality checks that would cast doubt on these claims.

Perhaps an obvious explanation is the conflict of interest. Are managers really incentivized to be honest with themselves and others about these risks? No doubt, that is a factor just as it was probably a factor in the assessments of risks taken by bank managers in 2008, whether or not it was consciously considered. However, individuals showed overconfidence even in situations where they had no stake in the outcome (trivia tests, etc.).

JDM research has shown that both the incentives and the amount of effort put into identifying possible surprises will make a difference in overconfidence.[10] Some of the sources of overconfidence would affect not only managers who depend on subjective estimates, but even those who believe they are using sound analysis of historical data. Managers will fail to consider ways in which human errors affect systems and will fail to consider common mode and cascade system failures.[11]

There may also a tendency to relax our concerns for infrequent but catastrophic events when some time passes without experiencing the event. Robin Dillon-Merrill, a decision and risk analysis professor at Georgetown University, noticed this tendency when she was studying the risk perceptions of NASA engineers prior to the *Columbia* accident. *The* Columbia *Accident Investigation Report* noted the following:

> The shedding of External Tank foam—the physical cause of the Columbia accident—had a long history. Damage caused by debris has occurred on every Space Shuttle flight, and most missions have had insulating foam shed during ascent. This raises an obvious question: Why did NASA continue flying the Shuttle with a known problem that violated design requirements?[12]

Dillon-Merrill considers each time that foam fell off the external tank of the Shuttle, but where the Shuttle still had a successful mission, to be a "near miss." Her proposal was that near misses are an opportunity to learn that is rarely exploited. She interviewed NASA staff and contractors about how they judged near misses and found two very interesting phenomena that in my opinion have important implications for risk management in general.

Perhaps not surprisingly, she found that near misses and successes were both judged much more favorably than failures. But were these near-miss events being rated more like a failure than a mission success? Did engineers take each near miss as a red-flag warning about an impending problem? Incredibly, just the opposite occurred. When she compared people who did not have near-miss information to people who had near-miss information, people with the near-miss information were *more* likely to choose a risky alternative.[13]

People with near-miss information were *more* likely to choose a risky alternative than people who did not have information about near misses.

Were managers looking at each near miss and thinking that because nothing had happened yet, perhaps the system was more robust than they thought? It might be more subtle than that. Dillon-Merrill found that when people have a known exposure to some relatively unlikely risk, their tolerance for that risk seems to increase even though they may not be changing their estimate of the probability of the risk.

Imagine that you are in an area exposed to hurricane risks. Authorities confirm that there is a 3% chance of injury or death each time you do not evacuate when ordered to for a hurricane warning. If you happen to make it through two or three hurricanes without harm, you will become more tolerant of that risk. Note that you are not actually changing your estimate of the probability of the harm (that was provided by authorities); you are simply becoming more numb to the risk as it is.

Now imagine the implications of this for Wall Street. If they have a few good years, everyone will start to become more "risk tolerant" even if they are not changing their underlying forecasts about the probabilities of a financial crisis. After mortgage uncertainty has settled for a decade or so, will all managers, again, start to become more tolerant of risks?

There are other effects to consider when examining the psyche of upper-level decision makers. Part of overestimating past performance is due to the tendency to underestimate how much we learned in the last big surprise. This is what Slovic and Fischhoff called the "I-knew-it-all-along" phenomenon. People will exaggerate how "inevitable" the event would have appeared before the event occurred. (News pundits talking about the mortgage crisis certainly make it sound as if it were "inevitable," but where were they before the crisis occurred?)

They even remember their previous predictions in such a way that they, as Slovie put it, "exaggerate in hindsight what they knew in foresight." I hear the "I-saw-that-coming" claim so often that, if the claims were true, there would be virtually no surprises anywhere in the world. Two lines of dialog in the movie *Wall Street* revealed Oliver Stone's grasp of this phenomenon. After "Bud" (Charlie Sheen's character) had his initial big successes as a broker, his boss said, "The minute I laid eyes on you, I knew you had what it took." Later, when Bud was being arrested in the office for the crimes he committed to get those early successes, the same boss said, "The minute I laid eyes on you, I knew you were no good." Kahneman sums it up:

> . . . when they have made a decision, people don't even keep track of having made the decision or forecast. I mean, the thing that is absolutely the most striking is how seldom people change their minds. First, we're not aware of changing our minds even when we do change our minds. And most people, after they change their minds, reconstruct their past opinion—they believe they *always* thought that.[14]

There is one other item about overconfidence that might be more unique to upper management or particularly successful traders. Some managers can point to an impressive track record of successes as evidence that a high level of confidence on virtually all matters is entirely justified on their part. Surely, if a portfolio manager can claim she had above-average market returns for five years, she must have some particularly useful insight in the market. An IT security manager who has presided over a virus-free, hacker-free environment much longer than his peers in other companies must have great skill, right?

Actually, luck can have more to do with success than we might be inclined to think. For example, a recent statistical analysis of World War I aces showed that Baron von Richthofen (aka "The Red Baron") might have been lucky but not necessarily skilled.[15] Two electrical engineering professors, Mikhail Simkin and Vwani Roychowdhury of the University of California at Los Angeles, examined the victories and losses for the 2,894 fighter pilots who flew for Germany. Together, they tallied 6,759 victories and 810 defeats. This is perhaps a suspiciously high win ratio already, but they showed that this still proves their point. They showed that, given the number of pilots and the win ratio, there was about a 30% chance that, by luck alone, one pilot would have got 80 kills, the number Manfred von Richthofen is credited for.

This might describe a large number of "successful" executives who write popular books on the special insight they brought to the table, but who then sometimes find they are unable to repeat their success. Given the large number of candidates who spend their careers competing for a small number of upper-management positions, it is likely that some will have a string of successes just by chance alone. No doubt, some of these will be more likely to hold upper-management positions. In the same manner, some will also have a string of successes in a coin-flipping tournament where there are a large number of initial players. But we know that the winners of this kind of contest are not just better coin-flippers. Sure, there is probably some skill in reaching upper management. But how much of it was more like winning a coin-flipping contest?

Inconsistencies and Artifacts: What Shouldn't Matter Does

No matter how much experience we accumulate and no matter how intelligent we are, we seem to be very inconsistent in our estimates and opinions. Often, our estimates of things change for random, unknown reasons. Other times, researchers know what causes a change in our estimates but it may be for reasons that should not have any logical bearing on what we think.

In 1955, a 52-year-old psychologist was building statistical models of how people made estimates and he found out how large the effects of our inconsistency really were.[16] Egon Brunswik was a troubled and tense professor of psychology at UC Berkley who challenged conventions in psychology. He promoted *probabilistic functionalism*, the idea that the psychology of organisms cannot be examined independent of uncertainties about their environments. He also developed innovative empirical methods and used the value of statistical descriptions of these thought processes, which included multiple variables. Brunswik would find that the models he created to describe certain human estimations were actually better at the estimates than the humans.

Brunswik's model is not difficult to test in almost any field. Suppose you are a loan officer at a bank and you are given a list of businesses, some information about each of them, and the size of loans they requested. The given information would include a general business category (e.g., manufacturing, retail, service, or other), the previous two years' revenue, the previous two years' profits, and current debt ratio. Suppose that based on that information alone you are asked to determine whether they would mostly likely default on the loan, be delinquent but not default, or pay back the loan on time.

Using Brunswik's approach, we would then perform what is called a *multivariate regression* to build a formula that approximates your judgments. Then when we compared the formula's predictions to your predictions, we would find that the formula was consistently better than you at predicting loan defaults. Remember, this formula was based *only* on your subjective judgments, not on an actual history of business loan defaults. If it were based on actual histories, chances are it would perform even better. Still, the observed improvement just by using Brunswik's so-called "Lens" method tells us something about human estimation skills. The key benefit of the formula was consistency. Experts had some good heuristics, but apparently could not apply them uniformely.

Brunswik's ideas were controversial for his time. He challenged methods developed by those whose names would eventually become much more well-known and respected than his own (R.A. Fischer, Karl Pearson, and others). This may have been the cause of his long struggle with hypertension and his eventual suicide just two months after publishing his final paper on the topic. So often, the tragedy of suicide is that better days would have come if he had chosen to live long enough to see them.

Since the 1990s, researchers have rediscovered Brunswik's works, hundreds of papers have cited him for his innovations, and "The Brunswik Society" meets annually to foster collaboration among researchers, who are still studying his methods.

In 1996, I started using Brunswik's Lens Method as a way to evaluate risks for a large number of information technology investments. Software development projects are known for high failure rates for a variety of reasons. Users may reject the new technology, rendering it shelfware. Projects to develop and implement the technology can be greatly delayed. Some software projects are canceled before any use is ever made of them.

I gave clients lists of hypothetical IT projects for which they would assess the probability of failure to be finished on time and on budget. For each project, I listed the projected cost and duration of the project, the department the project was meant to support, the level of the project sponsor (VP, director, etc.), whether it was a technology and vendor they had used before, and a few other facts the clients believed might tell them something about failure rates. This data was shown to them as a large spreadsheet table where each row was a project and each column was a particular data field (sponsor, projected costs, etc.). The list contained 40 hypothetical projects for them to review and for which to assess failure probabilities.

Unknown to the clients, I had duplicated two of the projects in the list so that the two projects each appeared twice in the list (two pairs). It took them 40 to 60 minutes to finish evaluating the list and by the time they got down to the 38th project on the list, they forgot that they had already

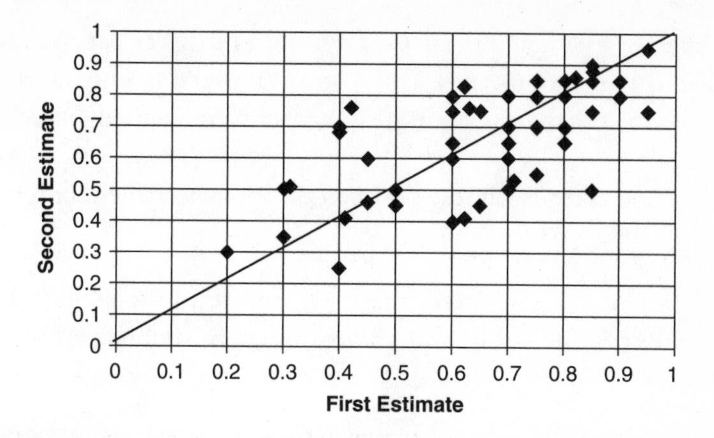

EXHIBIT 6.4 **Agreement between First and Second Estimates of IT Project Failure Probabilities**

evaluated an identical project earlier in the list. I plotted their first estimate and their second estimate for the same project on the chart in Exhibit 6.4.

What we see is that the second estimate was usually more than 10 percentage points different from the first estimate. Only 22% actually gave the same answer each time. In extreme instances, the second and first estimates differed by as much as 35%. (Note the point on the right of the chart, below the line, where the first estimate was .85 and the second was .5).

As we would expect, when I apply Brunswik's method, this inconsistency completely disappears. The formula produces an answer based only on the inputs and when the inputs are identical, the answers are identical. Like overconfidence, inconsistency is an error that can be completely removed.

But some inconsistencies may not be entirely random—they may be due to factors that should have no influence on our judgments, and yet do. Just such an effect appears in what Kahneman and Tversky called *framing*. The way that people are asked a question affects how they answer it. Like most other discoveries in JDM psychology, this should seem like common sense. But if it were common sense, why do none of the risk management methodologies mentioned earlier appear to take any steps to account for this?

Here is an example of framing in one of the experiments conducted by Kahneman and Tversky. In 1981, Kahneman and Tversky asked survey participants to choose between two treatment programs to try to help 600 people infected by a new and virulent disease. The survey participants were divided into two groups and each group was asked essentially the same questions as the other group, but the questions were worded differently.

Group 1 was asked to choose between these two treatment programs:

1. If program A is adopted, 200 people will be saved.
2. If program B is adopted, there is a one-third probability that 600 people will be saved, and a two-thirds probability that no people will be saved.

Group 2 was asked to choose between these two treatment programs:

1. If program A is adopted, 400 people will die.
2. If program B is adopted, there is a one-third probability that nobody will die, and a two-thirds probability that 600 people will die.

Note that program A in group 1 is identical to program A in group 2 (of the 600, 200 will be saved and 400 will die). Program B in each group is also just a different wording of the same option. In group 1, 72% of participants preferred program A. In the second group, 78% preferred program B.

Professional survey developers, of course, try to take great care to make sure that they don't inadvertently bias their findings by the arbitrary ways they happen to ask a question. Some of the things that seem to affect the responses of survey participants are so subtle that it takes some serious analysis to try to avoid it. When a study produces a response that is more of an effect of the survey method itself than the thing being studied, researchers call that an *artifact* of the study. For example, if the order of questions in a survey affects responses to the survey (which it apparently can), then survey designers have to build in controls to counter it—like giving different participants the same questions in a different order.

In any formal risk assessment approach, how much of the outcome is a mere artifact of the method of questioning, and how much is real? How much of the answers of the experts and managers were a function of overconfidence, logical errors, and random inconsistencies? Such questions have never been considered in most of the major best practice risk management methods. But it would seem highly unlikely that something makes these risk assessment tools particularly immune to these effects. There seems to be no way to conduct legitimate risk management practices without considering the psychology of risk and uncertainty.

Answers to Calibration Tests

These are the answers to the calibration questions earlier in this chapter. For additional practice, there are more calibration tests and answers in the Appendix.

Answers to Exhibit 6.1:

1. False
2. True
3. True
4. False
5. True
6. True
7. False
8. True
9. False
10. True

Answers to Exhibit 6.3:

1. 126 mph
2. 1687
3. 3.5 in
4. 1969
5. 1564
6. 2,451 miles
7. 78.5%
8. 88 years
9. 27.32 days
10. September 26, 1964

NOTES

1. A.H. Murphy and R. L. Winker, "Can Weather Forecasters Formulate Reliable Probability Forecasts of Precipitation and Temperature?," *National Weather Digest* 2, 1977, 2–9.
2. D. Kahneman and A. Tversky, "Subjective Probability: A Judgment of Representativeness," *Cognitive Psychology* 3, 1972, 430–454.
3. G.S. Tune, "Response Preferences: A Review of Some Relevant Literature," *Psychological Bulletin* 61, 1964, 286–302.
4. W. Feller, *An Introduction to Probability Theory and Its Applications* (New York: Wiley, 1968), p. 160.
5. E. Johnson, "Framing, Probability Distortions and Insurance Decisions," *Journal of Risk and Uncertainty* 7, 1993, 35.
6. D. Kahneman and A. Tversky, "Subjective Probability: A Judgment of Representativeness," *Cognitive Psychology* 4, 1972, 430–454.
7. D. Kahneman and A. Tversky, "On the Psychology of Prediction," *Psychological Review* 80, 1973, 237–251.
8. A. Tversky and D. Kahneman, "The Belief in the 'Law of Small Numbers,'" *Psychological Bulletin*, 1971.
9. R. Feynman, "Personal Observations on the Reliability of the Shuttle," Appendix IIF. In: Rogers, et al., 1986.
10. A. Koriat, S. Lichtenstein, and B. Fischhoff, "Reasons for Confidence," *Journal of Experimental Psychology: Human Learning and Memory* 6, 1980, 107–118.
11. P. Slovic, B. Fischhoff, S. Lichtenstein, "Societal Risk Assessment: How Safe Is Safe Enough?," 1980.
12. *The* Columbia *Accident Investigation Board Report*, Vol. I, p. 121.
13. R. Dillon and C. Tinsley, "How Near-Misses Influence Decision Making under Risk: A Missed Opportunity for Learning," *Management Science*, January 2008.
14. "Daniel Kahneman: The Thought Leader Interview," M. Schrage, www.strategy-business.com/press/article/03409?tid=230&pg=all 31.12.2003.
15. M. Simkin and V. Roychowdhury, "Theory of Aces: Fame by Chance or Merit?," *Journal of Mathematical Sociology* 30(1), 2006, 33–42.
16. E. Brunswik, "Representative Design and Probabilistic Theory in a Functional Psychology," *Psychological Review* 62, 1955, 193–217.

CHAPTER 7

Worse Than Useless: The Most Popular Risk Assessment Method and Why It Doesn't Work

Many are stubborn in pursuit of the path they have chosen, few in pursuit of the goal.

—FREDERICK NIETZSCHE

First, do no harm.

—AUGUSTE FRANÇOIS CHOMEL

Contrary to popular belief, the phrase, "First, do no harm," is not actually part of the Hippocratic Oath taken by physicians, although it is still a basic principle of medicine. The developers of the most popular risk management and decision analysis methods should also make this their most important principle. But because their efforts to develop these methods are often undertaken by practitioners isolated from the decades of academic research in decision-making and risk, this principle is routinely violated.

As I mentioned earlier, risk management is not just about reacting to the most recent disaster (which was, at the time I was writing this book, the

2008/9 financial crisis). If it were, the failures on which I would focus this entire book would be only the errors in the use of complex mathematical models in finance. We will discuss those, too, but not to the exclusion of some significant risks being assessed with some very different methods. Let's stay focused on the idea that risk management is supposed to be about all those disasters that haven't happened yet.

If you are one of the first three of the "Four Horsemen" of Risk Management discussed in Chapter 4, then you might not be at all familiar with some of the most popular risk management methods promoted by management consultants and international standards organizations. These methods often rely on some sort of "score" and they come in a variety of flavors. They are easy to create and to use and, therefore, they have a large and rapidly growing body of users.

These simple scoring methods are used to assess risk in terrorism, engineering disasters, and a range of business decisions. In certain issues, including information technology (IT) portfolio management or IT security, scoring methods are the majority of "structured" methods practiced. Scoring methods are used for almost any problem where promoters of scoring methods think scientific and quantitative solutions to risk management are impractical or impossible—which, as it turns out, covers many areas.

Unfortunately, any perceived benefit of this approach may be mostly a placebo effect. Even worse, the method itself may violate the "First, do no harm" principle of decision analysis by adding its own sources of error and making the decision worse than it would have been. Dr. Tony Cox, who holds a PhD in risk analysis from MIT, has researched these methods probably more than anyone else and has concluded that they are often "worse than useless." (We'll get back to him).

A Basic Course in Scoring Methods (Actually, It's an Advanced Course, Too—There's Not Much to Know)

As I mentioned before, scoring methods are easy to make, and require no special training or even any prior research. Anyone can develop his or her own scoring method for just about anything.

Almost all of them use some sort of simple *ordinal* scale—that is, a scale that indicates a relative order of what is being assessed, not actual units of measure. The ordinal scale that risk assessment scoring systems use might be a 1-to-5-point system or simply a high/medium/low rating system.

"Star" ratings used by film critics provide an ordinal scale in that they indicate rank order but not actual magnitudes. Two stars are simply better than one star, but not exactly twice as good. Therefore, as a rule, it's generally not a good idea to treat ordinal scales as you would measures of distance or mass. They don't really add or multiply like other measures. Four one-gallon containers of gasoline will pour exactly into one four-gallon gasoline tank, but Roger Ebert knows he would much rather watch one four-star movie than four one-star movies. Still, almost all scoring systems used in risk assessments add and multiply values on ordinal scales as if they were adding the prices of items in a grocery cart or computing an area by multiplying length and width.

There are a large number of specific scoring methods, but they all can be grouped into two broad categories: the additive *weighted scores* and the multiplicative *risk matrices*. Weighted scores may include several ordinal scales for items that are meant to be indicators of risk that are generally added up in some way to produce an aggregate score. Risk matrices, on the other hand, generally use just two ordinal scales (e.g., likelihood and impact), or three (e.g., threat, vulnerability, consequence), which are then multiplied together to get an aggregate score.

A simple example of an additive weighted score might be used in evaluating accounts receivable risk of corporate customers for large orders. That is, you might do a lot of billable work and ship a lot of goods, but, after the customer is invoiced, the customer can't or won't pay the bill. If you are evaluating the risks related to doing business with customers in developing countries, you could simply list several relevant factors, such as "currency risk," "political risk," "credit risk," and so on. These are normally perfectly reasonable factors to consider, but, here they are not defined in the probabilistic terms described in Chapter 6. Instead, they are reduced to an arbitrary ordinal scale such as a scale of 1 to 5. Each of the several risk factors would then be evaluated as a *1* or *2* or whatever value seems appropriate.

Currency risk might be considered to be fairly high, so the managers or their advisors might score it a *4*. Perhaps political risk (the possibility of interference by the government, civil conflict, etc.) is thought to be low, so it rates a *1* on this scale. But the order is large, so the order size risk gets a *5*. Continue for the remainder of the several risk factors. When finished, simply add the scores. Or, if you want to get a little fancier, choose a "weight" (e.g., .2, .6, .9, etc.) for each factor, so that you can make some factors more influential than others. When the weighted scores are added up, you might get an answer like a risk score of 22.5 or 39.1. Then, these values are usually compared to some table that gives general recommendations depending on the score. For example, the table might say "0–10: Low risk, proceed with the deal" and "40–50: Extreme risk, reconsider the size and conditions of the deal and/or offset risk with insurance." You get the idea.

In this version, the weighted score uses multiple independent scales. More than one alternative can be given a score of *2* on a given factor. One variation I've seen on additive weighted scores is where each factor among several alternatives is ranked from best to worst and the rank orders are used in the aggregation formula. In other words, one alternative is ranked *1* on a factor such as "cost," one is ranked *2*, and so on, for however many alternatives are considered.

The additive weighted score variety is used in prioritizing major project portfolios, evaluating new business ventures, and even for important public policy issues. Some use this for evaluating IT security or IT portfolios and it is used to determine funding priorities for toxic waste clean-ups. Another such weighted scoring method was actually developed by the U.S. Department of Health and Human Services as the basis for vaccine allocation in the case of a pandemic flu outbreak.[1] The U.S. Army developed an additive weighted score called "Composite Risk Management" for evaluating the risk of military operations.

The risk matrix approach (the kind that multiplies likelihood and impact) might be even more widespread. It certainly seems to get more attention from various international standards organizations. One example of this is the method developed by the National Institute of Standards & Technology (NIST) in a standard called *The Risk Management Guide for Information Technology Systems*[2] (NIST 800-30), as shown in Exhibits 7.1 and 7.2.

According to the procedure NIST describes, each of these is converted to points. For likelihood, *low*, *medium*, and *high* are converted to 0.1, .5 and 1.0, respectively. The impact is converted to a scale of 10, 50, 100. The product of these two produces another score, which is itself converted back to another and final low/medium/high scale. This final result is the "risk scale."

EXHIBIT 7.1 **LIKELIHOOD SCALE PROPOSED BY THE NATIONAL INSTITUTE FOR STANDARDS & TECHNOLOGY FOR IT SECURITY THREATS**

Likelihood	Likelihood Definition
High	The threat-source is highly motivated and sufficiently capable, and controls to prevent the vulnerability from being exercised are ineffective.
Medium	The threat-source is motivated and capable, but controls are in place that may impede successful exercise of the vulnerability.
Low	The threat-source lacks motivation or capability, or controls are in place to prevent, or at least significantly impede, the vulnerability from being exercised.

SOURCE: NIST 800-30, Table 3-4, p. 21.

EXHIBIT 7.2 **IMPACT SCALE PROPOSED BY THE NATIONAL INSTITUTE FOR STANDARDS & TECHNOLOGY FOR IT SECURITY THREATS**

Magnitude of Impact	Impact Definition
High	Exercise of the vulnerability (1) may result in the highly costly loss of major tangible assets or resources; (2) may significantly violate, harm, or impede an organization's mission, reputation, or interest; or (3) may result in human death or serious injury.
Medium	Exercise of the vulnerability (1) may result in the costly loss of tangible assets or resources; (2) may violate, harm, or impede an organization's mission, reputation, or interest; or (3) may result in human injury.
Low	Exercise of the vulnerability (1) may result in the loss of some tangible assets or resources or (2) may noticeably affect an organization's mission, reputation, or interest.

SOURCE: NIST 800-30, Table 3-5, p. 25.

This is actually the official position of the National Institute of Standards & Technology on measuring risk for IT security, and it is not fundamentally different from the methods developed by the standards of CobIT, *PMBoK* (mentioned in Chapter 4), or the major consulting firms. (In fact, the latter are frequently used as advisors on all of the standards development teams.) Sometimes these are called "5-by-5's" or "heat maps" (the latter name comes from color-coding methods that make the matrix look like a thermal image, with high risks shown in red and low ones in green).

Another variety of the multiplicative risk matrix uses three risk components: *threat*, *vulnerability*, and *consequence*. This is the basis of the model used by the Department of Homeland Security to evaluate terrorism threats. Like the other scoring methods, this method requires individuals to choose a score from an ordinal scale. But now they evaluate three items with each identified risk. Usually, the scores for threat, vulnerability, and consequence are simply multiplied together to get an overall "risk score" for each potential risk scenario.

Together, these ordinal scoring methods are the benchmark for the analysis of risks and/or decisions in at least some component of most large organizations. Thousands of people have been certified in methods based in part on computing risk scores like this. The major management consulting firms have influenced virtually all of these standards. Since what these standards all have in common is the use of various scoring schemes instead of actual quantitative risk analysis methods, I will call them collectively the "scoring methods." And all of them, without exception, are borderline or worthless. In practice, they may make many decisions *far* worse than they would have been using merely unaided judgments.

Scoring methods are virtually always developed in isolation from scientific methods in risk analysis and decision analysis. The developers in these areas tend to be experts in some particular problem domain, such as IT security or public health, but they are virtually never experts in risk analysis and decision analysis methods. There is no empirical evidence that these methods improve decisions at all. In fact, even considering the question of whether decisions are measurably improved seems to be completely absent from every one of the scoring methods I mentioned. The problems boil down to the following three main points.

Problems with the Scoring Methods

1. Since they are usually developed in isolation from research in this area, not one of these scoring methods considers the issues about perception of risks and uncertainties discussed in Chapter 6.
2. The qualitative descriptions of likelihood are understood and used very differently by different people, even when deliberate steps are taken to standardize the meanings.

3. The scoring schemes themselves add their own sources of error as a result of unintended consequences of their structure.

The first point is a failure to remove or address in any way a known existing source of error in subjective judgment of uncertainty. Not one scoring method even seems to be remotely aware of these phenomena—phenomena that should have profound bearing on any method that attempts to use subjective judgments in the analysis of risks. The fact that the people who are required to use these scoring methods are both extremely overconfident and inconsistent in their answers was not considered in the design of these methods. Since I addressed this previously, I won't elaborate further in this chapter.

The next two points are not just failure to remove error, they are sources of error on their own. The unnecessary introduction of ambiguity and other unintended consequences of ordinal scales detract from the quality of analysis so much that managers are often better off without it. That's exactly what caused Dr. Cox to call these methods "worse than useless" and even "worse than random."

Does That Come in "Medium"?: Why Ambiguity Does Not Offset Uncertainty

More than once, I've heard risk experts or managers comment that quantitative probabilities were too "precise" and that they lacked the knowledge to provide such precision. The default alternative is often to use some sort of scale of verbal expressions of likelihood, impact, or other factors. The use of these scales is based on certain assumptions about the users of the method and the nature of probabilities.

The following are misconceptions that are sometimes behind the arguments in favor of scoring methods:

- *Probabilities confuse managers.* I think it is quite possible that, instead, many risk consultants are confused about how to explain probabilities. The fact is that research in the calibration of probabilities (as explained in Chapter 6) indicates that most people are perfectly able to learn to comprehend and use unambiguous probabilities for forecasts that actually compare well with observed outcomes. Every manager I've trained to use explicit probabilities understands them very well and, furthermore, they overwhelmingly appreciate the clarity of the approach. Management decisions are made under a state of uncertainty, and speaking the language of probabilities is as basic to management as understanding "discounted cash flow" or "internal rate of return."

- *Verbal scales alleviate a lack of knowledge.* Many risk consultants and managers will say they don't have sufficient knowledge to use precise probabilities. First, the use of the term *precise* in probabilities seems to miss a fundamental point about probabilities. Probabilities are used to express uncertainty. This is especially important when one has a *lot* of uncertainty (the opposite of precision and accuracy). Furthermore, the use of these scales doesn't in any way alleviate the fact that one lacks much knowledge about the problem. If you adopt simple scales such as this, *you still lack as much knowledge as you did before.* So what is different? The only difference is the decreased clarity with which you view the problem.

Regarding this last point, I recently explained to another risk consultant that using verbal scales because we lack much knowledge is sort of like looking at our aging faces through a frosted lens. The wrinkles are still there, they just don't look as bad when the picture is blurred. Now imagine that you were considering the design of a suspension bridge. Suppose the bridge design has lots of engineering mistakes. In fact, when we look closely at the details, we determine that it is unlikely to stand on its own. Now look at the bridge design through a frosted lens. Those little flaws disappear and we may well convince ourselves that this is a fine bridge design. The "frosted lens" of simple scoring methods in no way alleviates the fundamental problem of limited information. It just makes you less aware of it.

Simple scoring methods in no way alleviate the fundamental problem of limited information. But the added ambiguity makes you less aware of it.

Let me add to the previous comment on what *precision* means in the context of a probability. Since probabilities are expressed as quantities, many people will confuse some of the characteristics of other quantified values with those of probabilities. If I state that someone is 187.36 centimeters tall, I've communicated a sense of precise knowledge I have about that fact. Certainly, I would not have given you that answer if I thought I could be off by 5 centimeters in my estimate. I might instead have said, "That person is about 190 cm tall."

But what am I saying about my confidence in an event if I say I would put a 37% probability on the occurrence of some uncertain event? Does this imply a sense of precision, as it would about other quantities? Not really; probabilities are used to convey our uncertainty about some other aspect of the world. If I say I have no idea whether it might rain tomorrow, I might say there is a 50% chance of rain tomorrow. Have I conveyed a high degree of precision in my probability by using the exact quantity of 50%? No; I communicated just the opposite. What I have conveyed is a high degree of uncertainty about tomorrow's weather. In fact, it's not possible for my uncertainty to be any higher about it.

If I had exact knowledge about the event, I wouldn't need probabilities at all. The event will occur or it will not. The probability is used to convey our uncertainty about the event, which is especially important when uncertainty is high. Similarly, when project managers are asked for a range of possible values for an uncertain quantity, like the cost to a construction project if a steelworkers' strike occurs at an inopportune time, they may resist by saying they can't know the *exact* range. But what they don't know exactly is the cost to the project. The range simply expresses how much uncertainty they have about it.

Several times in our careers, Sam Savage (The Stanford professor I introduced in Chapter 4) and I have run into people with profound confusions about this concept. Sam tells me of one manager being asked to estimate a project cost who said, "How can I tell you my 90% confidence interval of the cost if I don't even know the actual cost?" I've heard a graduate student at the London School of Economics say, "How can I give you a probability if I don't know what is going to happen?" These individuals are simply confused about the distinction between a point estimate of a quantity and uncertainty about that estimate.

Another risk consultant, one who sits on a panel of one of the standards organizations I mentioned earlier, explained that he is a "strong proponent of not having actuarial methods of risks" because it is "really impossible to have a number." Again, if we had an exact number, we wouldn't need what he calls "actuarial methods." In fact, I have 14 years of direct experience applying what he calls actuarial methods to IT projects. We use probabilistic methods *because* we lack perfect data, not in spite of lacking it.

We use probabilistic methods *because* we lack perfect data, not in spite of lacking it. If we had perfect data, probabilities would not be required.

The advantage that quantitative probabilities have is that they are unambiguous descriptions of our uncertainty, not a statement of precise, exact quantities. But because of misconceptions like these, many will prefer that uncertainties about some quantity or event be stated not as an unambiguous probability, but as a verbal scale of some kind. For example, a risk consultant might ask a manager to choose from the following:

An Example "Likelihood Scale":

- Very Likely
- Likely
- Unlikely
- Very Unlikely

These are actually some of the terms used in the scale developed by the Intergovernmental Panel on Climate Change (IPCC). Like the NIST method and some others, the IPCC report assigns specific probabilities to each of the levels of its scale. For example, in the IPCC report, the authors define "very likely" as meaning "greater than 90%" and "unlikely" as "less than 33%" (I wonder if these definitions were debated more than, or less than, the key findings of the report). Quite a few other verbal likelihood scales, however, do not even specify any probabilities at all. But, either way, the users of these methods will interpret the meanings very differently.

If you still think the use of a verbal scale somehow avoids the issue of a lack of precision, consider that verbal scales themselves actually add imprecision of their own. A JDM researcher, David Budescu of the University of Illinois at Urbana-Champaign, decided to see whether people even understood these statements in a common way. Budescu already knew that the literature on this topic showed that there are large differences in the way people understand such phrases, and that their use may lead to confusion and errors in communication.

He conducted an experiment where subjects read sentences from the IPCC report and assigned numerical values to the probability terms. He showed his subjects a series of statements from the IPCC report where these terms were used. For example, one statement from the IPCC report states, "It is *very likely* that hot extremes, heat waves, and heavy precipitation events will continue to become more frequent." Subjects were then asked to assign an equivalent probability to this event. For example, a subject may read the previous statement and estimate that "It is *95%* probable that hot extremes, heat waves, and heavy precipitation events will continue to become more frequent."

Budescu found that the respondents' assessments of the meaning of these terms varied widely. More surprisingly, he found they varied widely *even when they were given specific guidelines* for what these terms meant. For example, the word *likely* was interpreted in different contexts to mean anything from 45% to 84%. This wide range occurred even though subjects were informed that the guidelines specifically stated that *likely* should mean "greater than 66%" (see Exhibit 7.3).

Budescu says that this creates an "illusion of communication." When everyone "agrees" that some event is *very unlikely*, it turns out they are not

EXHIBIT 7.3 **VARIANCES IN UNDERSTANDING OF COMMON TERMS USED IN THE IPCC REPORT TO EXPRESS UNCERTAINTY**

Probability Phrase	IPCC Guidelines for Meaning of Phrase	Interpreted Meaning According to Subjects (Distribution of Actual Responses)		Percent of Responses that Violated Guidelines
		Minimum of All Reponses	Maximum of All Responses	
Very Likely	> 90%	43%	99%	58%
Likely	> 66%	45%	84%	46%
Unlikely	< 33%	8%	66%	43%
Very Unlikely	<10%	3%	76%	67%

Source: David V. Budescu, Stephen Broomell, and Han-Hui Po, University of Illinois at Urbana-Champaign.

agreeing at all. Some would be quite surprised as to how others interpreted that term. Apparently, detailed procedures for how those terms should be used is no guarantee that those rules will be followed in practice.

Often, the same person would even use a given term to mean completely different probabilities depending on the context of the usage. Here is one interesting example. I was talking to a client about a scoring method he had applied to risks related to a large project portfolio. Almost rhetorically, I asked one manager, "What does this mean when you say this risk is 'very likely'?" I pointed to a particular risk plotted on his "risk matrix." With little hesitation, he said, "I guess it means there is about a 20% chance it will happen." One of his colleagues was surprised by this response. When he asked for clarification, the first manager responded, "Well, this is a very high impact event and 20% is *too* likely for that kind of impact." A roomful of people looked at each other as if they were just realizing that, after several tedious workshops of evaluating risks, they had been speaking different languages all along.

A roomful of people looked at each other as if they were just realizing that, after several tedious workshops of evaluating risks, they had been speaking different languages all along.

But quite a few methods don't even bother to assign meaningful probabilities to their likelihood scales at all. Words like *probable* are meant to stand on their own and, presumably, are expected to be understood in the same way by all users. One example of this from the rules of the Financial Accounting Standards Board (FASB) was pointed out to me by Bob Clemen of Duke University. In the FASB rules regarding "Accounting for Contingent Losses," loss contingencies are sometimes recognized based on whether they are "probable," "reasonably probable," or "remote." These are each defined as:

- *Probable.* The future event is likely to occur.
- *Reasonably probable.* The chance of the future event occurring is greater than remote but less than probable.
- *Remote.* The probability the future event will occur is small.

In other words, the FASB has managed to define verbal expressions of likelihood entirely in terms of *other verbal expressions of likelihood.* The ambiguous nature of this rule means that different accounting firms could come to very different opinions. This encourages its own type of risk by incentivizing less than perfectly unbiased descriptions and actions. The impact of an unfavorable audit in this area can be significant for a corporation and there is an incentive to shop around for a better opinion. Even years after Enron and Sarbanes-Oxley, acquaintances in the accounting profession confirm for me that this still happens.

Ambiguity about "contingent losses" in FASB rules encourages optimistic valuations of risks in financial reporting. Corporations will shop around for the most favorably worded opinion.

Furthermore, this ambiguity turns out to have potentially greater implications when scales are applied to the *impact* of a risk. For most risky events, the reality of impact is that it has a wide range of possible outcomes, probably best represented by something like a 90% confidence interval. But the users of methods like NIST are forced to provide one particular evaluation of impact. For example, if you are evaluating the risk of a loss of customer data to hackers, the potential losses could include costs of recovering data, compensation to customers, legal costs, and/or the loss of customers. This could be anything from a trivial amount (the hacker was internal and was discovered before releasing the data) to the cost of major litigation while losing a large share of customers.

Tony Cox points out that in the case of evaluating an uncertain impact, an expert being asked to pick one category for impact may have to combine a subjective judgment of risk aversion along with her estimate of the actual impact.[3] In other words, suppose some event could result in a loss of $1 million to $50 million. If two different assessors were to explicitly discuss this loss, they might agree on this range. But because one assessor is more risk averse, she might think of this event as being "high" impact while another thinks of it as "medium."

Budescu's illusion of communication also applies. If they both did agree that the event would be "medium" impact, they might not realize that it is because a risk-tolerant person estimates a higher loss range and a risk-averse person estimates a lower loss range.

Unintended Effects of Scales: What You Don't Know Can Hurt You

Tony Cox lists even more problems with scoring methods. He finds that even simple-looking scales have peculiarities with their own unintended mathematical consequences. The errors left in popular scoring methods by being oblivious to biases like overconfidence, and the errors added by the ambiguity of the labels, should alone be reason enough to doubt the usefulness of most scoring schemes. But that's not the end of it. When we examine them closely, the arbitrary features of the scales themselves appear to add other sources of error. Should your assessments of the most important risks depend on nothing more than the fact that you happened to use one arbitrary scoring method and not another? Unfortunately, it does. I'll break these unintended consequences into three general types:

1. *Range compression.* Scoring methods inject imprecision by grouping a wide range of values under one category in a scale. This is magnified further by the fact that, even for 5- or 10-point scales, only a minority of the scale is used for a majority of the ratings given. If opinion slides a little, it can mean a big change in the standing of alternatives.
2. *Presumption of regular intervals.* Scores implicitly assume that the regular intervals of the "1-2-3-4-5" scales approximate the relative magnitudes being assessed.
3. *Presumption of independence.* None of the standard or popular scoring methods consider the effects of correlation (tendency to move together) among various factors and risks. This has significant implications for models with subjective scoring methods

Range Compression

The first item on the list comes from the fact that scoring methods often attempt to turn an otherwise meaningful and unambiguous quantity into a score with only a few possible values (usually 3 or 5). The NIST scale would apparently require both a 1% likelihood and an 18% likelihood to get "rounded off" to a 10% likelihood ("low"). Likewise, an additive, weighted scoring system I've seen applied to IT projects converts the return on investment (ROI) of a project to a 5-point scale so it can be added up along with several other factors. But the potential ROI range is so large that the value of *1* alone stands for any ROI between 1% and 299%. A *2* goes from 300% to 499%. Yes, a project with an ROI of 299% is judged the same as one with an ROI of 1%, but is only half as good as an ROI of 300%.

Tony Cox calls this *range compression*, and it is magnified when factors are multiplied together, as they typically are in risk matrices. Consider that NIST not only would lump together 1% and 18% likelihood, it requires users to lump together very different magnitudes of impacts. If a $100 million impact is considered "high," then so must be a $250 million impact (there is no higher category). A risk of 1% chance of losing $100 million would then be given the same ranking as an 18% chance of losing $250 million. The latter risk might even be a worse outcome than the ratios of the impacts would indicate. Even a "risk neutral" calculation (probability × loss) would show the second risk is 45 times greater. But a risk-averse manager would consider the difference to be even greater. Perhaps the $250 million loss would have resulted in bankruptcy, making the risk greater still. Yet, in the NIST framework, both of these—with a low likelihood and high impact—would be considered a "medium" risk. There is not enough resolution in this method to discriminate among some very different risks, which is critical to the intelligent allocation of resources to address the risks. The best description I've heard of this effect is from a sometimes-client and IT security expert Reed Augliere: "Garbage times garbage is garbage squared."

> "Garbage times garbage is garbage squared."
>
> —Reed Augliere, IT Security Expert

Range compression may be exacerbated further, depending on whether the users of the method "cluster" their scores. I looked at the score distributions of seven different scoring methods that all used 5-point scales (this

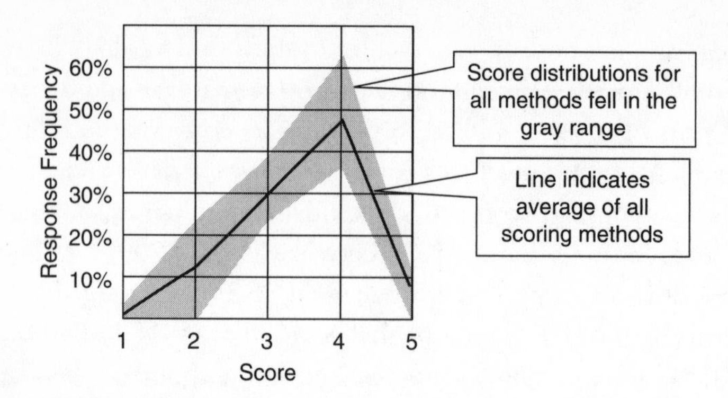

EXHIBIT 7.4 **Distribution of Scores from Seven Different 5-Point Scales**

is perhaps the most common scale). Each one required the valuation of several individual factors for a large number of projects or risk categories by subject matter experts (SMEs) so that the total was a hundred or more individual valuations for each scoring method. Other than the point-scale, the only thing they had in common was that a *5* always meant higher risk whether it was likelihood, impact, or some other factor in an additive weighted scoring system. Exhibit 7.4 shows the distribution of scores used by these seven scoring methods.

The chart clearly shows two things. First, the behavior of how the scores are actually used is very similar in each of these seven methods, developed by different people and used by different people. Second, two of the score choices—*3* and *4*—make up about 75% of all of the answers chosen. The implications of this for the scoring method are important. Since most of the chosen scores ended up being a choice between just two values, changing a *3* to a *4* (or vice versa) arbitrarily has a bigger impact on the priorities of the projects than if the scores were uniformly distributed. In other words, a chart that shows the final results of "risk rankings" or "project priorities" tends to have a large number in a small cluster, where small changes can make a big difference between ranks.

Since responses tend to be highly clustered, small changes in scores have a large impact on ranks of risks.

In experimenting with some of the scoring systems, I found that a change of one value from a *4* to a *3* could change the rank so much that it can make the difference in whether an item is in the "critical priority" list.

I found other very curious scoring behaviors when I looked at all of this data. There seemed to be patterns in responses of which the users of these scoring methods were themselves unaware. Apparently, extreme scores (*1* or *5*) were much more likely for risks that were evaluated much later in a long list of various risks that had to be evaluated. This effect appeared even though these were different teams answering different questions in different orders. By the time they get to the end of their list, do users start feeling obligated to use part of the scale they haven't used much? The data is not conclusive, but given how sensitive responses are to framing and other effects, it would not surprise me if it were true.

Presumption of Regular Intervals

Range compression is not the only source of error introduced by ordinal scales. When a scale is applied, there is an assumption that the numbers used in the scale at least roughly approximate the relative magnitudes of those items. Exhibit 7.5 shows one case where this simple assumption can be far from the truth. The exhibit shows relative values of "Level of Project Sponsor" in assessing IT project failure risk according to a 0-to-3-point scale originally used by one organization (a client of mine). Next to it are the relative magnitudes of the effect of the project sponsor based on actual

Relative Impact of IT Project Failure Rates Using a 0-to-3-Point Scale for "IT Project Sponsor" vs. Actual Historical Impact

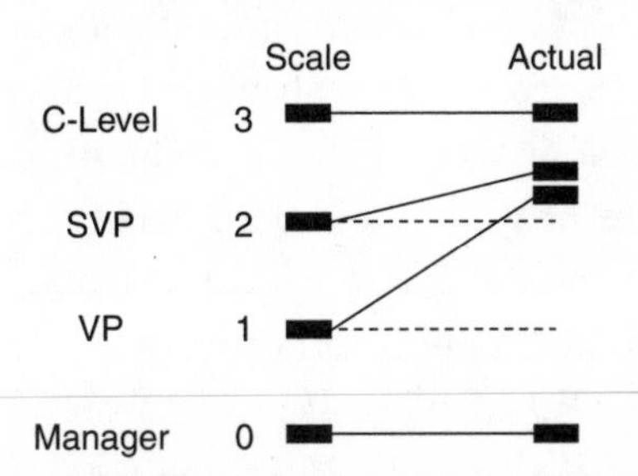

EXHIBIT 7.5 **Comparison of Scales versus Historical Data**

historical data of project failure rates in that organization (shown so that *3* is "maximum" for comparison to the original scale).

In the original weighted score shown on the left of Exhibit 7.5, having a senior vice president (SVP) as the champion of the project had literally twice the impact as has having a mere VP (the score is a *2* and *1*, respectively). A C-level executive such as the CEO, CFO, or CIO would be exactly three times as important for project success as the VP. But when I analyzed the actual completion-rate histories of the portfolio (which we were able to reconstruct for about 10 years of data), the differences between VP, SVP, and CEO were not nearly as stark, but they were all much better than a midlevel manager. Instead of being twice as important as a VP, an SVP was barely 10% more important. And the C-level executive, instead of being three times as important as a VP, was about 30% more important.

This example also illustrates how an arbitrary and seemingly minor change in the scoring system has a larger effect than the developers of the method apparently thought. If the scale were changed to 1 to 4 instead of 0 to 3, then the scale would have made an SVP 50% more important than a VP, not twice as important. And the C-level sponsor would have been twice as important instead of three times as important as the VP in ensuring project completion. Depending on how users distribute their scores, minor changes like this could have led to very different priorities.

Presumption of Independence

Finally, the issue of correlations among different risks and different factors is significant for all risk analysis, but universally ignored in scoring models. In multiplicative risk matrices, the correlation may be among different risks. Two or more medium-impact, medium-likelihood risks plotted on a risk matrix might be a much higher risk if they all happen together. If "loss of warehouse inventory due to natural disaster" and "interruption of manufacturing operations due to workforce unavailability" both occur as a result of a hurricane, then they can't really be modeled as two independent medium-impact events.

Losses can be interdependent in other ways, too. If the warehouse were located in Illinois instead of near the factory in Florida, then the same storm could not cause both events. But if the data center is in Florida, the warehouse in Illinois may have to sit idle just the same until the backup site is functioning. The best risk analysts using Monte Carlo models try to take care to include correlations and dependencies. They know that if they do not, different risks cannot be evaluated and compared.

Clarification of Scores and Preferences: Different but Similar-Sounding Methods and Similar but Different-Sounding Methods

Before I proclaim that all simple scoring models are completely useless (or worse), I need to qualify further the types of scores we are talking about and why they are being used. The scoring methods I was just describing use rather vague ordinal scales to rank components of risk. The actual use and accuracy of each such scale is not based on any kind of underlying probabilistic theory, and no statistics are collected showing that the methods work for truly improving decisions.

Now I'll introduce some methods that might be confused with these scoring methods, but that actually appear to work. I'll also discuss some decision analysis methods that are sometimes used in risk analysis. I'll discuss the difference between the two, and why some decision analysis methods can't apply to risk analysis.

They Sound Like Scores, but They Aren't (and They Work)

Some researchers have developed methods that might seem like one of the previous simple scoring methods, yet are not. For example, Egon Brunswik's model (mentioned in Chapter 6) ultimately produces a result based on *weighted* inputs, but remember that the weights were derived through a statistical regression, not subjectively chosen in a workshop. Also, the factors that were used were not reduced to ordinal scales. Real inputs of real measures are used (project cost, planned duration, loan amount, etc.).

Another JDM researcher I wrote about in my previous book was Robyn Dawes at Carnegie Mellon University. In 1979, he wrote a paper titled "The Robust Beauty of Improper Linear Models."[4] He showed that even very simple models can improve on results from unaided judges. But, like Brunswik, Dawes invents no predefined ordinal scales for his models and his claims of effectiveness are based on real measurements. Like

Brunswik's model, there can be several factors added up to get a value for something we are trying to evaluate—risks of a construction project, applicants for a job, or diagnoses of cancer patients. And, as is the case with Brunswik, the factors are items that a judge thinks should be considered in the evaluation.

But Dawes performs no *optimal fit* calculation as Brunswik did. He simply converts each factor into a *normalized* value so that the average of all the values in a given factor (say, the cost of a construction project in the model evaluating construction project risks) is represented by a zero. Then Dawes computes a standard deviation based on the "normal" probability distribution. If the project cost were just slightly above average, it might be +.5, or if it were far below average it might be −2.3. The sign depends on whether the judge thinks that more of that factor is a good thing. See the example spreadsheet for a Dawes linear model at www.howtofixriskmgt.com.

Dawes has published work that shows that this method can marginally outperform unaided decision makers. Once again, it is the empirical evidence shown by this research that makes it validated. According to Dawes, human judges seem to do well at identifying factors whether they are good or bad, but have a hard time considering multiple inputs. This is what his simple approach alleviates.

To summarize, the key differences between Dawes's model or Brunswik's model on the one hand and the models promoted by NIST, CobIT, *PMBoK*, and several major consulting firms on the other are as follows:

- Invalid scoring methods are developed in complete isolation from modern JDM research. Nothing in the scoring approach is designed to offset the known, measured human tendency to overconfidence and other biases.
- Invalid scoring models are not tested against reality. No evidence exists where outputs of the model are compared to a large sample of actual outcomes (project failures, credit defaults, security breaches, etc.).
- Brunswik and Dawes do not rely on human judgment alone for the inputs during the actual estimation effort—they are based on measurable units like cost or duration, some of which can be provided by objective measures. However, the invalid scoring methods attempt to elicit responses to vaguely defined concepts like "Rate the alignment with business strategy on a scale of 1 to 5."

- With the invalid scoring methods, otherwise-useful quantities are converted to an arbitrary scale with no consideration as to how the rescaling affects outcomes ("If project ROI is 0 to 50%, then score = 1, 51% to 100% = 2, etc."). The arbitrariness of the ordinal scale actually adds its own completely unnecessary and rather large *rounding error* to the decision.
- Invalid scoring methods do not assess user behavior and how sensitive the model may be to small changes in assumptions.

One scoring method that I do like was developed in 1964 by Fred J. Gruenberger, who was, at the time, with RAND Corporation. He proposed a "measure for crackpots" as a tongue-in-cheek way to evaluate the champions of bogus theories. A more current crackpot index was proposed by John C. Baez, a mathematical physicist (and cousin of folksinger Joan Baez). Gruenberger's original model and Baez's index are both geared toward detecting crackpots with new scientific theories, but the basic concept could be applied to popular risk management methods or, for that matter, popular business methods in general.

Both models give the most points for a lack of empirical verifiability of the claims. That is, if someone can't verify a theory by measurements of real observations, then he scores high as a crackpot. Baez mentions a few items that seem especially relevant for business fads. He gives extra crackpot points for each use of a term such as *paradigm shift* or invention of a new term without a clear definition. Both models include points for a martyr complex among the proponents of a new theory or method. It goes without saying that these are both "for entertainment value only" exercises, and neither, of course, is used to support major, risky decisions.

Methods that Aren't Exactly "Scoring," but Address (Necessarily) Subjective Preferences

There is quite a lot of respected academic work (not that I'm not using that as a sufficient indicator of validity) developed regarding the idea that if your preferences are at least *coherent* or *rational* (in various well-defined ways), then decisions based on them should be better (i.e., make preferred outcomes more frequent and undesirable ones less frequent). L.J. "Jimmie" Savage proposed a list of axioms for what is called "preference theory" in his 1954 text, *The Foundations of Statistics*,[5] which started a flurry of scholarly work on the topic that has flourished ever since. Even Kahneman and Tversky addressed this issue as part of Prospect Theory, for which Kahneman won the Nobel Prize in Economics.

The idea is that, even for choices that could be seen as purely subjective—where to have the company picnic, who was the better singer, and so on—some judgments are just more logical than others. An example of how Jimmie Savage would sometimes explain this idea was relayed to me by his son, Sam Savage. Jimmie asks us to imagine he is in a restaurant and he knows he wants either the duck or the prime rib lunch special. But first, he asks the waiter, "Do you have turkey, today?" The waiter says yes. Jimmie says, "In that case, I'll have the duck." Jimmie Savage's example is one of how we *don't* make decisions. The conversation violates one of Savage's proposed axioms of preference. Adding an irrelevant (not preferred) option to (or removing one from) the mix should not have any bearing on which of the remaining options you choose.

Here is a short list of such preference axioms:

- *No rank reversal* (the rule violated in Savage's example): If you prefer option A when given a choice among A, B, and C, then your choice should not change if C is dropped from the list or if another option, D, is added that is already inferior to one of the other options.
- *Transitivity:* If you prefer A to B and B to C, then you should prefer A to C. To say you prefer C to A is logically inconsistent with the first part of the statement.
- *Indifferent criterion independence:* If you are choosing alternatives based on two factors, and you end up preferring A, then adding a third factor for which all the alternatives are equally valued should not change your choice. For example, after ranking three alternatives for the company picnic based on size of the area and price, you choose Lincoln Park. Someone then decides "distance from office" should be added as a factor for consideration. You add it, but find that all three alternatives are exactly the same distance from the office, anyway. It should have no bearing on the outcome, right? But, if we don't think about some of the less obvious consequences of ranking and scoring schemes, it can.

These seem terribly obvious, but it is actually possible for risk managers to create or use scoring systems that violate these rules and not be aware of it. This comes up more often in scoring systems where all of the factors being considered are expressed as relative ranks. All of the logical consequences of these axioms and more are explored in Multi-Attribute Utility Theory (MAUT) and Multi-Criteria Decision Making (MCDM). These methods attempt to account for all sorts of tradeoffs between different items and work out the necessary, logical consequences.

I won't go into MAUT and MCDM in detail here, but there is one fundamental subjective tradeoff important to risk management. One tool of MAUT is to make a chart that documents how much of one thing a decision maker is willing to give up to obtain more of another. A key example of this is the *risk-versus-return* curve often used to evaluate financial portfolios. Harry Markowitz used one simple piece of utility theory when he developed Modern Portfolio Theory (MPT). He needed a way to quantify the risk aversion of an investor so that he could compute a recommended portfolio position.

Markowitz made a chart where one axis was the return on an investment and the other axis was the volatility of the investment. The investor could then state, by drawing on the chart, how much risk he or she was willing to accept for a given return. This is an example of a *utility curve*, showing how we are willing to trade off one item for another. Risk could also be expressed as, say, the chance of a negative return, or the benefit could be expressed as a net present value. But the essence is always the same—decision makers ultimately have to show how much risk they are willing to take for a given return. (See Exhibit 7.6.)

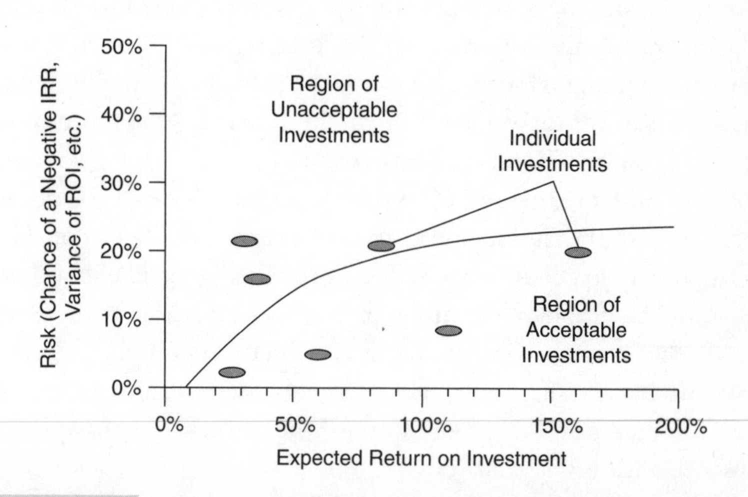

EXHIBIT 7.6 **Risk versus Return: The Investment Boundary**

At this point, we need to mention again (as first brought up in Chapter 5) the ambiguity introduced by the popular uses of the terms *risk management* and *risk analysis* and the established meaning of *decision analysis* and *analysis of preferences*. The analysis of decisions requires that we consider not only objective facts and quantitative estimates but also our preferred tradeoffs among different objectives. As earlier definitions made clear, risks boil down to the probabilities and magnitudes of possible losses that themselves can be quantified in a meaningful way.

Even if parts of this depend on subjective estimates, those subjective estimates are not the same as preferences. If you are expressing your uncertainty about the duration of a construction project using a subjective range estimate, you are attempting to estimate some real-world measurable quantity. You have not stated anything about what you *prefer* the project duration to be. But if you are considering different alternatives based on the net benefits versus the risks of a project, then you have an issue that fundamentally comes down to a subjective tradeoff or preference.

Decision analysis experts tend to think of risk analysis as something that provides input to decision analysis. Once the risk analysis is done, the decision analysis must, obviously, consider not just the risks of alternatives, but also their benefits and costs.

Since risk analysis cannot be just the application of preferences independent of real-world measurements, the application to risk analysis of methods meant specifically for assessment of preferences can be in error. Yet, some users have applied such methods as the primary method for risk analysis itself. Whatever the value of the methods may be, the most important thing to keep in mind is that risk analysis must in some verifiable sense be a *forecasting* or *predictive* method. This does not mean that each event must be predicted exactly, but it does mean that, on average, the results of risk analysis outperform unaided human judges at predicting the likelihood of various events. The problem with using preference-modeling methods for risk analysis is that none of these methods is a forecasting method: None predicts what is likely to happen. They are strictly for evaluation of fundamental preferences, not for prediction of the probable consequences of actions—the heart of risk analysis.

Here is a caveat that should apply to whatever application MAUT may have in risk management. I find that a good quantitative model finds very few fundamentally "competing objectives." A person may feel the need to "trade" between objective A and objective B, but in reality these are both just factors in a higher objective, C. For example, a utility curve showing the tradeoff between seeking an investment with better tax advantages or one that increases revenues should really be based on a financial calculation, not a subjective preference between tax advantages or revenues (but I have seen preference methods of MCDM and MAUT used this way). For most profit-oriented organizations, the basic tradeoff may boil down to simply risk versus return, not tradeoffs among a dozen or more objectives. If the real tradeoffs are this small of a set, a lot of the more elaborate methods may not apply.

They Don't Seem Like Scores, but They Are

I'll mention one more method that is not exactly in the scope of this book but (since it is very popular and some users have applied it to risk analysis) I feel forced to address briefly. The Analytic Hierarchy Process (AHP) is another method that attempts to help decision makers make rational tradeoffs between alternatives based only on stated preferences. AHP was developed by Thomas Saaty in the 1970s, and it employs a mathematical method to attempt to minimize the number of transitivity errors decision makers might make when considering problems with large numbers of competing objectives and tradeoffs among them. AHP is certainly successful, if we measure success by the number of passionate users and advocates (which I do not).

It resorts to a type of arbitrary score in the sense that users are asked to evaluate the relative "importance" of criteria, so that "slightly more important" means a *3*, "absolutely more important" means a *9*, and so on. (Some users are apparently unaware of this arbitrary conversion, since analysts can hide the actual scale from users who simply give verbal responses.)

AHP runs into problems in terms of violating Savage's axioms. It used to violate rank reversal, but proponents (who originally argued rank reversal is rational) have now "fixed" the problem (which they first argued was not a problem). But other logical problems with AHP have been discovered. It now appears to violate the indifferent criterion axiom.[6] Other problems are found with the mathematical methods themselves.[7]

Enthusiastic supporters of AHP claim that AHP is "mathematically proven" and enjoys a "broad consensus" among decision analysts. As I speak to decision analysis experts from around the country, I find this to be far from the truth. In fact, everyone I talk to seems to at least acknowledge the existence of serious controversy about the method. Robin Dillon-Merrill (from Chapter 6) is a longstanding member of the Decision Analysis Society and she observes, "Most decision analysis experts don't consider AHP a legitimate part of decision analysis." Tony Cox goes further, and was willing to go on the record with the following:

> AHP bears the same relation to decision analysis as alternative medicine bears to mainstream modern medicine: Its advocates passionately defend it, but mainstream practitioners note that there is no evidence that it works better than (or as well as) other methods, except in pleasing those who use it. Advocates point to the large numbers of satisfied users, and to publications extolling the supposed virtues of the methods, as evidence of respectability and efficacy; while critics object that the alternative methods lack a sound logical or scientific foundation and generate results that typically have not been demonstrated to compare favorably with those from mainstream methods.

I've reviewed a large number of the publications Cox refers to as "extolling" AHP. Every article I found was, in fact, merely a case study about the application of AHP to some problem—the question of whether the decision was any better than it would have been if other methods had been used is usually not even raised. I have more decision analysis experts willing to go on record denouncing AHP than I care to list, but you get the point.

I'm told some AHP proponents feel vindicated by Saaty's being recognized with the "Impact Prize" from Institute for Operations Research and the Management Sciences (INFORMS) in 2008. But the carefully worded award states, "This is not a research award. The awards committee is not judging the quality of a body of work. Instead, emphasis will be placed on evaluating the breadth of the impact of an idea or body of research." By that measure alone, I'm sure Saaty deserved the award. But that is not the same as evidence of the effectiveness of AHP, especially for risk management.

AHP proponents say it is evolving and some problems have been addressed. But Karen Jenni, a PhD decision analyst whose advisor was Baruch Fischhoff, sees little use in this. She asks, "Why keep fixing AHP when other methods already work that don't violate the axioms?" I agree. We are only being fair. All risk analysis methods (or misapplied preference analysis methods) must still be evaluated by the ultimate crackpot test: Does it actually improve forecasts of risk events and are decisions actually improved? More importantly, whatever the benefits of AHP and some of the other methods we discussed, they can't be the only tools used in risk management unless they can be validated as forecasting tools—which isn't their basic purpose.

NOTES

1. U.S. Dept. of Health and Human Services, *Draft Guidance on Allocating and Targeting Pandemic Influenza Vaccine*, October 17, 2007.
2. National Institute of Standards & Technology, *Risk Management Guide for Information Technology Systems,* NIST 800-30, 2002.
3. L.A. Cox, "What's Wrong with Risk Matrices?" *Risk Analysis* 28(2), 2008.
4. R.M. Dawes, "The Robust Beauty of Improper Linear Models in Decision Making," *American Psychologist* 34, 1979, 571–582.
5. L.J. Savage, *The Foundations of Statistics*, (Dover Prisee, 1954)
6. J. Perez et al., "Another Potential Shortcoming of AHP," *TOP* 14(1), June 2006.
7. C.A. Bana e Costa and J.-C. Vansnick, "A Critical Analysis of the Eigenvalue Method Used to Derive Priorities in AHP," *European Journal of Operational Research* 187(3), June 16, 2008, 1422–1428.

CHAPTER 8

Black Swans, Red Herrings, and Invisible Dragons: Overcoming Conceptual Obstacles to Improved Risk Management

In theory there is no difference between theory and practice. In practice, there is.

—YOGI BERRA

Even if every argument I made up to this point were accepted by all managers, there would still be some serious conceptual obstacles to overcome from some corners. Risk management may, for a number of reasons, not be considered feasible. Most of these objections to risk management boil down to some fundamentally different ideas about basic concepts like the nature of probability and predictability.

Here I need to give a bit more context for the eventual solution I propose. I'm proposing that quantitative risk modeling similar to what is used in engineering risks, insurance, nuclear power, and oil exploration is part of the solution. We need to modify the existing methods, but the ideal approach is a version of quantitative modeling of risks. In fact, the definitions I gave for risk and uncertainty in Chapter 5 were chosen in part because they lend themselves to quantitative modeling and are consistent with quantitative methods in decision science.

I propose that the probabilities and consequences of events can be measured in a meaningful way. In my previous book, *How to Measure Anything*, I argue that *measurement* is simply observation-based uncertainty reduction about a quantity. The objective of measurement is to improve (even just slightly) our current knowledge about an unknown quantity that is relevant to some decision. By this standard, the objective of quantitative assessments of risk is to *improve* on the unaided intuition of managers, not to attain perfect clairvoyance. We quantify the probabilities and losses from various events and use these values in calculations (quantitative models) that will reduce the error of managers and allow them to make better "bets."

The obstacles I'm about to discuss are strongly held opinions about quantitative modeling of risk. Some object to the very idea that quantitative risk management is *ever* possible in *any* situation. Others accept that quantitative methods are possible in some fields, but not in their specific industry or organization. Some base these objections on the fact that some unusual events could never have been predicted or that their problems are too complex or immeasurable. Each of these ideas may result in a potential source of resistance to improved risk management.

In my interviews and research, I was sometimes surprised to find out how passionate some people were about their positions on the topics of probability and risk. You might even think that we were talking about one of the more controversial issues in religion or politics and not the nature of risk. But even though, for whatever reason, this seems to be a touchy subject with some people, we need to be aware of these opposing views and learn to navigate among them.

Risk and Righteous Indignation: The Belief that Quantitative Risk Analysis Is Impossible

Some will argue that there is simply no way to measure risks. Paradoxically, this specific position on the topic of risk is promulgated by some people who make their living as "risk experts." They are not swayed by the fact that the very existence of the insurance industry and actuarial science alone would seem to contradict this belief, as would many other experts of higher caliber. But the label of *expert* should never impress a scientifically minded skeptic (as all risk managers should think of themselves). The reason I know that experts can be wrong is that they don't even agree with each other. Since some must be wrong, any could be wrong.

Many of these experts seem to employ a similar type of objection to measuring risk: There exist extraordinary events that no model could have predicted. The events of September 11, 2001, the unexpected rise of Google, major stock market crashes, and various engineering disasters, are cited as evidence for this point. In other words, if a particular method failed to predict this specific event, then the method failed and should be abandoned. This line of reasoning has fundamental logical errors. My goal here is to point out these errors so that the risk manager can address them when confronted with them and get on with his or her job.

To that end, I'll introduce you to two actual risk management "experts" who commit these fundamental logical errors. I will use pseudonyms for them, because it is not my objective to expose them individually. They merely represent a large class of people with similar opinions. Let's call them John and Jerald.

Both John and Jerald make their livings as risk management consultants. Both have PhDs. John's is in philosophy and Jerald's is in engineering—not in the decision sciences, statistics, actuarial science, or any field related to risk management. Both have written books but, according to their Amazon rankings, they sell very few. Both rail against the more quantitative risk management methods and propose their own, softer methods, instead. I don't believe they have met, but each would probably entirely disagree with the method employed by the other. They both become extremely agitated when their methods are questioned.

When I first talked to these experts, they each pointed out several historical disasters and used them as evidence of the impossibility of risk analysis. (In Chapter 1, I mentioned this problem; certain high-profile risk experts have learned that they can engage audiences though a variety of interesting stories about disasters.) In the course of discussing their approaches to risk management, I could tell they relied heavily on these stories as part of their standard shtick in front of audiences. It is a very successful tactic for some people, especially if they have a gift for storytelling. The stories enthrall audiences, but this does them very little good. It is not just the knowledge of the details of these catastrophes that is important, but the interpretation of these events for risk managers.

John, for example, pointed out that the 1940 Tacoma Narrows Bridge collapse in Tacoma, Washington, is an example of the failure of quantitative risk analysis. The first Tacoma Narrows Bridge has become a famous case study of engineering disasters due (in this case) to *aeroelastic flutter.* The winds in the Tacoma Narrows valley caused the bridge to swing, the swings amplified the aerodynamic effects, and the aerodynamic effects amplified the swings. For the few months that the bridge was in use, it got the nickname "Galloping Gertie" for this easily noticeable swinging. But on November 7, 1940, the swings became so severe they tore the bridge apart. It was used right up to the point of its destruction, where one man barely escaped with his life.

But do these examples of surprising disasters really tell us, as John claims, anything about the effectiveness of quantitative risk analysis? John claims that quantitative risk analysis was used in the construction of the bridge and concludes that "ipso facto, quantitative risk analysis failed." He goes on to list Three Mile Island, Chernobyl, the downfall of Enron and Arthur Andersen, and many more examples. In each case, only superficial details are mentioned and each is meant to be one more piece of evidence against whatever risk management method was used. And, since the methods being used didn't prevent these disasters, presumably his alternative approach (a very soft, nonquantitative method) should be preferred. There are at least four major fallacies in this thinking:

Fallacy #1: Presume some particular method was used. What "quantitative risk analysis" is allegedly debunked in the cited events? The construction of the Tacoma Narrows bridge predates most of the more sophisticated methods available today, including basic computer simulations. Likewise, was the problem at Chernobyl, Three Mile Island, or Katrina really because of a quantitative risk analysis method or the lack of it? He presumes that the occurrence of the event is somehow evidence against some specific type of analysis, even though the analysis method varied from one event to the next.

Fallacy #2: Anecdotal evidence is sufficient. The occurrence of a single unlikely event is not evidence that the previously computed odds against the event must have been wrong. This is the *anecdotal fallacy*. A casino, for example, correctly computes that a bet on a single number in the game of roulette has only a 1 in 37 chance of winning for the player (a loss for the casino). If a player bets a large amount on a single number and wins, was the casino wrong about the 37-to-1 odds against it? No; even if we allow for the possibility that the wheel is biased, that single spin doesn't prove the odds were wrong. Only a large number of spins could conclusively show that the wheel might be biased and the assumed odds were wrong. One spin—or one disaster—is not conclusive proof one way or the other. The expert gives several examples of such disasters, but it is a biased sample of disasters. Only examples that seem to support the point are selected from a very large set of possibilities. In the same way, one could list selected anecdotes to "prove" any stereotype or prejudice of any group of people. Listing anecdotes of unlikely disasters is not a valid argument against any particular method of risk analysis.

Fallacy #3: Even extremely unusual events must be exactly predicted for a model to be of any use. This is like saying that, in order for my insurance company to compute the premium for my life insurance, it cannot just compute the odds of my death in a given period of time. Instead, it must predict the exact circumstances of my death, which, for all I know, may be an extremely unlikely event. For example, there is a tiny chance my cause of death will be due to being hit by a falling airplane while lying in bed. If I were killed in this way, should anyone challenge the actuaries and say "*Aha*—you could never have predicted that, so actuarial science is a fraud"? No, actuarial science is in no danger of being debunked because, like the casino, the objective is to make good bets over time, not predict individual causes of death.

Fallacy #4: The false choice. Even if there is a legitimately proven flaw with one method it does not necessarily follow that some other method is automatically preferred. The alternative method must be subject to the same standard.

Jerald, our other expert, also commits this fourth fallacy of the false choice. Jerald told me point blank in a phone interview that he is a "staunch enemy of risk analysis." No kidding—he makes his living in risk management and he said that. While he says risk analysis is a waste of time, he is, surprisingly, a big booster for risk management. He simply believes that one can be done without the other. When I asked him how he chooses which risks to focus on managing, he explained his version of a simple risk map, as shown in Chapter 2, using subjective "high/medium/low" categories for risks. I pointed out to him that this is still an attempt to analyze risk, he is just not doing it quantitatively or, for that matter, with any method that has any kind of track record of actually improving decisions.

The false dichotomy from both of these experts is that if one method couldn't predict some specific event, then you must instead prefer the alternative methods they propose. But, in each of these cases, alternative methods would also have failed to predict the specific event. John insisted that the Tacoma bridge example was proof that quantitative methods failed and that, therefore, we should rely only on subjective methods such as his. I pointed out that the methods associated with quantitative analysis today—such as probabilistic computer simulations—were not available then and they couldn't be to blame.

I then pointed out that the subjective intuition was available to engineers at the time (as it always has been) and that subjective methods also failed to predict the disaster. Remarkably, he countered that he knew that subjective methods were not used. *What?* I told him that the engineers had access to their subjective instincts (i.e. common sense) the entire time and that only some kind of radical, experimental brain surgery could have denied them that.

Unlike the quantitative methods that came later, subjective, intuitive methods always have been available and, by this standard, these disasters are as much evidence against qualitative methods as against quantitative methods. The correct way to choose among alternative methods is to look at complete track records of sufficiently large samples—not selected anecdotes—of all of the proposed methods whether they are quantitative or qualitative. A single anecdotal disaster isn't evidence for or against any method if all methods failed to predict it. As with the casino or the life insurance company, we ask whether we would be better off over a large number of random scenarios. Applying the same standards to all, we can select the best.

A Note about Black Swans

The de facto standard-bearer of critics of methods used in risk analysis is Nassim Nicholas Taleb, author of the popular books, *Fooled by Randomness* and *The Black Swan,* as well as an earlier technical book on derivatives. He is a mathematician and former Wall Street trader who has challenged some fundamental dogma about risk management in finance.

Taleb explains that the impact of chance is unappreciated by mostly everyone. He sees the most significant events in history as being completely unforeseeable. He calls these events *black swans*, in reference to an old European expression that went something like "That's about as likely as finding a black swan." The expression was based on the fact that no European had ever seen a swan that was black—until Europeans traveled to Australia. Until the first black swans were sighted, black swans were a metaphor for impossibility. Taleb puts September 11, 2001, stock market crashes, major scientific discoveries, and the rise of Google in his set of black swans. Each event was not only unforeseen but *utterly unforeseeable* based on our previous experience.

A heretic of financial convention, Taleb has written that Nobel Prize–winning tools in economics—such as Modern Portfolio Theory and Options Theory—are fundamentally flawed and are in fact no better than astrology. He believes that the Nobel Prize in Economics is itself an intellectual fraud (after all, it was not established in the will of Alfred Nobel, but by the Royal Bank of Sweden 75 years after Nobel's death). He claims that once, in a public forum, he riled up one such prizewinner to the point of red-faced, fist-pounding anger.

Taleb is certainly passionate about his cause and exudes frustration at those who run against it. Taleb seems to tirelessly promote a scientific view of risk analysis—all the while, making several unscientific generalizations about many groups of people, who include, I'm sure, many of his readers. A read of Taleb's books would reveal that Taleb—a Wharton MBA—seems to despise MBAs as well as people who lack sophisticated appreciation of opera. He wants to be away from areas "polluted by persons of commerce." In *Fooled by Randomness*, he even berates one unnamed individual for not being "well bred." After quite a lot of name-calling, he finishes out that book by saying that he likes to poke fun at those who take themselves too seriously but, by that point, the reader is hard pressed to accept that he was just joking.

I'm probably one of Taleb's hated "persons of commerce." I have an MBA (and not even an ivy-league MBA, like Taleb), I have seen exactly three operas in my entire life, and none of my ancestors I knew (farmers from Kentucky and South Dakota) would call themselves "well bred." But when I look past the rather unscientific and emotional personality judgments he makes, I can't help but defend part of what he says.

I find that reading Taleb is like making a quick survey of many of the topics that have fascinated me most over the past 20 years or so. He touches on chaos theory, fractals, experimental psychology, decision science, and Monte Carlo simulations. He admires some of the same mathematicians as I do, and as much as Taleb sneers at economists, he points out some economists he admires (but not the Nobel Prize winners). He admires some Nobel Prize winners (especially if the winner was not an economist). Some have characterized Taleb as being against quantitative analysis of risks, but nothing could be further from the truth. Taleb is a quantitative analyst; he just doesn't accept models uncritically regardless of how popular they might be—which is the only truly scientific position on the topic.

Taleb's abrasiveness aside, as a fellow skeptic, I think it is important to know where Taleb makes a good point about challenging the current dogma in finance. I also think, as a fellow skeptic, that it's good to challenge Taleb where his reason and evidence fall short. First, here are two broad themes present in all of Taleb's work where he is absolutely correct:

1. *The impact of randomness in success and failure is underrated.* People will routinely confuse luck with competence and they will presume that the lack of seeing an unusual event to date is somehow proof that the event cannot occur. They will also commit what Taleb calls the *narrative fallacy*. That is, they retroactively explain the "causes" of events that were just random. Managers, traders, and the media seem to be especially susceptible to these errors. Because of the large number of managers, some managers will have made several good choices in a row, by chance alone. Such managers will see their past success as indicators of competence and, unfortunately, will act with high confidence on equally erroneous thinking in the future. In other words, he appears to agree with everything I described in Chapter 6.

2. *Certain highly respected models are wrong.* Taleb points out (as have quite a few economists) that many of the most lauded tools in finance, especially some of those that won the Nobel, are based on some assumptions that we know to be false by simple observation. Nobel Prize–winning theories such as Options Theory and Modern Portfolio Theory assume a particular distribution of potential returns and prices that makes extreme outcomes appear much less likely than we know them to be. These theories use an otherwise-powerful tool in statistics and science known as a *Gaussian* or *normal probability distribution.* But applying this distribution to markets seems to be a bad idea. Using this distribution, a one-day drop of 5% or greater in the stock market should have been unlikely to have occurred *even once* since 1928. I looked at the history of the Dow Jones index from 1928 to the end of 2008 and found that, instead, such a drop occurred 70 times—9 times just in 2008. We will also be discussing this more later in the book. Models have to be tested empirically, regardless of how advanced they appear to be. Just because a quantitative model allegedly brings "rigor" to a particular problem (as the Nobel Prize committee stated about one award), that is no reason to believe that it actually works.

But, as much as I support Taleb in these observations, he also makes some errors, or at least some points that require slightly different arguments than he provides or some clarification:

- Taleb presumes certain methods were being used when major black swans occurred and that, therefore, those specific methods must have been proven wrong (John and Jerald's Fallacy #1). He argues, for example, that the downfall of Long Term Capital Management (LTCM) disproves Options Theory (discussed briefly in Chapter 4). Options Theory won the Nobel Prize for Robert Merton and Myron Scholes, both of whom were on the board of directors for LTCM. The theory was presumably the basis of the trading strategy of the firm. But an analysis of the failure of LTCM shows that a big reason for its downfall was the excessive use of leverage in trades—an issue that isn't even part of Options Theory. Taleb also states that the crash of 1987 disproved Modern Portfolio Theory (MPT), which would seem to presume that at least some significant proportion of fund managers used the method. I find fund managers to be tight-lipped about their specific methods, but one fund manager did tell me how "learning the theory is important as a foundation but 'real-world' decisions have to be based on practical experience, too." (However, even if everyone had been using these methods consistently, the same result could have easily occurred.)

- Taleb argues that single events effectively disprove a probabilistic model. This sounds like Fallacy #2 from the prior list, but there are conditions when it can be correct. The first black swan, of course, did conclusively disprove the notion that there were absolutely (100% confidence) no black swans. But if someone had computed that there was a 90% chance that there were no black swans, does the first sighting of one conclusively show the calculation to be in error? Not necessarily, but there may be situations where a single event may actually support Taleb's point. Various fund managers have said that fluctuations in 1987 and 2008 were an extreme case of bad luck—so extreme that they were effectively far more unlikely than one chance in a *trillion-trillion-trillion*.[1] But if there is even a 1% chance they computed the odds incorrectly, bad math on their part is *far* more likely. In this case, the fact the event occurred even once is sufficient to cause serious doubt about the calculated probabilities. Now, if the fund managers had instead said that the events that occurred were simply unlikely (e.g., a 5% chance), then the single event would not suffice to dispute the estimate (more about that in Part Three of this book).
- Taleb uses the apparent unforeseeability of specific events as evidence of a flaw in risk analysis. The implication is that if risk analysis worked, then we could make exact predictions of specific and extraordinary events such as 9/11 or the rise of Google (John and Jerald's Fallacy #3). Yes, the rare events—black swans—are individually impossible to predict precisely. But, as with my cause of death being due to falling plane parts, that's not even the point. Taleb says he admires the mathematician Edward Thorp, who developed a mathematically sound basis for card counting in blackjack in the 1960s. Now, if the objective of card counting was to predict every hand, even the most extraordinarily rare combinations as Taleb would seem to require,

then Ed Thorp's method certainly fails. But Ed Thorp's method works—that's why the casinos quit letting him play—because his system resulted in better bets on average after a large number of hands. Taleb is also a fan of the mathematician Benoit Mandelbrot, who uses the mathematics of *fractals* to model financial markets. Like Thorp and Taleb, Mandelbrot is equally unable to predict specific extraordinary events exactly, but his models are preferred by some because they seem to generate more realistic patterns that look like they *could* be from real data. Taleb and others cannot set the bar for "success" in risk analysis so high that they would have to reject the very alternatives they promote.

- Taleb assumes that if some model is flawed, he must, therefore, resort to his "common sense" (John and Jerald's Fallacy #4). Taleb stated in an interview for *Fortune* that "We replaced so much experience and common sense with 'models' that work worse than astrology, because they assume that the Black Swan does not exist." True enough, in far too many cases. He goes on to state, "No model is better than a faulty model."[2] I stated earlier that in the spectrum of risk management methods, some methods are certainly worse than applying no formal process at all. But this is not quite the same as what Taleb just said—having "no model" is never a choice for anyone and finding fault in one model does not automatically favor another model. Taleb's model is his "common sense," which is, as Albert Einstein defines it, "merely the deposit of prejudice laid down in the human mind before the age of 18." Of course, we develop these rules because usually they are fairly effective for most problems we have to deal with. But, as with every other model, common sense has its own special errors. In fact, another one of Taleb's own chosen heroes (a very exclusive group, indeed) is Daniel Kahneman, who (as described in Chapter 6) made an impressive career out of identifying the various faults in human common sense. By the way, Kahneman, an experimental psychologist, is someone that Taleb has called one of the only "real scientists" ever to win the Nobel Prize in Economics.
- Taleb does not appear to apply his own (admirable) standards of empirical evidence to his preferred methods. As we discussed in the previous point, Taleb cannot merely show that one model is

flawed to argue in favor of another model (e.g. his common sense). He must show that his common sense is *less flawed* than the other models and that requires empirical evidence. Taleb also claims that some of the methods he and his fellow traders use outperform the "Nobel" Prize–winning tools (Taleb often puts the "Nobel" in quotes when referring to the prize in economics to differentiate it from the "real" Nobel prizes), but he does not offer specific empirical evidence of this. Like most traders, Taleb may be understandably secretive about his specific methods, but if he expects his claims to be taken as scientifically valid, he needs to offer the data for all of us to examine. One data point we do have for effectiveness of his approach is the fact that his investment firm, Empirica Capital LLC, closed in 2004 after several years of mediocre returns.[3] He had one very good year in 2000 (a 60% return), because while everyone else was betting on dot-com, he bet on *dot-bomb*. But the returns the following years were far enough below the market average that the good times couldn't outweigh the bad for his fund. However, Taleb's trading strategy, if he had continued with it, would have done very well during the crisis of 2008. We just needed a little more data to be sure. We wouldn't want to use the crisis of 2008 as anecdotal evidence, either.

- Taleb rightly points out that historical analysis is no guarantee of future outcomes. He shows several examples of when history is a poor indicator—like the relatively good life of a turkey right before Thanksgiving. But there is a fundamental paradox in many of the objections to analyzing historical data by looking at examples of when historical data was wrong. They are assessing the validity of using historical examples by using *historical examples!* What Taleb and others prove with such examples is merely that what I will call a "naïve" historical analysis can be very misleading. Taleb demonstrates his points about the turkey by looking at previously known examples of turkeys. He uses what you could call a "history of histories," or *meta-historical analysis*, to show how wrong naïve historical analysis can be. The error in historical analysis in, for example, a stock price is to look only at the history of *that* stock and only for recent history. If we look at all historical analysis for a very long period of time, we find how often naïve historical analysis can be wrong. Furthermore, Taleb's own "experience," as extensive as it might be, is also just a historical analysis (just a very informal type with lots of errors in both recall and analysis, as shown in Chapter 6). No thinking person can ever honestly claim to have formed any idea totally independent of previous observations. It just doesn't happen.

- Finally, Taleb seems to make a variety of other points that, like the previous points, seem at least a little inconsistent. Explaining the outcomes in terms of the narrative fallacy committed by others is sometimes itself a narrative fallacy. Arguing that "experts" don't know so much is not supported by quoting other experts. He argues that rare events defy quantitative models, but then gives specific examples of computing rare events with quantitative models (he shows the odds of getting the same result in a coin flip many times in a row, and argues the benefits of Mandelbrot's mathematical models in the analysis of market fluctuations). But not all of these points are directly related to our topic, so I'll leave it to other readers to compile an exhaustive list.

It's also worth noting that Taleb's views on risk management, while he tries to keep the topic broad, are really based on his experience in the world of financial markets—not the other aspects of risk management, like operational risks. Some underlying phenomena of the financial markets might be entirely random and all we can do with purely random processes is to attempt to describe the distributions of various outcomes. But even if it were true that the underlying mechanisms of financial markets are impossible to model explicitly, this may not be the case in many examples in risk analysis of internal business processes, engineering structures, or the weather. In many of these cases, detailed quantitative models outperform unaided human judgment.

I'll make one final comment on the errors of these experts. Remember, all of our previous experts seemed to have assumed that if we find any fault at all in a model, then we reject it without consideration as to whether the alternatives have more faults or less. But I argue that "better is good" and I'll use a widely known parable to bring home the point. It's a well-worn example, so bear with me if you've heard it. Two men are preparing to go hiking. While one is lacing up hiking boots, he sees that the other man is forgoing his usual boots in favor of sporty running shoes. "Why the running shoes?" he asks. The second man responds, "I heard there are bears in this area and I want to be prepared." Puzzled, the first man points out, "But even with those shoes, you can't outrun a bear." The second man says, "I don't have to outrun the bear, I just have to outrun you."

Frequentist versus Subjectivist

One particularly odd, esoteric problem that creeps into some discussions about risk management is the debate between the *frequentist* or *objectivist* view of probability on one hand and the *subjectivist* view of probability on the other. Even if you have heard of this debate, it may seem like an obscure issue to raise, but the ideas related to it permeate business under different names more often than you might think.

You might come across this issue when you hear phrases like "How do we know the *real* probability?" or "How can we compute uncertainty *objectively*?" People who say this reveal that they hold a particular view of probability. They hold that probability is a measurable feature of the world, like how many pounds a particular black swan weighs. Unless one is familiar with this particular philosophical argument, one might not even know that there is another view on the issue.

What is the probability that a coin flip turns up heads? 50%? There is apparently room to debate this. What if I already flipped the coin, and simply didn't tell you the result? Is the probability that it is heads still 50%? Some would say no. The coin is already either heads or tails and probability simply doesn't apply. It is either heads or tails; you just don't know the result.

Some people, particularly some mathematicians, will go further and say that a probability applies only in a "true" random processes. These processes have to be "strictly repeatable," that is, the conditions that produced the random result have to be exactly identical in every iteration or the process is not really random. Furthermore, the frequentists' view of *probability* is that the only useful meaning of the term is the ratio of the frequency of occurrences over a very large number (actually, an infinite number) of independent trials. But is risk based on any *true* random processes? Do we ever really have "infinite trials"? What if we can't compute an objective probability? Is it even possible for real-world events to be strictly repeatable? It would seem that *probability* is an esoteric term to be used only in the abstract and that the probability of real-world events can never be computed. Therefore, real-world risk can never be computed.

But there is an alternative to this philosophical quagmire. One equally valid view of probability is the subjectivist view. This view is that all probabilities are simply a quantified expression of our uncertainty about a thing. This holds that there is no uncertainty independent of an observer. It doesn't matter whether the coin was already flipped, whether the flip was "strictly repeatable," or whether coin flips are "true randomness." The fact is that we are uncertain of the outcome and our uncertainty is best described by saying that we put a 50% probability on heads.

This subjectivist view is also often called the *Bayesian* view. Bayes's Theorem is a particularly useful tool in statistics developed by the Reverend Thomas Bayes and published three years after his death in 1761. But Bayes himself didn't take a position on this issue of frequentist-versus-subjectivist interpretations of probability. Bayes's Theorem gives the same answer to a given problem, like every other formula in probability theory or statistics, whether the user is a frequentist or not, and I believe calling subjectivism *Bayesianism* is a source of confusion to some about this powerful tool (more to come on Bayes later).

Which of these is right—the frequentist's view or the subjectivist's view? I propose what I think is the only pragmatic position. At one level, who cares? No formula in probability theory or statistics actually asks one to specify whether one is a subjectivist or objectivist regarding probability. Although some will argue that probability theory and statistics implies one of these answers, the fact is that this claim is not testable either way. In this sense, the entire issue is what Carl Sagan would call an "invisible dragon":

> Now, what's the difference between an invisible, incorporeal, floating dragon who spits heatless fire and no dragon at all? If there's no way to disprove my contention, no conceivable experiment that would count against it, what does it mean to say that my dragon exists? Your inability to invalidate my hypothesis is not at all the same thing as proving it true. Claims that cannot be tested, assertions immune to disproof are veridically worthless, whatever value they may have in inspiring us or in exciting our sense of wonder.[4]

Sagan, like Taleb, was a fan of the philosopher Karl Popper and his views on science. If some distinction mattered at all, it should be observable in some way. If it mattered to decision makers who make choices under uncertainty whether a probability was "objective," then it should be possible to design a game or even a real business decision that would be different if you had already "flipped the coins." But no such game or real-life problem exists. If there is an optimal action for the manager, then the optimal action is the same under both conditions.

If a manager considers betting on whether a project will finish on time to be just as desirable as (not better or worse than) betting the same amount on a coin flip, then that manager is effectively saying that he believes there is a 50% probability the project will finish on time. Any rational analysis of his choices would consider, for all practical purposes, his subjective probability of 50% to be equivalent to an objective probability of 50%. There is no problem set where it should make a difference to the decision maker whether the probability was *truly random* or not. In fact, the existence of true randomness is not even a testable claim according to the standards of Popper and Sagan. All we can test for is our uncertainty. Consider the following strings of numbers:

- 1582662204348132742253364306751213233459
- 5897932384626433832795028841971693993751

Which is random? If I told you that one was generated with rolls of a 10-sided die and that the other was based on a well-known constant (and therefore deterministic), would it matter if you were betting on what the next digit would be? Unless you are able to figure out which constant I'm talking about, you should be equally uncertain about the next digit in both strings.

On a side note, the position that the concept of "probability" does not apply to uncertain events that have already occurred (e.g. a coin that has already been flipped but is not revealed to you) is the basis for another esoteric controversy among statisticians. Some statisticians argue that the phrase "90% confidence interval" (as described it in Chapter 6) does not really mean there is a 90% probability that the interval contains the value in question. They claim, "Given any two numbers, the parameter . . . , since it is a constant, is either between such numbers or not between such numbers."[5] But in a review of 20 statistics texts I easily find more sources (both basic and advanced, including several classics) that explicitly define a confidence interval as having the stated *probability* of containing the answer.[6,7,8] Those that take the former position (some rather vehemently) are simply starting with the frequentist view whether they know of this debate or not. When they describe what "90% confidence interval" means in the absence of probability, they will claim it means that after a large number of such tests, the true value will have fallen within the stated interval. In other words, it's exactly the same test I would apply if it *were* a probability. This is a distinction no different than the distinction between Sagan's invisible dragon and no dragon at all.

In reality, *true randomness*, *strict repeatability*, and *objectiveness* of a probability are all untestable and irrelevant to us in the real world. Some uncertainty may be fundamentally *irreducible*, but we could never prove that. To a manager, all that really matters is her uncertainty and whether further attempts at uncertainty reduction might be fruitful, regardless of whether all uncertainty is reducible. This leaves us with no choice in the debate. To real-world decision makers, the only useful meaning of the word *probability* is that of the subjectivists. We will use probabilities as an expression of our uncertainty.

We're Special: The Belief that Risk Analysis Might Work, But Not Here

For a risk manager or chief risk officer (CRO), there is usually not a wholesale rejection of the notion that risk can be assessed and managed (the claim some make, but which none actually live by). But it is common to argue that any methods that might have more quantitative validity, for some reason, just don't apply to their environment.

Many managers see their own environments as somehow uniquely complex. I've applied quantitative methods in nuclear power, insurance, mass media, military logistics, software projects, large construction projects, security, and issues of public health and safety. Yet, I still periodically hear, "Yes, but none of those are exactly like our business." True; but none of any of the previously mentioned applications are exactly like the others, and we still used quantitative models effectively.

If I point out the usefulness of conducting some aspects of risk management more like an actuary might conduct them, I may hear the objection, "But the insurance industry has a lot of data—we have none." Here, I'll reiterate a few more points from my first book, *How to Measure Anything*:

- Whatever your measurement problem is, it's been done before.
- You have more data than you think.
- You need less data than you think.
- Getting more data (by direct observation) is more economical than you think.
- (An addition to the original list): You probably need completely different data than you think.

Each of these assumptions is much more productive than the typical set of assumptions that people start with (that is, the very opposite set of the assumptions above). If we simply assumed, as most people usually do, that we don't have enough data or that this has never been measured before, then the enquiry will stop at that point. But resourceful managers will not stop at that imagined barrier.

When people say they don't have enough data, have they actually determined how much they need and what can be inferred from the data they have (no matter how little it is)? Did they actually determine—or even consider—the cost of getting new data based on new observations? Did they determine that the data they think they need even applies to the problem, or that some other more obvious measurement would be more relevant? When I ask these questions, the answers are the results of specific calculations (which I will discuss in more detail later). When people make these claims, it is virtually guaranteed that they have done *none* of this math.

One 2001 book on environmental risk analysis characterized *actuarial risk* as being limited to "provid[ing] only aggregate data over large segments of the population and for long time duration."[9] There are at least two errors in this claim. The first actuary I asked about this disagreed (apparently the authors of the book didn't ask any actuaries about this definition). Christopher (Kip) Bohn, the actuary from Aon whom I quoted previously, said, "I wouldn't agree with that at all. Ideally, actuaries would like to have lots of data but sometimes that's just not the case. Even when there is historical data, there are things that have changed and the data that you have is no longer applicable."

Yes, it is true that insurance companies have quite a lot of data on insurance claims and this information is critical to computing risks. But they also have to include information on which they have very little data and that is often in the areas where they have the greatest exposure. For example, the mortality tables in insurance are based on a great deal of data about the deaths of men and women at various ages, degrees of healthiness, and so on. But how much data do they have about a pandemic virus or a major change in health trends that may affect their risks of offering life insurance?

Bohn says, "For a while, we were seeing people getting older, but now we see people getting more obese and the life span trend begins to turn." If an insurance company offers a life insurance product that has a fixed premium as long as the policy is active, then future changes in mortality trends may mean that they pay life insurance claims far too frequently and too soon. Unfortunately, this risk can't be diversified by selling more life insurance to more people.

And, unknown to some people, insurance companies insure fairly rare events for which they have little if any historical data:

- *Major event insurance.* The International Olympic Committee and cities where the Olympics were held have taken out insurance to protect against cancellations due to terrorism or other disasters. Since the modern revival in 1896, the games have been canceled only three times—once due to World War I and twice during World War II.
- *Prize insurance.* The $10 million "X-Prize" for the first privately funded manned flight of a reusable vehicle to an altitude of 100 km was insured in case someone won it (which someone did). The premium cost $5 million—which the insurer would have kept if no one had claimed the prize.
- *Coupon insurance.* For risk of "overredemption" of coupons, retailers buy this insurance just in case far too many people decide to redeem a coupon. Retailers know that only a small percentage of coupons will be used but that a large number have to be distributed just to reach those who would use it. But there is a risk that a promotion might be unexpectedly successful (or that hard economic times force more coupon clipping) and that the retailer might lose money on it.

- *Credit risk insurance in developing or high-risk nations.* Some insurers underwrite credit risks (the risk of receivables not getting paid) in developing economies or high-risk regions, including war zones, where there is risk of government default or intervention. Such insurance is called *confiscation, expropriation, nationalization, and deprivation (CEND)* insurance.

How much data do these insurers have for such policies? How many data points are there for civil wars in *any* country? There may be many data points for product promotions, but isn't every product promotion different? We will see later that quantitative methods are useful in many areas even where there is much complexity, unknown unknowns, and an apparent lack of data.

We have only scratched the surface of a comprehensive list of the main fallacies, misconceptions, and cognitive obstacles to understanding risks and risk management methods. I was recently talking to a government agency manager about quantitative methods for risks of certain kinds of terrorist attacks. The manager said, "We can't compute the odds of an event that never happened." That was from an authoritative source, he said—a "respected PhD." Yet, other respected PhDs go right on doing exactly that—they compute the odds of events that have never occurred. The nuclear power industry, for example, uses quantitative models to assess the odds of "1-in-100-year" or even "1-in-500-year" events—which is, of course, much longer than the nuclear power industry has been in existence. The methods for doing this simply involve knowing the probabilities of failures of each component in a system (for which the industry has extensive historical failure data) and building quantitative models.

This is just one more example of what I'm sure is a very long list of illusionary obstacles to quantitative risk management. By the end of this book, I hope to overturn a few more of these misconceptions.

NOTES

1. Some analysts indicated that the crash of 1987 was "13 standard deviations" from the norm. In a normal distribution, such an event is about one chance in about 10^{39}. Others indicated it was a 16 or 20 standard deviation event—one chance in 10^{58} and 10^{89}, respectively.

2. E. Gelman, "Fear of a Black Swan: Risk Guru Nassim Taleb Talks about Why Wall Street Fails to Anticipate Disaster," *Fortune,* April 3, 2008.
3. S. Paterson, "Mr. Volatility and the Swan," *Wall Street Journal Online,* July 13, 2007.
4. C. Sagan, *The Demon-Haunted World: Science as a Candle in the Dark* (Ballantine Books, 1996).
5. L. Smith, D. Williams, *Statistical Analysis for Business: A Conceptual Approach* (Wadsworth Publishing Company, 1976) pg. 303.
6. G. Weinberg, J. Schumaker, *Statistics; An Intuitive Approach, 2nd Edition* (Wadsworth Publishing Company, 1962 pp. 183–4).
7. D. Raj, *Design of Sample Surveys*, McGraw Hill Series in Probability and Statistics 1972, pg 17.
8. A.A. Sveshnikov, *Problems In Probability Theory, Mathematical Statistics and Theory of Random Functions*, (Dover Publications, 1958).
9. C.C. Jaeger, O. Renn, and E.A. Rosa, *Risk, Uncertainty, and Rational Action* (Earthscan, 2001).

CHAPTER 9

Where Even the Quants Go Wrong: Common and Fundamental Errors in Quantitative Models

There is perhaps no beguilement more insidious and dangerous than an elaborate and elegant mathematical process built upon unfortified premises.

—THOMAS C. CHAMBERLAIN, GEOLOGIST (1899)

When it comes to improving risk management, I'm an unrepentant bigot for quantitative methods in the assessment, mitigation, or deliberate selection of risks for the right opportunities. I think the solution to fixing many of the problems we've identified in risk management will be found in the use of more quantitative methods—but with one important caveat. In everything I've written so far, I've promoted the idea that risk management methods should be subjected to scientifically sound testing methods. We should hold even the most "quantitative" models to that same rigor. They get no special treatment because they simply seem more mathematical or were once developed and used by highly regarded scientists.

The idea that the mere use of very sophisticated-looking mathematical models must automatically be right has been called *crackpot rigor* and a risk manager should always be on guard against that. Unfortunately, the rapid growth in use of sophisticated tools has, in many cases, outpaced the growth in the skills to use these tools and the use of questionable "quantitative" methods seems to be growing out of hand.

I'm a fan of science and scientific method. But science has evolved to its current advanced state in part because some scientists have always questioned other scientists, and the stature of any individual or institution could never in the long run withstand contradictory findings in repeated, independent tests. This chapter is an introduction to some of the quantitative methods in risk management and how they fair under empirical testing.

Introduction to Monte Carlo Concepts

This book is meant for managers from all sorts of backgrounds who need to get involved in risk management. For those who are not familiar with *Monte Carlo simulations* (mentioned in Chapter 4), I will provide a very basic introduction to the concept before going further.

When business managers consider possible investments in new products, technologies, or facilities, or any other use of capital, they might sit down with a spreadsheet and think through the costs and benefits. They might say the new equipment will produce one million widgets with a per-unit profit of $2 each. For now, we'll keep this very simple, but in business school the managers were taught to also include the life of the equipment, tax implications, interest rates, inflation, annual growth rates, and more. They would use this to compute some exact value for the return on investment (ROI). For now, let's just say we have an all-maintenance-included lease of $1 million for a year and we have to make at least that much to break even.

Managers might treat each of the values as a "best guess" even though they know they don't know any of these values exactly and the ROI they just computed is also highly uncertain. The demand for the new product will not generate exactly $2 million per year but some range of possible values. The machine has the capacity to produce enough, 1.25 million, widgets per year but the manager "conservatively" assumed it would work at only 80% capacity. Let's say we think we could be off by as many as 750,000 widgets per year—either under or over—on our demand for this product. If the average of all possible demands is one million widgets per year at $2 per widget and we can be off by three-quarters of a million, what is the average profit per year? It's not $2 million.

The belief that the average revenue is $2 million in this case is what Stanford professor Sam Savage calls the "Flaw of Averages." Because managers may not explicitly try to account for their uncertainties, it can lead to some bad decisions. Because of the constraints, the average of possible outcomes will be something less than the $2 million. If we weren't running into the machines' capacity as an upper bound, then the higher-than-expected demand might average out the lower-than-expected demand. But if the demand were 1.7 million widgets per year, we could still produce no more than 1.25 million. However, the only lower bound on the capacity is zero. Because we bump into the ceiling of 1.25 million widgets no matter what the demand is, but demand could go as low as zero, the average production level is not the average demand and, therefore, the average revenue is something less than $2 million.

One way to more realistically account for this uncertainty is to generate a large number of possible scenarios. We can randomly generate the demand and apply the capacity constraints. We can even generate possible values for the profit per widget. Let's say that our estimates are not point estimates but ranges, as follows:

- *Demand.* 250,000 to 1,750,000 widgets per year
- *Profit per widget.* $1.50 to $2.50

We'll call these ranges 90% CI with a normal distribution (first mentioned in Chapter 6). Keep in mind that this means there is a 5% chance the value would be above the upper bound and a 5% chance it would be below the lower bound. Now, what does the annual profit look like considering that we can't produce less than zero or more than 1.25 million? I show a simple Monte Carlo solution to this in a spreadsheet available on www.howtofixriskmgt.com.

The simulation shows 10,000 scenarios, where one scenario might show a demand of 800,000 widgets at $2 per widget, for a gross profit of $1.6 million. Another might show a demand of 1.4 million widgets, an actual production of 1.25 million (the capacity of the machine), and a profit of $2.2 per widget for a gross profit of $2.75 million per year.

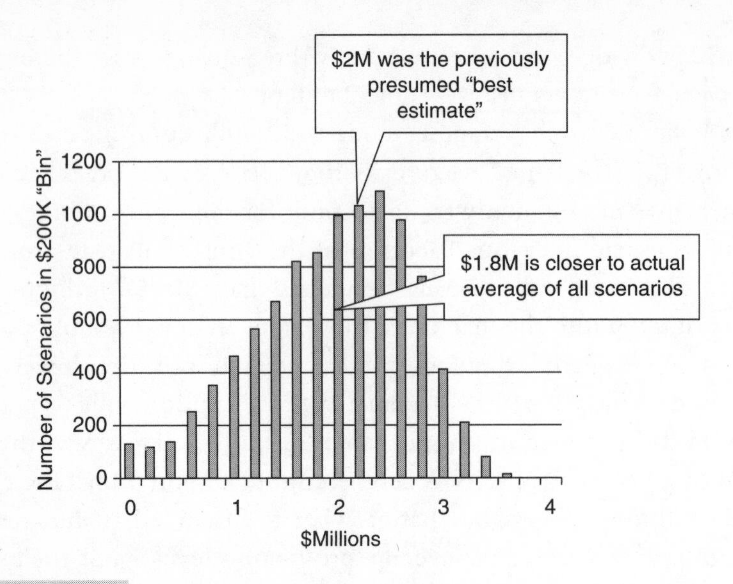

EXHIBIT 9.1 **Histogram of Outcomes**

Exhibit 9.1 shows how those outcomes are distributed by counting the number of results that ended up in a series of "bins," which I defined in intervals of $200,000 (one bin is the range of $600K to $800K, another is $800K to $1 million, etc.). Charts that show the number of instances in each of a series of ranges of values is called a *histogram*. Of the 10,000 scenarios simulated, about 450 came out between $800,000 and $1 million. About 210 landed between $3 million and $3.2 million. The total count in each of these bins is represented as the height of the bar in the exhibit.

This is obviously a very simple example. We can simulate uncertainties about other items such as periodic downtime with the piece of equipment (which affects our capacity), the lifespan of the piece of equipment, or even the possibility that the product produced will be obsolete before the end of the life of the equipment and demand will vanish. If we had determined that because of the lease and of other costs of doing business we'd have to generate at least $1 million per year to break even, then we can compute the risk of losing money on this equipment.

Since about 1,500 of our 10,000 scenarios generated less than $1 million per year for us, we can say that the chance of losing money is 15%. We can also say that there is about a 1% probability of making no revenue at all and

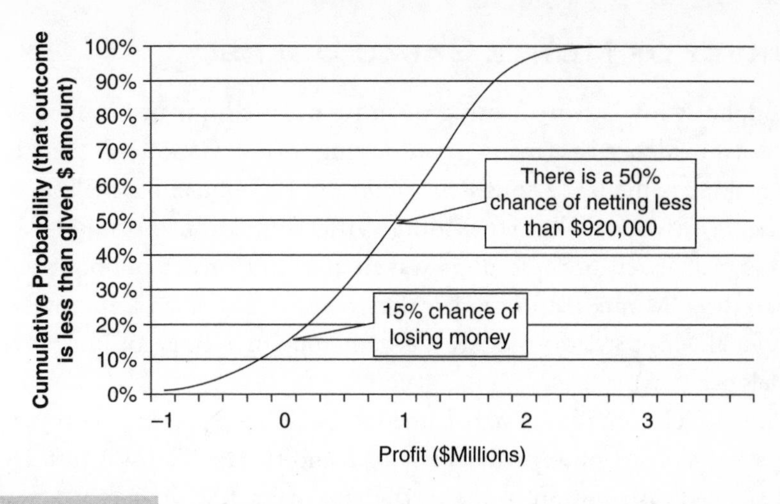

EXHIBIT 9.2 **Cumulative Probability**

losing the entire $1 million lease. Now we are speaking about risk in useful terms. Another way of looking at this is what is sometimes called a *cumulative probability* chart, as shown in Exhibit 9.2.

Without this simulation, it would have been very difficult for anyone other than mathematical savants to assess the risk in probabilistic terms. Imagine how difficult it would be in a more realistically complex situation. Imagine we were simulating all the components of a supply chain, with inventory levels at each stage, possible interruptions from vendors, and unplanned downtime in the factory, along with variations in demand. We could break each simulation into small time units to show how some events could cascade in a way that causes other problems. It would seem impossible to legitimately assess these risks without such simulations. In fact, the Nuclear Regulatory Commission and oil companies in high-risk exploration investments believe there is no other valid way to assess these risks.

But the availability of Monte Carlo tools for PCs has both pros and cons. Availability makes Monte Carlo simulations much more practical for a wide variety of problems. But it also brings a much larger body of users who might not use the disciplines that have evolved in industries that have used Monte Carlo simulations for decades. Let's examine how two popular Monte Carlo tools are actually used and confront these issues.

Survey of Monte Carlo Users

Throughout my career in using quantitative methods in business, I had anecdotal evidence that many persons using Monte Carlo tools were probably making some fairly consistent errors. So I conducted a small survey of 35 users of two well-known Monte Carlo simulation tools, @Risk and Crystal Ball. Each of these users was then asked for details about the last one to three Monte Carlo models they constructed. Data for a total of 72 individual Monte Carlo models was gathered (an average of just over two models per user).

The modelers in the survey claimed to be fairly experienced on average. The average years of experience was 6.2 and the median was just 4 years (this skewed distribution is due to the fact that a few people had over 15 years of experience but there were many at the bottom end of the scale). Most of the models were not terribly complicated—73% had fewer than 50 variables. Those surveyed worked on a variety of Monte Carlo applications including:

- Business plans
- Financial portfolio risks
- Sales forecasts
- Information technology projects
- Mining and oil exploration
- Pharmaceutical product development
- Project schedule and budget forecasts
- Engineering and scientific models such as radar simulations and materials strength
- Competitive bidding
- Capital investments in the steel industry
- Alternatives analysis on supply chains and inventory levels
- Building construction risks
- Product variations in manufacturing

I asked them questions about where they got their data from and about quality control on their models. Here is what I found:

- There were a lot of subjective estimates but *no* calibration of probabilities. An overwhelming majority of those surveyed—89%—used some subjective estimates in models. On average, the percentage of variables in all models that were subjective estimates was 44%. However, not one of the modelers ever used—*or had even heard of*—calibration training. As discussed in Chapter 6, this would mean that almost all estimates were overconfident and all of the models understated risks.

- When I asked about validating forecasts against reality, only one respondent had ever attempted to check actual outcomes against original forecasts. This question produced a lot of "hand-waving" and carefully qualified statements from the other respondents. The one person who claimed he did do some validation of original forecasts could not produce the data for it. Instead, he offered only anecdotal evidence.
- While 75% of models used some existing historical data, only 35% of the models reviewed used any original empirical measurements gathered specifically for the model. Furthermore, only 4% ever conducted an additional empirical measurement to reduce uncertainty where the model is the most sensitive. In contrast, I find that, based on sensitivity analysis and computing the value of further measurements, all but 2 of the 60 models I've personally developed in the last 14 years required further measurement. It appears that most modelers assume that they can model only on subjective estimates and the existing data they are given. The idea of conducting original empirical research is almost completely absent from Monte Carlo modeling.

The most disturbing finding of all the survey results was that while most modelers used subjective estimates, none surveyed had ever used calibration training prior to asking subject matter experts to provide estimates. The problem is exacerbated further by the fact that the very models that focused on the biggest, riskiest issues used even more subjective estimates and the very items that required subjective estimates were often the most sensitive in the model.

I could have made this a much larger sample if I had included the clients I had trained myself, but I didn't want to bias the sample by including them. However, when I asked those I trained about models they built before I met them, the results were the same. Of those who did build quantitative models based even partly on subjective estimates, none had used or even heard of calibration. This includes large groups of economists and statisticians who routinely performed Monte Carlo simulations on a variety of critical government policy decisions.

Also, the general lack of outward-looking empirical methods and of checking the quality of past models were critical issues for Monte Carlo modeling. Even the fact that I had to conduct this survey says something about the industry. Just as doctors are said to make the worst patients, those who measure things such as risk are among the least likely to measure themselves. It appears that broad scholarly work in investigating how Monte Carlo simulations are used is virtually nonexistent. There is more research in how people make impulse purchases at a checkout counter than in how users of Monte Carlo models assess critical risks of major organizations.

There is more research in how people make impulse purchases at a checkout counter than in how users of Monte Carlo models assess critical risks of major organizations.

These findings complement or may even explain several other key problems with how some of the most sophisticated risk analysis tools are being used or misused.

The Risk Paradox

Jim DeLoach at the risk management consulting firm Protiviti observed, "Risk management is hopelessly buried at the lowest levels in organizations. I see risk analysis focus on the chance that someone will cut off a thumb on the shop floor." The paradox in risk management that I've observed anecdotally over the years, and that seems to be observed by many risk experts I talk to, is that the most sophisticated risk analysis methods used in an organization are often applied to low-level operational risks, whereas the biggest risks use softer methods or none at all.

THE RISK PARADOX

The most sophisticated risk analysis methods used in an organization are often applied to low-level operational risks, whereas the biggest risks use softer methods or none at all.

My standard anecdote for the *risk paradox* comes from the 1990s, when I was teaching a seminar on my Applied Information Economics (AIE) method to what I thought was an audience of chief information officers (CIOs) and IT managers. I asked if anyone had applied Monte Carlo simulations and other quantitative risk analysis methods. This was almost entirely a rhetorical question since I had never seen anyone raise a hand in any other seminar where I asked that question. But this time, one manager—from the paper products company Boise Cascade—raised his hand. Impressed, I said, "You are the first CIO I've ever met who said he used Monte Carlo simulations to evaluate risks in IT projects." He said, "But I'm not a CIO. I'm not in the IT department, either. I analyze risks in paper production operations." I asked, "In that case, do you know whether they are used in your firm on IT projects?" He responded, "No, they are not used there. I'm the only person doing this in the firm." I then asked, "Which do you think is riskier, the problems you work on, or new IT projects?" He affirmed that IT projects were much riskier, but received none of his more sophisticated risk analysis techniques. Here are just a few more examples of the risk paradox:

- As mentioned in Chapter 1, Baxter, like many other pharmaceutical companies, uses quantitative risk models on stop-gate analysis—the assessment of the decision to move ahead to the next big phase in the development of a new product. The reason sophisticated methods are justified for that problem is the same reason they are justified in oil exploration—it is a large capital outlay with a lot of uncertainty about the return. But the legal liabilities from the heparin case may (as of the writing of this book) still turn out to be much larger than the capital investments in the next phase of a new drug.
- During and before the 2008 financial crisis, banks that routinely did some quantitative risk analysis on individual loans rarely did any

quantitative risk analysis on how economic downturns would affect their entire portfolio.

- Long Term Capital Management (LTCM) used the Nobel Prize–winning Options Theory to evaluate the price of individual options, but the big risk was the extent of the leverage they used on trades and, again, how their entire portfolio could be affected by broader economic trends.
- Insurance companies use advanced methods to assess the risks accepted by insurance products and the contingent losses on their reserves, but major business risks that are outside of what is strictly insurance get little or none of this analysis—as with AIG and their credit default swaps.
- There are some risk analysis methods that have been applied to the risks of cost and schedule overruns for IT projects. But the risks of interference with business operations due to IT disasters are rarely quantified. A case in point is the enterprise resource planning (ERP) system being installed at Hershey Foods Corp. in 1999. Meant to integrate business operations into a seamless system, the ERP project was months behind and the cost ran up to $115 million. They attempted to go live in September of that year but, over the all-important Halloween season, they were still fixing problems with order processing and shipping functions of the system. Business was being lost to competitors and they posted a 12.4% drop in revenue. This risk was much greater than the risk of the ERP cost overrun itself.

This sequestration of some of the best risk analysis methods causes problems with the further evolution of risk management. The relative isolation of risk analysis in some organizations means that different analysts in the same organization may work in isolation from each other and build completely inconsistent models. And the lack of collaboration within firms makes another important step of risk management almost impossible—a cooperative initiative to build models of industrial economics and global risks across organizational boundaries.

The Measurement Inversion

For the simple widget simulation we discussed earlier in this chapter, imagine that you had an opportunity to reduce your uncertainty about either the demand or the per-unit profit. Which one would you measure first and how much would you be willing to spend? For years, I've been computing the value of additional information on every uncertain variable in a model.

As mentioned in the earlier example, we would find that about 1,500 of our 10,000 scenarios we generated for the widget-production opportunity failed to make enough money to pay for the one-year lease. For each of those scenarios, we lost some amount of money. If we decide to go ahead with this lease and we get one of these undesirable scenarios, the amount of money we would lose is the *opportunity loss (OL)*—the cost of making the wrong choice. If we didn't lose money, then the OL was zero. We can also have an opportunity loss if we decide not to sign the lease but then find out we *could* have made money. In the case of rejecting the lease, the OL is the difference between the lease and the money we made on the widgets if we would have made money—zero if the equipment did not make money (in which case we were right to reject the idea).

The *expected opportunity loss (EOL)* is each possible opportunity loss times the chance of that loss—in other words, the chance of being wrong times the cost of being wrong. In our Monte Carlo simulation, we simply average the OL for all of the scenarios. For now, let's say that given the current level of uncertainty about this equipment investment, you still think the lease is a good idea. In each scenario the OL is either 0 (if we made money) or the cost of the lease minus the money we made (in those cases where we didn't make money). We would find that the EOL is about $60,000.

The EOL is equivalent to another term called the *expected value of perfect information (EVPI)*. The EVPI is the most you would reasonably be willing to pay if you could eliminate all uncertainty about this decision. While it is almost impossible to ever get "perfect" information and eliminate all uncertainty, this value is useful as an absolute upper bound. If we can reduce the $60,000 EOL by half with a survey that would cost $8,000, then the survey is probably a good deal. If you want to see a spreadsheet calculation of this and a more elaborate EVPI problem, these can be found on www.howtofixriskmgt.com under this chapter on the reader downloads page.

This becomes more enlightening when we compute the value of information for each variable in a model, especially when the models get very large. This way we not only get an idea for how much to spend on measurement, but also which specific variables we need to measure and how much we might be willing to spend on them. I have done this calculation for 60 models where most had about 50 to 100 variables (for a total of over

4,000 variables). From this I've seen patterns that still persist every time I add more analysis to my library. The two main findings are:

1. Relatively few variables require further measurement—but there are almost always *some*.
2. The uncertain variables with the highest EVPI (highest value for further measurement) tend to be those that the organization almost never measures, *and* the variables they *have* been measuring have, on average, the lowest EVPI.

I call this second finding the *measurement inversion*, and I've seen it in IT portfolios, military logistics, environmental policy, venture capital, market forecasts, and every other place I've looked.

Everybody, everywhere, is focusing on the least valuable measurements at the expense of the most valuable measurements.

Everybody, everywhere, is systematically measuring all the wrong things. It is so pervasive and impactful that I have to wonder how much this affects the Gross Domestic Product. Organizations appear to measure what they know how to measure without wondering whether they should learn new measurement methods for very-high-value uncertainties.

Where's the Science? The Lack of Empiricism in Risk Models

The measurement inversion is related to a broader issue of the general lack of empiricism in most Monte Carlo models. Let me reiterate and expand on some findings from the Monte Carlo survey and other observations:

- *Subject matter experts (SMEs) are not calibrated.* Input is used from SMEs without any knowledge of their past performance in making estimates and forecasts. All subjective inputs are very likely systematically overconfident, and therefore risk is greatly understated.

- *Models that are built are rarely back tested.* Comparing models to history is not itself a conclusive validation, but models that do not fit historical reality at all are very likely flawed. If anyone had done this on certain financial models, they would have known the 2008/9 a financial crisis was much more likely than the models indicated.
- *Only a small fraction of Monte Carlo models make use of new empirical measures specifically made for highly uncertain and sensitive variables in the model.* The few empirical measures that are used tend to be those already available to the risk analysts. It rarely occurs to a risk analyst to conduct original research to reduce uncertainty about some part of the model, even though the EVPI calculation mentioned previously would for most big decisions easily justify the additional expense for most big decisions.
- *Opportunities for marginal uncertainty reduction are overlooked.* For highly uncertain variables, even a few empirical observations can significantly reduce uncertainty.
- *There is a pervasive lack of incentive to follow up on previous forecasts to see how well they did.* Each model often has dozens of individual estimates and they add up quickly after a few models. I've done 60 models in the past 14 years and they total to over 4,000 variables. Many of these are variables where we would know exact quantities after the fact (e.g., comparing the actual cost of a project to its originally forecasted range). As difficult as it sometimes is (given that some clients I had years ago have moved, or that some didn't track a metric as recommended), the follow-up effort is always enlightening. It confirms some parts of models and indicates the need for refining other parts of models. It is the only way to consistently improve. But I find almost no colleagues who attempt this.

But there are solutions. In my previous book, *How to Measure Anything*, I explained how many things that might seem to be immeasurable really aren't. Some experts with strong quantitative backgrounds are among those who make this mistake. For example, there is sometimes an assumption that "we don't have enough data" to measure a variable. This belief is usually based on several fallacies. The fact is that the amount of data you need, what can be derived from existing data, and what kind of data is needed are all the result of specific calculations using both the prior state of uncertainty and the data that is gathered. I find it's always the case that the ones claiming they didn't have the data, didn't do the math to prove that claim.

Contrary to what is taught to some first-semester statistics students, there is no standard "minimum acceptable" level of data one needs for "statistically significant" findings. In Chapter 11, I'll describe some methods that can squeeze useful measurements (i.e., uncertainty reductions) out of very few observations and, again, I'll point you to spreadsheets on the book's website. For now, know that the right math shows that when a variable is highly uncertain, even a few observations can significantly reduce uncertainty. Uncertainty reduction is the goal of a measurement and, without doing the math, we shouldn't presume how much uncertainty reduction we can get from some simple observations or how much that uncertainty reduction is worth relative to the cost of the measurement.

Another imagined obstacle to the use of more empirical methods is the belief that separate events are so unique that literally nothing can be learned about one by looking at another. It is said that each IT project, each construction project, each merger is so special and unique that no previous event tells us anything about the risks of the next event. This would be like an insurance company telling me that they cannot even compute a premium for my life insurance because I'm a completely unique individual. Although we know insurance companies don't let that stand in the way of good risk analysis, many other fields are not immune to this misconception. Even some scientists, such as geologists who study volcanoes (volcanologists), seem to have woven this into their culture. This is the very reason why the risk of a catastrophic eruption of Mount St. Helens in 1980 was ignored by volcano experts. (See The Mount St. Helens Fallacy inset.)

THE MOUNT ST. HELENS FALLACY

Fallacy: If two systems are dissimilar in some way, they cannot be compared. In effect, this fallacy states that if there are any differences at all, there can be no useful similarities.

On May 18th,1980, Mount St. Helens in the Cascade Range of Washington State exploded, in the most destructive volcanic event in U.S. history. Over 50 people were killed, 250 homes were destroyed, and over 200 square miles of forest was leveled.

Prior to the eruption, rising magma had formed a bulge on the north side that protruded so far it became unstable. At 8:32 am the huge bulge slid off and "uncorked" the magma column resulting in a "lateral" explosion (meaning it exploded out of one side).

Scientists who previously studied the volcano found no geological evidence that a large lateral explosion had ever occurred on Mount St. Helens before . . . and therefore ignored the possibility. A U.S. Geological Survey geologist Richard Hoblitt stated, "Before 1980, the volcanic-hazards assessment for a given volcano in the Cascade Range were based on events that had previously occurred at that volcano. The 1980 directed blast showed that unprecedented events are possible and that they need to be considered."[1]

Scientists had to ignore even the basic physics of the system to conclude that, because it had not happened before, it could not happen now. There is no way the bulge could have been stable and a landslide had to release pressure. Hopefully, unprecedented events are now considered systematically, but that message has not sunk in for everyone. In a Discovery Channel special on volcanoes, one volcanologist said "No two volcanoes are exactly alike. So in order to study a volcano you really have to study the history of *that* volcano." Put another way, this is Taleb's turkey—by looking at *that* turkey it would never be apparent that its about to be killed. We only know this from looking at the history of other turkeys.

But, actually, looking at other volcanoes does tell us something about a particular volcano. (If not, then what exactly is the *expertise* of a volcano expert?) Furthermore, from a risk analysis point of view, volcanoes not only have something in common with other volcanoes, they have a lot in common with forest fires, power outages, wars and stock markets. That's the next topic.

Financial Models and the Shape of Disaster: Why *Normal* Isn't So Normal

A common probability distribution used by many Monte Carlo modelers is the *normal* or *Gaussian* distribution. It is used because it seems to fit a range of observed phenomenon from physics, manufacturing errors, and certain

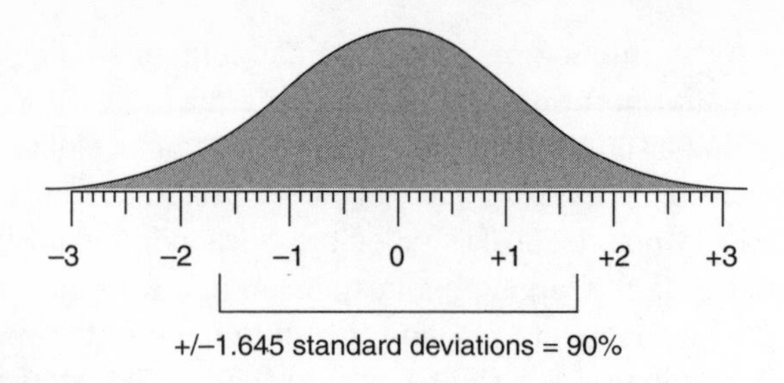

EXHIBIT 9.3 **The Normal Distribution**

actuarial data. It is also the fundamental assumption behind Options Theory and Modern Portfolio Theory, two influential methods in finance that won the Nobel Prize for their creators—and may have contributed to the ruin of some the methods' adherents.

The normal distribution is a bell-shaped symmetrical probability distribution that describes the output of some random or uncertain processes. The *bell* shape (see Exhibit 9.3) means that outcomes are more likely to be near the middle and very unlikely at the tails. The shape can be fully described by just two dimensions—its *mean* and *standard deviation.* Since this is a symmetrical and not a skewed (i.e., lopsided) distribution, the mean is dead center. The standard deviation represents a kind of *unit of uncertainty* around the mean.

SIMPLE RANDOM SURVEY EXAMPLE USING A NORMAL DISTRIBUTION

If you haven't thought about normal distributions lately, here is a very simple example. The math for this and a more detailed explanation can be found at www.howtofixriskmgt.com.

Normal distributions are useful for showing the error in a random sample. If a random survey of commuters says drivers on average spend 25 minutes each way in a commute to work, then that means the average of all the responses in the survey is 25 minutes. But to determine how far from reality this survey result could be, the standard deviation of the "error of the estimate" is computed, which can then be used to determine a range with a given confidence. To communicate how far off the mean of the survey might be from reality (which he could only know if he surveyed all commuters), the statistician often computes a *confidence interval (CI)*—a range that probably contains the real average of the entire population of commuters. The width of this range is directly related to the standard deviation. Let's say the statistician determines the standard deviation of the error of the estimate is 2 minutes and that he decides to show this range as a "90% confidence interval" (meaning he is 90% confident that the range contains the true answer). By referencing a table (or an Excel function), he knows the upper bound of a 90% CI is 1.645 standard deviations above the mean and that the lower bound is 1.645 standard deviations below the mean. So he computes the upper bound of the range as $25 + 1.645 \times 2 = 28.3$ and the lower bound as $25 - 1.645 \times 2 = 21.7$. *Voilà*, the survey shows with 90% confidence that the average commute is between 21.7 minutes and 28.3 minutes.

The normal distribution is not just any bell shape, but a very particular bell shape. If you are saying that the distribution of hits around a bull's-eye of a target on a firing range is "normal," then you are saying that—after a sufficiently large number of shots—68.2% of the shots land within one standard deviation of the center, 95.3% are within two standard deviations, 99.7% are within three, and so on. But not all distributions exactly fit this shape. To determine whether a normal distribution is a good fit, statisticians might use a mathematical method called the *Kolmogorov-Smirnov test (K-S test)* to determine *goodness of fit* for a normal distribution. This test is probably the most popular—but probably the least relevant for risk analysis.

The main concerns for risk analysts are at the tails of the distributions, and the K-S test is very insensitive to how "fat" the tails are. I mentioned in Chapter 8 how this might not work well. If we apply the normal distribution to Dow Jones daily price changes from 1928 to 2008, we would find a standard deviation of about 1.157% for a daily price change (as a percentage relative to the previous day). Since the bounds of a 90% CI are

1.645 standard deviations away from the mean, that means that about 90% of daily price changes would be within 1.9% of the previous day. In reality, about 93% fell within this range, but it's close. But when we get further out from the "average" trading day, the normal distribution drastically understates the likelihood of big drops. As first mentioned in Chapter 8, a normal distribution says that a 5% price drop from the previous day should have had a less than 15% chance of occurring *even once* during that 80-year period while in reality it happened 70 times.

But, since the K-S test focuses on the main body of the distribution and is insensitive to the tails, an analyst using it would have determined that normal is a pretty good assumption on which to base a financial model. And for a risk analyst who worries more about the tails, it is wrong by not just a little, but a lot. With the Dow Jones data, the likelihood of even more extreme events—like a 7% single-day price drop—will be underestimated by a factor of a *billion* or more. Note that this distribution is the basic assumption, however, for the Nobel Prize–winning theories of Modern Portfolio Theory and Options Theory—two very widely used models. (*Note:* A technical person will point out that absolute price changes are actually the *log-normal* cousin of a normal distribution, but since I expressed the data in terms of price changes as a ratio relative to the previous day, I can apply the normal distribution.)

What shape do financial crashes really take? It turns out that financial disasters take on a distribution more like the distribution of volcanic eruptions, forest fires, earthquakes, power outages, asteroid impacts, and pandemic viruses. These phenomena take on a *power-law distribution* instead of a normal distribution. An event that follows a power law can be described as following a rule like this: "A once-in-a-decade event is *X* times as big as a once-in-a-year event," where *X* is some ratio of relative severity. If we plot events like this on a log/log scale (where each increment on the scale is 10 times greater than the previous increment), they tend to look like straight lines. In Exhibit 9.4 you can see the power-law distribution of fatalities due to hurricanes and earthquakes. In the case of earthquakes, I also show the Richter Scale measurement (which is already a log-scale—each increment on a Richter Scale indicates an earthquake 10 times more powerful than the previous increment).

From the chart you can see that power-law distributions are closely represented by a straight line on a log-log chart of frequency versus

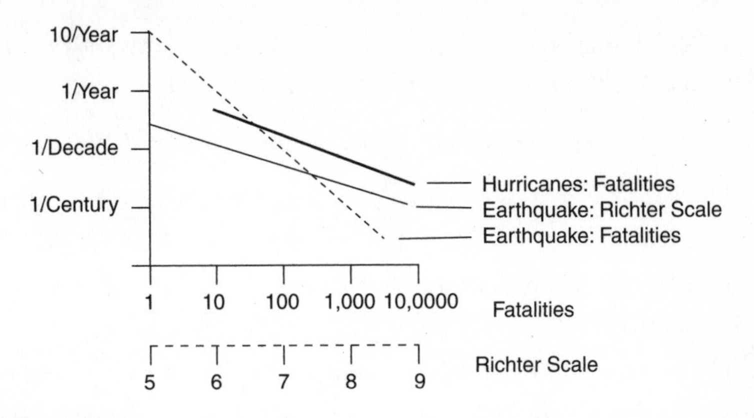

EXHIBIT 9.4 **Power-Law Distributions of Hurricane and Earthquake Frequency and Severity**

magnitude. A once-in-a-decade worst-case earthquake would kill about 100 people. That's about 10 times the damage of an earthquake that happens about every year. This means that *X* in the rule above would be 10 in this case. The same ratio applies as we move further down the line. An earthquake that would kill a thousand people (in the United States only) is a once-in-a-century event.

Many of the systems that seem to follow power-law distributions for failures are the kinds of stressed systems that allow for both common mode failures and cascade failures. Forest fires and power outages, for example, are systems of components where a single event can affect many components and where the failures of some components cause the failures of other components. Hot, dry days make everything more likely to burn and one tree being on fire makes its neighbors more likely to catch fire. Peak energy user periods strain an entire power grid and power overloads in one electrical subsystem cause strain on other subsystems. Likewise, the avalanche on Mount St. Helens unleashed a high-pressure column of magma beneath it.

Unfortunately, many of the systems that matter to business have a lot more in common with power grids and volcanoes than with systems best modeled by normal distributions. In fact, normal distributions seem to apply only to systems with a large number of individual and independent components. If you are rolling a hundred dice or flipping a thousand coins, the normal distribution is your best bet for modeling your uncertainty about the outcome. But financial markets, supply chains, and major IT projects are complex systems of components where each of the following occurs.

Characteristics of Systems with Power-Law Distributed Failures:

- The entire system can be stressed in a way that increases the chance of failure of all components.
- The failure of one component causes the failure of several other components (i.e. a common mode failure).
- The failure of those components in a system, start a chain reaction of failures (cascade failure)

Let's look at how close the history of financial market is to the power laws. Exhibit 9.5 shows how the frequency and magnitude of daily price drops on the S&P 500 and Dow Jones Industrial Average (DJIA) appear on a log-log chart. The solid lines show actual price history for the two indices and the dashed lines show the Gaussian approximation of them. In the range of a drop of a few percentage points, the Gaussian and historical distributions are a moderately good match. For both indices, price drops of 1% are slightly overstated by the Gaussian distribution and between 2% and 3% price drops, the historical data matches Gaussian. The K-S test would look at this and determine that the normal distribution is close enough. But once the price drops get bigger than about 3% from the previous day's closing price, the two distributions diverge sharply.

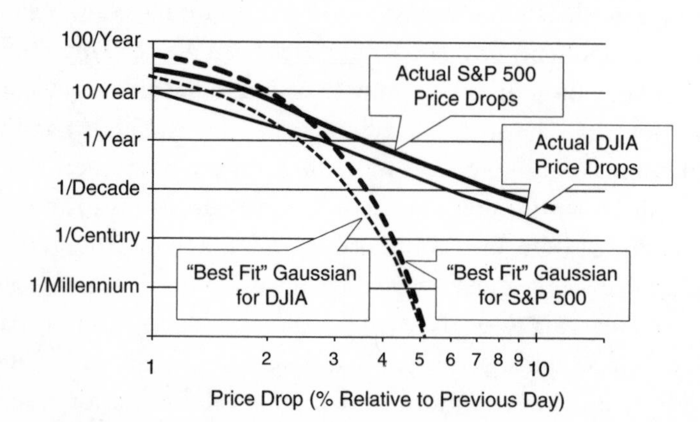

EXHIBIT 9.5 **Frequency and Magnitude of Daily Price Drops in the S&P 500 and DJIA (Log-Log Chart)**

Clearly, the real data from either index looks a lot more like the downward-sloping straight lines we see on the log-log frequency and magnitude charts for hurricanes and earthquakes. The more strongly curving normal distribution applied to the same data indicates here that the normal distribution of these price drops would put a 6% or greater drop in a single day at something less frequent than a one-in-10,000-year event.

But, in the actual data a price drop that large has already occurred many times and probably would occur at something closer to once every few years. After the 1987 crash, where both indices lost over 20% in a single day, some analysts claimed the crash was something on the order of a once-in-a-million year event. The power law distribution puts at closer to once in a century or so. Or, to put it another way, it has a reasonably good chance of occurring in a lifetime.

Although I'm a booster for the firms that developed powerful tools like Crystal Ball, the most popular products seem to have one major omission. Of all the wide assortment of distribution types they include in their models, most still do not include a power-law distribution. But they aren't hard to make. I included a simple random power-law generator in a spreadsheet on www.howtofixriskmgt.com.

Another interesting aspect of stressed-system, common-mode, cascade failures is that if you model them as such, you may not even have to *tell* the model to produce a power-law distribution of failures. It could display this behavior simply by virtue of modeling those components of the system in detail. Computer models of forest fires, flu epidemics, and crowd behavior show this behavior naturally. The use of the explicit power law will still be required for any model that is a simple statistical description of outputs and not a model of underlying mechanisms. Therefore, financial models either will have to replace the normal distribution with power-law distributions or they will have to start making more detailed models of financial systems and the interactions about their components.

Following Your Inner Cow: The Problem with Correlations

Many systems we want to model are like herds of cattle—they tend to move together but in irregular ways. Cattle do not move together in any kind of formation like marching soldiers nor do they move entirely independently of each other like cats. Trying to describe the way in which one cow follows another with one or two numbers—like "10 feet behind"—is sure to leave out a lot of complexity. Yet, this is exactly what is done in many quantitative risk models.

When two variables move up and down together in some way we say they are *correlated.* Correlation between two sets of data is generally expressed as a number between +1 and −1. A correlation of 1 means the two variables move in perfect harmony—as one increases so does the other. A correlation of −1 also indicates two perfectly related variables, but as one increases, the other decreases in lockstep. A correlation of 0 means they have nothing to do with each other.

The four examples of data in Exhibit 9.6 show different degrees of correlation. The horizontal axis could be the Dow Jones and the vertical axis could be your revenues. Or the horizontal axis could be number of mortgage defaults and the vertical axis could be unemployment. They could be anything we expect to be related in some way. But it is clear that the data in the two axes in some of the charts is more closely related than the data

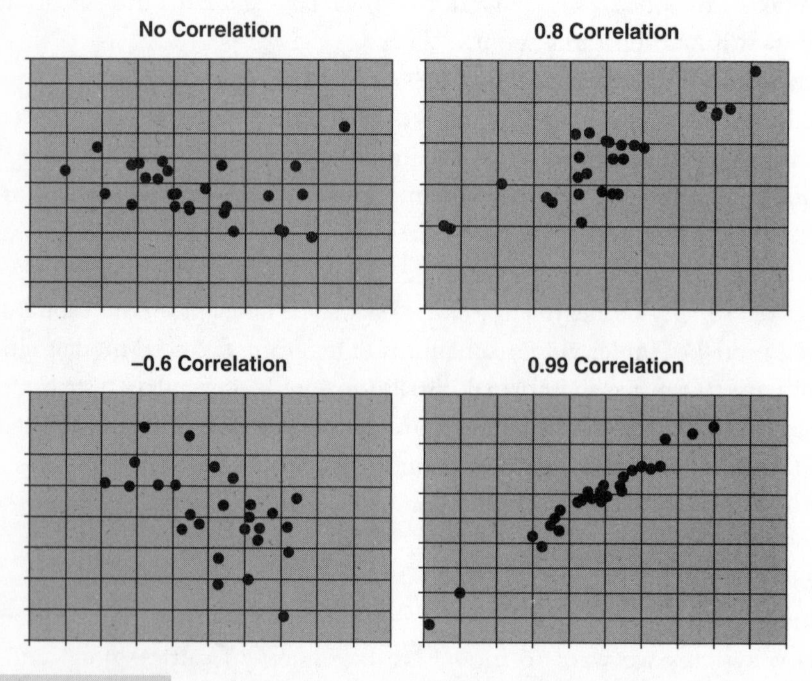

EXHIBIT 9.6 **Examples of Correlated Data**

in other charts. The chart in the upper-left-hand corner is just two independent random variables. The variables have nothing to do with each other and there is no correlation. In the lower-right-hand corner, you can see two data points that are very closely related.

Correlated random numbers are not difficult to generate given a coefficient of correlation. We can also use a simple formula in Excel (= correl()) to compute the correlation between two data sets. See the spreadsheet in www.howtofixriskmgt.com for simple examples that both generate correlated numbers and compute correlations among given data. Tools like Crystal Ball and @Risk allow the modeler to specify correlations between any combination of variables.

But one common error regarding correlations is that many modelers will ignore them. This will almost always lead to a systematic underestimation of risks. If you are considering the risks of a construction project and you build a Monte Carlo with ranges for detailed costs for each part of a major facility, these costs may be correlated. If the costs of one part of the building rise, it is probably for reasons that would affect the costs of all parts of the multibuilding facility. The price of steel, concrete, and labor affects all of the buildings in a facility. Work stoppages due to strikes or weather tend to delay all of the construction, not just one part.

If the costs of different buildings in a facility were being modeled as independent variables, they would, like rolling a dozen dice, tend to average each other out. It would be unlikely for a dozen independent variables to all move up and down together by chance alone. But if they are correlated at all, then they do tend to move up and down together, and the risks of being over budget on one building are not necessarily offset by another building being under budget. They tend to all be over-budget together.

Correlation significantly increases the risks, but even the savviest managers will ignore this. In a January 15, 2008 press release from Citigroup, CEO Vikrim Pandit explained the reported $9.83 billion loss for the fourth quarter of 2007: "Our financial results this quarter are clearly unacceptable. Our poor performance was driven primarily by *two factors* [emphasis added]—significant write-downs and losses on our sub-prime direct exposures in fixed income markets, and a large increase in credit costs in our U.S. consumer loan portfolio."

But these are not two independent factors. They are more like one factor. The housing market affects both of these. They would tend to move up and down together more often than not, and any risk model that treated them as independent significantly understated the risk. Another respected financial expert, Robert Rubin, secretary of the Treasury under Clinton, described the 2008 financial crisis as "a perfect storm" and said, "This is an extremely unlikely event with huge consequences."[2] *Perfect storm* seems to imply the random convergence of several independent factors—which probably was not the case.

The other big error in correlations is not the exclusion of relationships among variables but modeling them with a single correlation coefficient. Consider the two data sets shown in Exhibit 9.7. Although the movement of the vertical axis data with the horizontal axis data is obviously different in the two charts, the typical calculation of a correlation would give the same coefficient for both. The one on the right could be approximated by a single "best fit" correlation and the error around it, but the one on the left is both more complex and more precise. If we tried to model correlations that are historically related in the way the left-hand chart shows by using a single correlation coefficient, the Monte Carlo would generate something that looks like the chart on the right.

A correlation is a gross approximation of the relationship between two variables. Often, the relationship between two variables is best described by a more complex system than a single number. It's like the difference between knowing someone's IQ and knowing how the brain actually works.

In fact, simple correlations are not even close to being constant and, because the reasons for their correlations are not known, the correlations

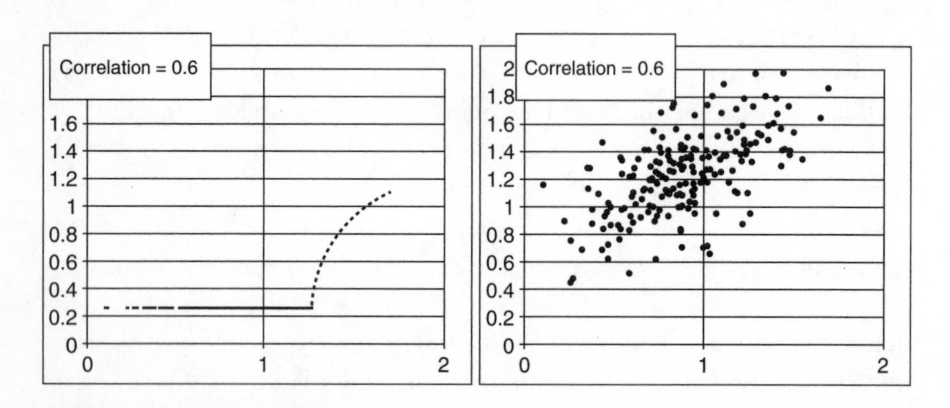

EXHIBIT 9.7 **Same Correlation Coefficient, Very Different Patterns**

change without warning. John Joseph, a commodity trading advisor and principal with Sema4 Group in Dallas, PA has found that currency correlations change suddenly even after years of what seems like a consistent correlation. He points out that the correlation between the British Pound and the Japanese Yen relative to the dollar was positive from 1982 until 2007. Then it swung in one year from a +0.65 correlation to −0.1. Most analysts modeling currency risk based on a years of data would state with high confidence the correlation between the Yen and the Pound and that it would probably continue. But in reality they have no basis for this confidence since this level of analysis explains nothing about the underlying system.

There is an alternative to using that single coefficient as a basis for correlation. When we model our uncertainties about the construction costs of a facility, we know that the price of steel, other materials, and labor affects all of the costs of all of the buildings. This can be modeled explicitly without resorting to correlation coefficients and it will be a much more realistic model. It is like basing risk analysis of Mount St. Helens on the physics of systems of rock structures, pressure, and gravity instead of basing it on just the history of that volcano. The types of models that would also show power-law distributed failure modes by explicitly modeling things like common mode failures do not need to resort to the very rough approximation of a coefficient of correlation (more on that later).

"That's Too Uncertain": How Modelers Justify Excluding the Biggest Risks

Perhaps the risk paradox is partly a function of some persistent confusion I mentioned in earlier chapters. There is a culture among some otherwise-quantitative modelers of excluding things from risk analysis *because they are uncertain.*

When I spoke with the head of a university "collaborative" for modeling risks, this particular issue caused strain among the team. The director of this interdisciplinary effort mentioned some of her frustration in dealing with what she called the "modelers." She explained that "Modelers are saying that because we can't estimate the actions of people, we have to leave those variables out." I thought this was odd, because as a modeler I routinely include so-called "people variables." When I model the risk and return of implementing some new information technology in a firm, I often have to include uncertainties like how quickly users will begin to effectively use the new technology. I've even made models that include uncertainties about whether particular bills would pass in Congress or the action of an enemy in Iraq.

I came to find that when she said "modeler" she was talking about a group of bridge construction engineers who, for some reason, put themselves in charge of building the Monte Carlo simulations for the risks the group assessed. To the engineers, only variables about the physical parameters of the bridge seemed "real enough" to include. Those whom the director referred to as the "modelers" and "non-modelers" didn't talk to each other, and there were people on her staff who had what she called a "professional divorce" over this. In her world, modelers are typically coming from engineering and hard sciences and non-modelers are coming from political science, sociology, and so on. Non-modelers are arguing that you have to put in the people variables. Modelers are saying that because (they believe) they can't measure the people variables, they have to leave them out of the model. The modelers are saying the important things are the tensile strength of materials, and so on.

This presents two important issues. First, why would one group of subject matter experts presume to be in charge of building the Monte Carlo model as opposed to some other group? I would generally see engineers as just one other type of SME involved in a modeling issue that requires multiple types of SMEs. But more to the point, why leave something out because it is uncertain? The whole point of building a Monte Carlo model is to deal with uncertainties in a system. Leaving out a variable because it is *too* uncertain makes about as much sense as not drinking because you are too thirsty.

A similar exclusion of variables that are considered "too uncertain" sometimes happens in models made for oil exploration. When analysts estimate the volume of a new oil field, they build Monte Carlo simulations with ranges for the area of the field, the depth, the porosity of the rock, the water content, and so on. When they run this simulation, they get a range of possible values for how much oil is in the field. But when it comes to modeling one of the most uncertain variables—the price of oil—they sometimes don't use ranges. For the price of oil they may use an exact point.

The reason, I've been told, is that the geologists and scientists who run the Monte Carlos are either "too uncertain" about the price or that management simply gives them an exact price to use. But this means that when management is looking at the output of a risk of an oil exploration project, they really aren't looking at the actual risks. They are looking at a hybrid of a proper risk analysis based on ranges and an arbitrary point estimate. They undermine the entire purpose of the Monte Carlo.

They further violate the output of a Monte Carlo in other ways. Sometimes, analysts producing Monte Carlos are told to collapse their perfectly good distributions to a single point for "accounting purposes." You can't give them the range that represents your uncertainty—so you're told—so you have to pick one number. If you have an oil field that has somewhere between 2 and 6 billion barrels, should you tell the investors it has 4 billion?

The executives know that the cost of overestimating the amount of oil in their reserves can be *much* higher than the cost of underestimating reserves. So, since they would rather underestimate than overestimate, they tend to pick a number that's in the lower end of the range. Steve Hoye, prior to starting his current job at Crystal Ball, was in the oil business for 20 years starting in 1980. As a young geophysicist, he saw this firsthand. He points out other incentives that affect how distributions are converted to points:

> There are benefits to underestimating and sometimes serious consequences for overestimating. Shell had a 20% write down in 2004 on their reserves. They had to go back to investors and tell them they didn't have as much reserves as they thought. It's a great study in the cost of being wrong. In Texaco, where I worked, they had a big write down in the 1970s and senior management was reshuffled as a result.

That's understandably conservative. But now imagine every manager is doing this for every oil field. One study found that, because of the practice of systematically converting distributions to conservative points and then adding the points together, oil reserves are systematically underestimated.[3]

One study found that, because of the practice of systematically converting distributions to conservative points and then adding the points together, oil reserves are systematically underestimated.

Usually, big oil does a good job of quantifying risks. As Hoye puts it, "There are enormous risks in oil, huge capital outlays and multiple years before a payoff. The success rates are 1-in-8 in exploratory projects. And that's the good rate." But the strong incentive to model risks well may be undercut when the results are communicated. "Oil companies are dealing with an asset they cannot touch but they have to make public pronouncements of the value of these assets," says Hoye. Perhaps the best way to deal with it is to share the actual uncertainty of the distribution with investors. A range has a chance of being right while a point estimate will almost always be wrong.

John Schuyler with Decision Precision is another longtime expert at Monte Carlo simulations for oil exploration who sometimes sees odd hybrids between deterministic and stochastic models. He observes, "Many people might run a Monte Carlo, take the mean and put it in a deterministic model or reduce [the ranges] to 'conservative' or 'optimistic' points. . . . All of this is coming up with a horribly contrived result." Schuyler adds, "All that good Monte Carlo simulation upstream is kind of going to waste."

This attitude of excluding uncertainties because they are too uncertain is pervasive in many industries. In mid-2008, I had a lengthy discussion with an economist who made a living doing business case analyses for luxury home developments. He indicated that his business was not going to be affected much by strains on the mortgage system because, he claimed, the high-end houses and "second home" market were less affected.

Although he was familiar with Monte Carlo simulations, I was very surprised to learn that, even with the risks and uncertainties in real estate, he conducted a deterministic, fixed-point analysis of the developments. I said risk has to be a major component of any real estate development investment and he would have to include it somehow. His position was that it would be too difficult to determine ranges for all the variables in his models because he just didn't have enough data. He saw no fundamental irony in his position: Because he believed he didn't have enough data to estimate a range, he had to estimate a point.

He saw no fundamental irony in his position: Because he believed he didn't have enough data to estimate a range, he had to estimate a point.

This is based on the same misconception about "precision" and probabilities I discussed regarding scoring models in Chapter 7. If modelers exclude something because it is more uncertain than the other variables, they will invariably exclude some of the most important sources of risks in a model. Taken to the extreme, some analysts exclude probabilistic models altogether and choose models based on point estimates. Until we can begin to see that probabilistic models are needed exactly because we lack information, we will be unable ever to conduct a meaningful risk analysis.

Is Monte Carlo Too Complicated?

One issue with the adoption of Monte Carlo–based methods for addressing risks is the concern that Monte Carlos are too complex. Even those who use fairly quantitative methods in other ways may see the Monte Carlo as abstruse.

A book published in 1997, *Value at Risk*, expressed one reservation about this "weakness" of the Monte Carlo method.[4] After acknowledging that "Monte Carlo is by far the most powerful method to compute value at risk," it goes on to say, "The biggest drawback of this method is its computational cost. If 1,000 sample paths are generated with a portfolio of 1,000 assets, the total number of valuation calculations amounts to 1 million. When full valuation of assets is complex this method quickly becomes too onerous to implement on a frequent basis."

I've been running Monte Carlo simulations on a variety of risk analysis problems regularly since 1994. Most of my models had 50 or more variables and I routinely ran 50,000 scenarios or more. That's a total of 2.5 million individual values generated, conservatively, each time I ran a Monte Carlo. But I don't recall, even on the computers of the day, a simulation taking much more than 60 minutes. And I was running on uncompiled Excel macros—hardly the best available technology. My notebook now has a processor that is more than 15 times faster than my 1994 notebook and I have about 100 times as much RAM. Sam Savage further improves these calculations speeds by the use of a fast distribution calculation that would run calculations like that in seconds.

Think of how much additional computing power would really cost if you wanted faster simulations. If Monte Carlos are "by far the most powerful method" (with which I agree), how much better off would you be if you were managing a large portfolio slightly better? Would it justify spending an extra few thousand dollars on a high-end PC? Even a top-end workstation would certainly be justified for some simulation problems. Spending money on computing power for just one machine used by your risk analyst is trivial for virtually any risk analysis problem that would justify hiring a full-time person. The idea that Monte Carlo simulations today are onerous at all is some kind of retro-vacuum-tube thinking. Steve Hoye agrees: "In the old days, Monte Carlo was a big mainframe, but now with Excel-based tools those assumptions are no longer applicable."

Aside from the computing power issue, the idea that it is just too complex is also unfounded. Hoye goes on to point out "Some people will argue that Monte Carlos are justified only for special cases. I think a lot of people have a misperception that it is difficult to understand and academic, therefore it's in their best interest not to have to deal with it." Every time I've seen analysts object to Monte Carlo simulations, they were never talking from experience. In each case they knew very little about the method and had no basis for judging whether it was too complex.

Complexity, after all, is relative. I've always stated that my most complex Monte Carlo models were always *far* simpler than the systems I was modeling. I would model the risks of a software development project with more than a million lines of code. My model was one big spreadsheet with fewer than a hundred variables. And it would take less time and money than even the most trivial parts of the project I was analyzing.

My most complex Monte Carlo models were always *far* simpler than the systems I was modeling.

Here is a rule of thumb I use for estimating costs of a good quantitative risk/return analysis with a major project. I start at about $30,000 to analyze the risks of project investments that are about a $1 million outlay. Then for each 10-fold increase in the investment costs, I approximately double the price of analysis (e.g., a $10M investment costs $60K to assess; at $100M it's $120K, etc.). I modify these figures based on scheduling constraints, the availability of client staff, and the extent of the deliverable. In the scheme of things, this is a trivial amount, especially for investments that turn out to be very risky.

Even a $10M investment gets analyzed for less than one-tenth of a percent of its cost. If the chance of a negative return or, worse yet, total loss of the investment is anything more than 10% (which is typically the case in every IT investment of that size, and is certainly the case with any new product development, venture capital investment, etc.), then the value of the analysis based on the information value calculation is easily many times the cost of the analysis.

NOTES

1. R. Carson, *Mount St. Helens: The Eruption and Recovery of a Volcano,* (Sasquatch Books, 2002), pg 69.
2. Interview with Fareed Zakaria, *CNN,* October 26, 2008.
3. "Have We Underestimated Total Oil Reserves?" *New Scientist,* June 11, 2008.
4. P. Jorion, *Value at Risk,* (Irwin Professional Publications, 1997).

How to Fix It

CHAPTER 10

The Language of Uncertain Systems: The First Step Toward Improved Risk Management

The most important questions of life are, for the most part, really only problems of probability.

—Pierre Simon de Laplace, 1812

Part Two of this book, the "Why It's Broken" part of the failure of risk management, at this point might seem overwhelming. We discussed several issues with current approaches:

- How different areas of risk management evolved very different solutions and none were complete solutions (but some were much further from the mark than others).
- Differences in the definition of *risk*, leading to confusion in the industry
- Systematic problems with how experts assess uncertainties and risks
- Popular but worse-than-useless solutions to risk analysis and risk management
- Conceptual obstacles to adopting better methods

- Common errors even the quantitative analysts make, including lack of consideration for common errors in subjective estimates, lack of empirical testing of models, focusing on all the wrong measurements, ignoring correlations or modeling them in an oversimplified way, and excluding the biggest risks

Most of the key problems with risk management are focused primarily on the problems with risk analysis. That is, if we only knew how to analyze risks better we would be better at managing them. For the broader risk management component, I'll offer suggestions that will help support the organization, implementation, and desired scope of risk analysis.

Fortunately, I think explaining how to fix the problems will be simpler than explaining what is wrong with existing methods. Thanks to a little input from Professor Sam Savage, I was able to boil all the solutions down to three basic steps:

The Three Key Improvements to Risk Management

1. *Adopt the language and the philosophy of modeling uncertain systems.* Use calibrated probabilities to express your uncertainties and use those uncertainties in Monte Carlo models of your organization as a system.
2. *Be a scientist.* Be outward looking with the modeling and the quality control of the model. Models need to be compared to history, forecasts need to be validated once actual events occur, and empirical observation should be used in models where the information value justifies it.
3. *Build the community as well as the organization.* In the short term, lobby for a high-level position for analysis, incentive structures that support good analysis and forecasting, and a quality control process for a single, evolving organizational model. Produce the equivalent of a "Statement of Actuarial Opinion" for your firm expressed in probabilistic terms. Beyond your own organization, support the professional certification of analysts and collaborative models across organizations, industries, and governments.

This means first and foremost speaking the language of *probabilities*—and that means getting rid of the risk analysis methods that do not speak that language. The softer scoring methods and half-baked, hybrid deterministic methods are of no value—stop using them. Begin the switch to probabilistic modeling methods immediately. Do not continue to use your previous methods while you make a gradual transition to better methods. Go cold turkey. Don't continue to use the previous methods in parallel with better methods simply because "that's what management understands." Abandon them altogether. Do not hang onto an ineffectual method simply because it took time and money to develop and everyone is vested in it. Write it off as a complete loss. The feeling that it was working was a placebo effect, a mirage. Adopt better methods now, or your risk management efforts will continue to be a failure.

If you quit wasting effort in the methods I've spent much of this book debunking, you will more quickly be able to develop the replacement method. Learning the language of the new method has two components: (1) getting calibrated and (2) modeling systems. Calibration will help organizations develop an *intuition* for probabilities and risk in the same way that they intuitively handle costs of projects. The model of your organization and its environment is what this new language will help us build.

Getting Your Probabilities Calibrated

Calibration training not only measurably improves the expert's ability to assess odds, it forms the basis of and intuition for understanding probabilistic models in general. In my experience, the sorts of objections found in Chapter 8 have effectively evaporated by the time subjects go through calibration training.

The most important part of calibration is repetition and feedback. In an intense, half-day workshop, I give a series of tests to subject matter experts (SMEs) on whom we will rely for estimates. You saw examples of such tests in Chapter 6, but that was just a toe in the water. In the Appendix, you will find additional, longer tests. As with the sample tests in Chapter 6, these include both true/false questions as well as 90% confidence interval questions.

Let's start by evaluating your performance on the each of the small tests in Chapter 6 by comparing your expected results to your actual results. Since the range questions asked for a 90% confidence interval (CI), you should expect 90% of the actual answers to be within your ranges. However, if you are like most people, you got less than that within your stated bounds at first. Granted, these are very small samples so the test can't be used to measure your calibration precisely, but it's a good approximate measure. Even with this small sample, if you are getting less than 70% of the answers within bounds, then you are probably overconfident. If you got less than half within your bounds (as most people do), then you are very overconfident.

Now, you need to compute the expected number correct for your binary questions. For each of the answers, you said you were 50%, 60%, 70%, 80%, 90%, or 100% confident. Convert each of the percentages you circled to a decimal (i.e., 0.5, 0.6 . . . 1.0) and add them up. Let's say your confidence in your answers was 1, .5, .9, .6, .7, .8, .8, 1, .9, .7 making your total 7.9. So your "expected" number correct was 7.9. Again, 10 is a small sample, but if your actual number correct was 2.5 or more lower than the expected correct, you are probably overconfident.

If you are like most people, you did not do well, even for these small tests in Exhibits 6.1 and 6.3. But before we start to practice with more calibration tests (provided in the Appendix), we can learn a few simple methods for improving your calibration.

First, we can exploit the fact that most people are better at assessing odds when they pretend to bet money. Without looking up the answer, provide your 90% CI estimate for the average weight of a six-foot-tall, American male. Now, suppose I offered you a chance to win $1,000 in one of the two following ways:

Option A. You will win $1,000 if the true answer turns out to be between the numbers you gave for the upper and lower bounds. If not, you win nothing.

Option B. You draw a marble at random from a bag of nine green marbles and one red marble. If the marble is green, you win $1,000. If it is red, you win nothing (i.e., there is a 90% chance you win $1,000).

Which do you prefer? Drawing the marble has a stated chance of 90% that you win $1,000, and 10% chance you win nothing. If you are like most people (about 80%), you prefer to draw from the bag instead of betting on your answer. But why would that be? The only explanation is that you think you have a higher chance of a payoff if you draw from the bag. The conclusion we have to draw is that the "90% CI" you first estimated is really not your 90% CI. It might be your 50%, 65%, or 80% CI, but it can't be your 90% CI. You have overstated your confidence in your estimate. You express your uncertainty in a way that indicates you have less uncertainty than you really have.

An equally undesirable outcome is to prefer option A; you win $1,000 if the correct answer is within your range. This means that you think there is *more* than a 90% chance your range contains the answer, even though you are representing yourself as being merely 90% confident in the range.

The only desirable answer you can give is if you set your range just right so that you would be indifferent between options A and B. This means that you believe you have a 90% chance—not more and not less—that the answer is within your range. For an overconfident person (i.e., most of us), this means increasing the width of the range until options A and B are considered equivalent.

You can apply the same test, of course, to binary questions such as those shown in Exhibit 6.1. Let's say you said you were 80% confident in your answer to the question about Napoleon's birthplace. Again, you give yourself a choice between betting on your answer being correct or drawing a marble at random. In this case, however, there are 8 green marbles and 2 red marbles in the bag for a payoff 80% of the time. If you prefer to draw, that means you are probably less than 80% confident in your answer. Now let's suppose we change the marbles in the bag to 7 green and 3 red. If you then consider drawing a marble to be just as good a bet (no better or worse) as betting on your answer, then you should say that you are really about 70% confident that your answer to the question is correct.

In my calibration training classes, I've been calling this the "Equivalent Bet Test." As the name implies, it tests to see whether you are really 90% confident in a range by comparing it to a bet that you should consider equivalent. There is research that indicates that betting money significantly improves a person's ability to assess odds,[1] but even pretending to bet money improves calibration significantly.[2]

Since most JDM researchers use an urn in this example, they call it the *equivalent urn (EQU)*. But this has also been done with examples of cards, dice, and dials as the analyst sees fit. I have an example of a spinning dial on an Excel spreadsheet for the equivalent bet on the book's website, www.howtofixriskmgt.com.

You can improve your performance on each test by practicing other methods as well. Several researchers suggest that one reason for lack of calibration (which is usually overconfidence) is failing to think about the ways in which one can be wrong—in other words, questioning basic assumptions and presumptions. Sarah Lichtenstein suggested correcting for this by spending some time thinking of why your range should contain the answer and why it might not. Think of two "pros" and two "cons" for each estimate.

Another corrective method involves a way to avoid *anchoring*. Kahneman and Tversky first discovered anchoring among subjects in estimating experiments. They described it as a tendency to adjust from some previously acquired point value—even when the previous number was randomly chosen or unrelated. In one experiment, Kahneman and Tversky discovered that subjects' estimates of the number of physicians on the island of Manhattan were influenced by the previous number elicited on the test—the last four digits of the subject's social security number.

Kahneman and Tversky found that it is natural for many estimators to think of a single "best estimate" first, then to attempt to determine some kind of error around it. For example, if an SME is asked to estimate a range for next quarter's sales, it may be natural for her to think of one best number ($20 million) and then to imagine how far off she can be ($5 million, resulting in a range of $15 to $25 million). But this tends to cause SMEs to provide narrower ranges than they need to be realistically represent uncertainty. Kahneman and Tversky found that the best way to elicit this estimate is ask for the probability that sales will be over a particular amount. Then ask for the chance that it will be over some higher amount. By iteration, you can find two sales values that the expert believes there is a 95% of exceeding and a 5% chance of exceeding. Those two values are equivalent to the 90% CI.[3]

Take the tests in the Appendix and try applying each of the methods listed above in each test. It will take practice, but if you apply these methods by habit your calibration will improve. The tests in the Appendix are longer than the examples in Chapter 6 (20 questions), but the same process of evaluation we used on the small example tests applies. You become calibrated when your expected number correct comes very close to your actual number correct. That is, you are calibrated when you get about 90% of the answers within your 90% CI for the range questions. For the binary questions, you are calibrated when the sum of the assessed probabilities of being correct is about the same as the actual number correct.

This will go a long way to developing the basic skills of thinking about risk probabilistically, even for management with no statistical training. In

SUMMARY OF METHODS TO CALIBRATE PROBABILITY ESTIMATES

1. *Repetition and feedback*. Take several tests in succession, assessing how well you did after each one and attempting to improve your performance in the next one. Continue to track performance after training is complete.
2. *Equivalent bets*. For each estimate set up the equivalent bet to test whether that range or probability really reflects your uncertainty.
3. *Consider two pros and two cons*. Think of at least two reasons why you should be confident in your assessment and two ways you could be wrong.
4. *Avoid anchoring*. Think of range questions as two separate binary questions of the form "Are you 95% certain that the true value is over/under (pick one) the lower/upper (pick one) bound?"

my own calibration workshops, where I have trained people with a variety of technical and nontechnical backgrounds, I find that group of all participants actually reach calibration within a statistically allowable error. Another 20% improve significantly but don't quite reach calibration, whereas just 10% seem to resist any calibration at all.

But the good news is that the people we were going to rely on most for estimates were almost always within the group that achieved calibration. Those that resisted calibration were generally not the SMEs we were going to count on for estimates. The individuals who were not successfully calibrated were often lower-level support staff rarely involved in making or supporting managerial decisions. The explanation may be a lack of motivation to do well since they knew they would not be called on for input for the real decision being analyzed. Or, perhaps, those who routinely made risky decisions for the firm were already going to be more receptive to the idea of calibration.

One more item will go a long way to producing an organization that can think about risk probabilistically. A formal system that documents forecasts made by SMEs, tracks the results, reports them, and provides incentives to continue improving will fundamentally change the way an organization thinks about decisions under uncertainty. I will explain more about creating this "calibrated culture" in the last chapter.

The Model of Uncertainty: Decomposing Risk with Monte Carlos

After calibration, the single best method to adopt and master for the analysis of uncertainties is the Monte Carlo simulation. While we need to take care to avoid the problems I explained in Chapter 9 regarding Monte Carlo models, it is the single best hope for mastering the analysis of risk in your organization or any other. There is a good reason why Monte Carlo simulations are routinely adopted for the analysis of the biggest risks, including nuclear power safety, oil exploration, and environmental policy. The fact is that when it comes to risks that big, the best risk analysts trust nothing else.

The incentive to perform Monte Carlo analysis was so high for some of these areas that they were the earliest adopters of Monte Carlo simulations, even when Monte Carlos were run on mainframes with punch cards. But the availability of PC-based simulation tools makes Monte Carlo simulation practical for more moderate risks that most organizations would encounter. As I mentioned in the previous chapter, I find a very high degree of acceptance of these tools. The objections that Monte Carlos are complex, academic, or require too much computing power are all hollow defense mechanisms used by people who simply are unfamiliar with how to use Monte Carlos on practical problems. I find the acceptance of Monte Carlo simulations to be even higher after calibration training of the individuals we use as estimators. It seems that once they realize they can learn to assess odds quantitatively, then they seem to have the right intuition for understanding the Monte Carlo approach.

There are plenty of good Monte Carlo tools to pick from (see Exhibit 10.1). The total number of users for all of the various Monte Carlo

EXHIBIT 10.1 SOME AVAILABLE PC-BASED MONTE CARLO TOOLS

Tool	Made by	Description
Crystal Ball	Oracle (Previously Decisioneering, Inc., purchased by Oracle) Denver, CO	Excel-based; a wide variety of distributions; a fairly sophisticated tool. Broad user base and technical support. Has adopted Savage's SIPs and SLURPS and Dist utility (details in Chapter 12).
@Risk	Palisade Corporation Ithaca, NY	Excel-based tool; main competitor to Crystal Ball. Again with many users and technical support.
XLSim	Stanford U. Professor Sam Savage, AnalyCorp	An inexpensive package designed for ease of learning and use. Savage also provides seminars and management protocols for making Monte Carlo methods practical in organizations.
AIE	Hubbard Decision Research Glen Ellyn, IL	Excel-based set of macros; also computes value of information and portfolio optimization; emphasizes methodology over the tool and provides consulting for practical implementation issues.
Risk Solver Engine	Frontline Systems Incline Village, NV	Unique Excel-based development platform to perform "interactive" Monte simulation at unprecedented speed. Supports SIP and SLURP formats for probability management.
Analytica	Lumina Decision Systems Los Gatos, CA	Uses an extremely intuitive graphical interface that allows complex systems to be modeled as a kind of flowchart of interactions; has a significant presence in government and environmental policy analysis
SAS	SAS Corporation Raleigh, NC	Goes well beyond the Monte Carlo; extremely sophisticated package used by many professional statisticians.
SPSS	SPSS Inc. Chicago, IL	Goes far beyond the Monte Carlo; tends to be more popular among academics.
Mathematica	Wolfram Research Champaign, IL	Extremely powerful tool that does much more than Monte Carlo; used primarily by scientists and mathematicians, but has applications in many fields.

software tools is in the tens of thousands and chances are that somebody is already applying one of these tools to problems very similar to yours.

Modeling the uncertainty of a system is a skill that most people seem to adopt well just by learning one of these tools. The introductory training courses are generally on the order of a few days, not weeks, but users can get as advanced as they feel they need to. If you are already familiar with basic tools of management in business (certainly a prerequisite for a risk manager), then you are probably going to understand how to use these tools for assessing risk. I find that those who already know how to build a spreadsheet to compute net present value or return on investment for a project with several benefits and costs probably have the basic thinking skills required for this.

Modeling is much more intuitive than some might first think. The beginning of all modeling simply comes down to some form of *decomposition*. That is, we want to find the parts of a system that contribute to the behavior of the whole, build relationships among them, and aggregate them. If you are building a deck for your backyard, you can think of estimating the components. When we estimate the net value of some new project, we don't just pull a number out of the air right away. We think of several benefits, several costs, and total them up.

Paul Meehl, an influential JDM researcher who worked on statistical models that outperformed humans in clinical judgments, performed a lot of research that made a very strong case for decomposing problems to get better answers. He, along with Robyn Dawes, found that human judges were good for lots of things but when it came to considering multiple factors in a judgment, some relatively simple mathematical models that combined several factors did better at assessments on several topics (review Chapter 7 if you need to see how these models were different from the ordinal scales that have been debunked). Meehl makes an obvious but useful observation when thinking about estimating odds:

> When you check out at the supermarket, you don't eyeball the heap of purchases and say to the clerk, "Well it looks to me as if it's about $17 worth. What do you think?" The clerk adds it up.[4]

The same is true when we assess risks. Instead of doing the math in our heads, we just document the estimates and events we know about that influence some outcome we want to estimate. Consider assessing the risk of a negative return on investment for a new major investment in information technology for an insurance company that wants to provide additional assistance to brokers.

You may make the following estimates:

1. The productivity savings of your insurance company's staff will be $3 to $8 million per year, assuming 100% adoption by the brokers at current sales levels.
2. The actual adoption rate among brokers will be 10% to 60%.
3. Current sales levels can change by –20% to +35% each year, over the next 5 years.
4. The initial investment will be $2 million to $4 million and it will take 8 to 16 months to develop.
5. For projects of this duration and these costs, there is a historic rate of cancellation prior to implementation of 8%.
6. If the project is canceled, 10% to 100% of the expected investment will have been made and will be an unrecoverable loss.

Should I just say that the chance of a negative return is about 12%? No, I would be better off modeling each of these uncertainties—which should have all come from calibrated estimators or valid empirical data—in a Monte Carlo simulation and letting the model add them up for me. We can also make the model even more elaborate by including uncertainty about the lifespan of the new technology and the possibility that the rollout could interfere with normal business operations.

Research shows that decomposing a problem this way is an effective method of improving estimates, especially for the most uncertain quantities.[5] When estimates are extremely uncertain, such as the revenue losses due to a major product recall, it makes sense to decompose the problem into a few quantities that might be easier to estimate: How big is one batch of the recalled product? Historically, what has been the effect of a product recall on sales of other products in our firm or similar firms? What is the cost of the recall campaign? How would these change if it were a simple quality defect or a child-safety defect? In my experience, when estimators start identifying what they *do* know about a problem, they can better estimate something they were convinced they *couldn't* know.

If this kind of simulation seems difficult, don't be deterred. The best way to get started is to *start.* Furthermore, don't assume you have to do it on your own. I find the industry of well-trained Monte Carlo developers to be large and eager. Start by picking a tool, going to the training (or sending someone), or just using Google to find an expert for hire with tool-in-hand.

Decomposing Probabilities: Thinking about Chance the Way You Think about a Budget

For some reason, even though most people seem to intuitively think of decomposing cost estimates (maybe our daily lives predispose us to that), they rarely think of decomposing probability estimates. But probabilities can be decomposed just as easily as costs.

Here is a very simple one-level, one-factor decomposition for a single probability applied to the chance of a major supplier going bankrupt. Suppose you previously thought the chance was about 10%. We write that as P (bankruptcy) = 10%.

But you know that a bankruptcy is less likely if the cost of steel decreases next quarter. If the cost of steel decreases, you put the chance of bankruptcy at just 5%. This is a *conditional probability* in that the probability of one thing has changed based on some other condition. We can write that as P(bankruptcy|steel_goes_down) = 5%. But if the price of steel does not decrease, you think bankruptcy has a 35% chance. You also put the chance of a decrease in the price of steel to be 40%. We would combine these factors as:

$$P(\text{steel\_goes\_down}) \times P(\text{bankruptcy}|\text{steel\_goes\_down}) +$$
$$(1 - P(\text{steel\_goes\_down})) \times P(\text{bankruptcy}|\text{steel\_does\_not\_go\_down}) =$$
$$P(\text{bankruptcy})$$
$$\text{Or} \quad 40\% \times 5\% + 60\% \times 35\% = 23\%$$

In other words, considering how we estimated the conditional probabilities, the original estimate of a 10% chance of bankruptcy might be a little optimistic. But if the probability seems obviously too high, then perhaps you should reconsider the conditional probabilities. Iterate this process until you reach an equilibrium state—that is, all the probabilities seem agreeable to a well-calibrated expert.

There are other basic rules in probability that allow us to decompose a probability in other ways. Again, we estimate some items that seem easier to estimate in order to better estimate something that seems hard. We can decompose them according to known sufficient and necessary conditions. Here are a couple more examples of a decomposition of a probability:

- If we know that event X will occur if both of two other events, A and B, occur, then the probability of the event occurring is $P(X) = P(A) \times P(B)$.
- If we know that event X will occur if either one of two other events, A and B, occurs, then the probability of the event occurring is $P(X) = 1 - (1 - P(A)) \times (1 - P(B))$.

These simple calculations can all be done without a Monte Carlo simulation, but often they need to be considered along with ranges of possible losses and other continuous quantities. For example, if we lose this supplier, it will take 5 to 15 days to replace them with other suppliers and we will lose $1 to $2 million per day until we are back up to full production. Now we need to go back to the Monte Carlo simulation.

A Few Modeling Principles

Modeling complex, risky problems with quantitative methods like Monte Carlos has been going on so long that several good principles have evolved. Here are a few concepts I've come across over the years. I would like to credit Sam Savage for pointing out a few of these to me:

- "Models are to be used, not believed," said Henri Theil in *Principles of Econometrics*. We need to find a way to practice modeling without worshiping models. I'll add to that what statistician George Box has said: "All models are wrong; some models are useful." There is a tendency to treat a model, once it is made, as the "truth," as in "It came from the model; it must be right." It seems that it must be hard for most organizations to build models that they then constantly doubt. Yet, this is the most reasonable and scientific approach. Modelers must be pragmatists—each model is only as good as the validity and usefulness of its output.

- "The perfect is the enemy of the good," said Voltaire. As I pointed out earlier, the idea is that we outperform the existing method, which in many cases comprises the subjective, uncalibrated risk assessments of people. Taleb's statement that common sense is better than the wrong model ignores the fact that common sense is also a model that is wrong—the question is which one is *less* wrong when we track results against reality. Start tinkering.
- "Build a little, test a little," says Burt Rutan, the aerospace engineer whose company, Scaled Composites, was the first private company to send a human above Earth's atmosphere. As with building a new spacecraft, building a model of a system should be an evolutionary process where we check each step along the way against reality. This is similar to the position of Alan Manne, a Stanford energy economist, who said, "To get a large model to work you must start with a small model that works, not a large model that doesn't work."
- Don Knuth, a Stanford computer scientist, proposed five stages of model development. If Rutan and Manne were proponents of *gradual* evolution, Knuth is more along the lines of *destructive* evolution. He proposes the following:
  1. Decide what you want the model to do.
  2. Decide how to build the model.
  3. Build the model.
  4. Debug the model.
  5. Trash stages 1 through 4 and start again, now that you know what you really wanted to model in the first place.
- "A successful model tells you things you didn't tell it to tell you," said Jerry Brashear, a consultant in DC. I thought I had heard this in other forms from other sources, but Mr. Brashear seems to be the source of this insightful quote. I always find that the most useful model must produce some surprise. When I built the Monte Carlo simulation for battlefield fuel forecasts used by the Marine Corps, we were all surprised to find that road conditions on the main supply routes were much better predictors of fuel use than the chance of enemy contact. Such revelations are even more profound (and helpful) when we use empirical measurements that themselves had surprising results.

- "Everything should be made as simple as possible, but not simpler," said Albert Einstein. Complexity itself is not a benefit, just the opposite. But don't be afraid of complexity if the individual components are well-founded.
- "Plans are worthless; planning is everything," said Dwight D. Eisenhower. This must be a bit of hyperbole needed to make a point, but I see a near corollary in modeling. The modeling process itself has value, but there is a caveat. Many risk management methods claim that the modeling alone is the key benefit. Regardless of whether the methods are based on any scientific rigor, they will say, "At least the modeling is helping us think about the problem better." Any of the risk management methods could claim that. It's as if the General would conclude that his statement means that all planning processes are equally good—which I seriously doubt. I will argue that a probabilistic modeling method forces us to think about risks in a way none of the other methods would. And the benefits have to be measured by a track record of better forecasts and decisions—not just a better way of *thinking* about decisions.
- Finally, always attempt to model the components of a system, not just the system's behavior. A model of the components of the system—the "structural model"—is has a good chance of improving forecasts and, therefore, decisions. It exploits our explicit knowledge about how events are related. This is "modeling the mechanism."

Modeling the Mechanism

Sometimes modelers start a modeling process with a simple statistical description of the issue. This gives the probability of an event or the range of outcomes, but nothing else. It is like doing weather forecasting using merely the historical percentage of rainy days or the historical distribution of different temperatures. The inner mechanisms of the system are not part of the model.

This is not unlike what some financial models do. There is no attempt to explain or even connect things in any way, just to show how the market has done in the past. Some would argue that since the market is random, this may be the best anyone can do. If that's the case, we should at least check that our description matches reality—which is not the case when some distributions are applied to the market. But for most models in business, especially operational issues, we can do better.

The next best state is to show at least how different components in a model are correlated using the coefficient of correlation. If there are several costs in a construction project but some are correlated, a Monte Carlo would underestimate the uncertainty about the cost if we excluded the correlations. Most of the Monte Carlo tools available allow users to specify how different variables in a model are correlated. This certainly improves the performance of the model but it doesn't really explain much. In science, the discovery of these correlations is usually just the beginning of a question, not the answer. For example, a cancer researcher may find that people in one part of the country are more likely to get stomach cancer, but they don't know why. So they begin an investigation and find that it is a particular diet or something in the environment.

Using correlations to improve models is key to Modern Portfolio Theory. For the investments in a portfolio, each investment will have a *covariance* with each other investment, building up to a *covariance matrix*. These covariances are usually based on trends seen in historical data. If one stock tends to match the movement of another stock very closely, then the covariance between them will be very close to 1. If they move completely independently, covariance will be zero, and if they tend to offset each other the covariance will be closer to –1. Again, the risk here is that we don't really understand why the covariances are there and why some are higher than others.

For the investment portfolio modeled with a covariance matrix, all we know is that they *have* been moving together in these ways, not why. Since the mechanism of the system is not explained to us, there is a danger of some big surprise. I've met many Monte Carlo users who assume that excluding correlation coefficients is a big error. True; if we know of the correlations and can do no better, then we should include them. But as pointed out in Chapter 9, correlations themselves can be a gross oversimplification of a complex relationship. Fortunately, there is a better way.

The best case for the weather forecaster is not just a description of the historical frequency of rainy days, or to show how rain and temperature are correlated. The best solution would be to have an actual model of the weather, the storm fronts, the ocean currents, lake effects, and so on.

When we think of modeling correlated variables in a construction cost estimate, we generally know why they are correlated and it would be a big error to exclude this knowledge or to minimize it with a gross approximation using a single coefficient.

In the previous chapter, I alluded to how correlated construction costs could be modeled better than with a coefficient of correlation of the costs between the different buildings in a facility. When the engineer says that the costs of buildings B and C should be correlated, he generally knows why. We want to exploit that particular knowledge, not ignore it. The reason they are correlated is because, as he knows, they are both mostly steel buildings with a concrete foundation. The costs of steel, concrete, and labor will affect both of them. But the engineer also knows that building A will use much less steel and though it uses labor it uses hardly any ironworkers. He also knows that the road construction is not related to the cost of steel or ironworker labor at all. (See Exhibit 10.2.)

This can be further decomposed, of course. We find a historical relationship between the price of steel and concrete and the movement of an energy index. We could apply the same principles of structural decomposition to this relationship, but that may begin to get outside of our engineer's knowledge base. If that truly were a high-value measurement to make, we might further investigate the mechanisms underlying the energy/concrete/steel correlations just as we did the building cost

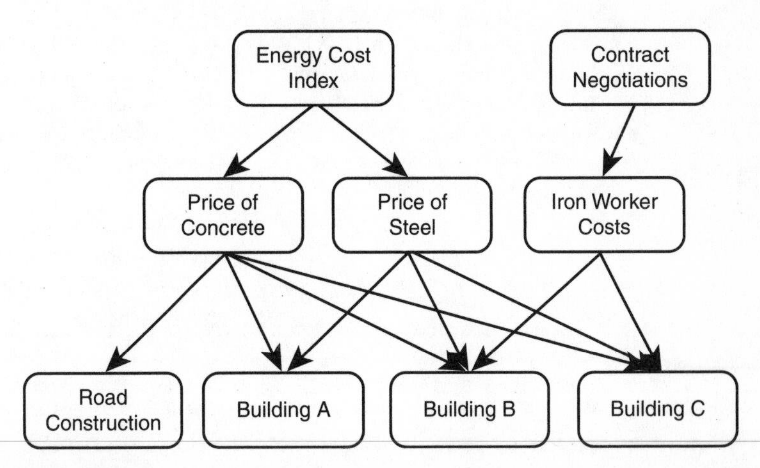

EXHIBIT 10.2 **Example Structural Model of Correlations between Costs of Buildings in a New Facility**

EXHIBIT 10.3 **THREE MATURITY LEVELS FOR MODELS**

	Maturity Levels of Model	Examples
Better than Qualitative	*Level 1:* Just describe the basic behavior of the system in terms of a distribution. This tells us the least about the system and is not correlated in any way to other events or systems.	"Based on historical data, there is a 90% chance that there will be between 2 and 7 days of unscheduled factory interruptions next year."
Even Better	*Level 2:* List other factors that historically correlated with the event you are trying to model. This tells you something that might be useful and it is probably an improvement on the first-order description. But it doesn't explain *why* the correlation exists. It may also greatly oversimplify the relationship because correlations are simple, linear approximations.	"There is a correlation of .43 between the frequency of factory disruptions and the number of days hotter than 100F."
Best	*Level 3:* Build a structural model. Structural models explicitly list the components in a system and describe *why* they are related. This approach generates the most realistic models. These models are also easier to validate since they involve potentially several individual forecasts that can each be validated against reality. Correlations will appear simply as a function of how you described the way that the components interact.	"On high-temperature days, there is a 6% chance of a power brownout lasting 6 to 48 hours. If one occurs, there is a 95% chance backup power will avoid interruption." "Absenteeism will increase to 10% to 40% if an outage from the previous day persists. More than 20% absenteeism will force a shutdown." "Accidents increase by 15% to 42% on days over 100F. 20% of accidents force a shutdown."

correlations. But we may have already gone far enough for a significant improvement in assessing the risks. For a recap of these three "Maturity Levels of Models," see Exhibit 10.3.

Even William Sharpe, a former RAND economist who won the Nobel Prize in Economics together with Harry Markowitz in 1990, sees a better solution than the Level 1 and 2 approaches (as I call them) he and Markowitz promoted for finance. In his most recent publication, Sharpe suggests a fairly ambitious-sounding Level 3 model for economics and finance:

> Instead of formulating complex algebraic models . . . one can build a computer model of a marketplace, populated by individuals, have them trade with one another until they do not wish to trade any more, then examine the characteristics of the resulting portfolios and asset prices.[6]

This has already begun in the application of *agent-based* models to a variety of problems. Agent-based models have been developed for traffic, crowd control, terrorism, and even financial markets. The most striking feature of many of these models is that they already seem to display the power-law distribution of failures without having to program in that explicit calculation. More work is being done, and true validation against reality is not achieved for most of them. But the move toward Level 3 is on its way.

NOTES

1. A. Hoerl and H. Fallin, "Reliability of Subjective Evaluations in a High Incentive Situation," *Journal of the Royal Statistical Society* 137(2), 1974, 227–230.
2. S. Lichtenstein and L. Phillips, "Calibration of Probabilities: The State of the Art to 1980," *Judgment Under Uncertainty: Heuristics and Biases,* 1982.
3. D. Kahneman, P. Slovic, and A. Tversky, *Judgment Under Uncertainty: Heuristics and Biases,* (Cambridge University Press, 1982).
4. P.E. Meehl, *Journal of Pers. Assess.,* 1986, 50, 370.
5. D. MacGregor and J.S. Armstrong, "Judgmental Decomposition: When Does It Work?" *International Journal of Forecasting* 10(4), December 1994, 495–506.
6. W. Sharpe, *Investors and Markets: Portfolio Choices, Asset Prices and Investment Advice,* (Princeton University Press, 2007).

CHAPTER 11

The Outward-Looking Modeler: Adding Empirical Science to Risk

The test of all knowledge is experiment. Experiment is the sole judge of scientific truth.

—RICHARD FEYNMAN, *FEYNMAN LECTURES ON PHYSICS*

Too often, a model of reality takes on a reality of its own. The users of the model are likely eventually to adopt it as "the truth." The philosophers Plato (an *idealist*) and Benedict de Spinoza (a *rationalist*) were similar in that respect. That is, they believed that all knowledge had to come from their "models" (reason) alone—that everything we know could have been deduced without observation. In a way, they believed, the need to resort to observation merely shows the weaknesses and flaws in our ability to reason.

David Hume in contrast, was an empiricist. The empiricists doubt even the most rigorous, rational models and prefer to get their hands dirty with observation and real-world facts. They insist that reason alone would be insufficient for the basis of our knowledge even if our ability to reason were perfect. In fact, the empiricist says, much of what we call *reason* could not have been known without observation first.

But the best combination appears to be skill in theory and in observation. The Nobel Prize–winning physicists Enrico Fermi and Richard Feynman were competent theorists as well as consummate observers. They had a knack for checking just about any claim with observations much simpler than one might expect were necessary. Fermi used a sprinkling of a handful of confetti to estimate the yield of the first atom bomb. Feynman became known to the public for a simple, widely broadcasted experiment with ice water to show that the O-ring material on the boosters of the Space Shuttle *Challenger* was sensitive to cold weather. The materials for these experiments had trivial costs, yet the findings were extremely realistic and useful.

However, I would say that most modelers, whether they really thought about this or not, are closer to Plato and Spinoza than Hume. The survey I conducted of Monte Carlo modelers shows that most of them are *outward looking* only to the extent that they bring subject matter experts (SMEs) into a workshop to discuss the model and their estimates. But we found that calibration is virtually nonexistent among models that use subjective inputs. They never measure how good the sources of their subjective estimates are.

On its own, calibration is an introduction of *empiricism* into modeling. It requires that an analyst measure—and improve—how well the estimators estimate before they are asked for input. But that is just a start for empiricism in modeling risks.

Even idealist and rationalist philosophers like Plato and Spinoza might not have done what I see organizations are guilty of. Plato and Spinoza may err in their faith of a model reached by reason alone without the aid of observation. But they at least understood the model of reason they were referring to. Some managers may not even do that much. I'm referring to the tendency to believe not just the product of our reason, but the output of a computer. In this case, they put their confidence neither in the observation nor in the soundness of the reasoning, but in the *technology* that produced the answer.

We need to make empiricists out of modelers everywhere. We can start by addressing these three problems and their solutions:

1. Analysts don't consider unexpected behaviors from the model.
2. Models are far too rarely improved with empirical observation (and one particularly powerful empirical method is rarely seen).
3. Many models are not checked against historical data.

Why Your Model Won't Behave

Stephan Wolfram is perhaps the most prolific developer of computer models in the world. At the age of 16, he published an important paper in particle physics, and, at 20, received his PhD in particle physics from Caltech. His company, Wolfram Research, developed *Mathematica,* the powerful PC-based tool for mathematicians, scientists, and modelers.

His interest lately has been in the surprising behavior of what should be simple models. He found so much to say about the behavior of some of the simplest possible iterative computer programs that he wrote *A New Kind of Science,*[1] a massive text that describes numerous classes of fascinating behavior of these simple programs. This is particularly important for systems of several interacting components (such as what we are calling *structural models* or *agent-based systems*) and where there is an iterative time component. That is, the simulation generates a scenario for one time increment. Then, using the previous time increment as an input, it generates another time increment. If you ran a model such as this for distribution operations, you might generate a new iteration for every day or even every minute or second. Your model would show how a disruption in the supply chain at a factory would adversely affect the operations at a port the next day, which would then affect inventory levels in regional warehouses the day after that.

In mathematics, this is called a *Markov process* (originally developed by the mathematician Andrey Markov in the 19th century). A Markov process is one where the probability of the next state of an iterative system is determined entirely by the current state. This is effectively how system models of the weather, nuclear power plants, or aerodynamics are developed. Most structural models of financial systems would have to be modeled with a type of Markov process. Each outcome of the model is really a series of sequential scenarios playing out in the market—perhaps down to the minute.

But this is where Wolfram finds that models don't behave. They don't necessarily find equilibrium or follow a repeating pattern. And Wolfram is talking about models that are completely deterministic—no random number generation. And, of course, Wolfram is talking about models that don't have mistakes in them (which a lot of models developed by business analysts would).

Wolfram told me, "If you have a reasonably simple program, it should be easy to figure out what could happen. The surprising discovery is that in a great many of simple models, you can't work out what will happen more efficiently than running a simulation. What modeling shows is an unexpected chain of consequences." He calls this being *computationally irreducible*, and it appears to be a feature not merely of most complex systems in the real world, but also of the models we make of those systems.

This complex behavior of structural models is not a bad thing. It is part of what makes structural models more realistic. Real systems do behave in this way. But that is why models need to be tested against reality.

Empirical Inputs

The survey of Monte Carlo modelers (see Chapter 9) found that of the 72 models I reviewed, only 3 (4%) actually conducted some original empirical measurement to reduce uncertainty about a particular variable in a model. This seems inconsistent with my experience, but, then again, I'm computing the value of additional information and using that to decide whether and what to measure further.

Of the 60 models I've completed up to this point, only 2 have shown that further measurement was *not* needed. In other words, I'm finding that additional empirical measurement is (easily) justified about 97% of the time, while most modelers in the survey employed additional measurements about 4% of the time. I won't bother to show you the sampling error (both samples might be slightly biased, anyway) because, by any measure, empirical measurements are far too rare.

As I said, one key reason for this may be that most analysts are not actually computing the economic value of additional information. So, let me recap this calculation. As discussed in Chapter 9, the *expected value of perfect information (EVPI)* for some uncertain decision is equal to the *expected opportunity loss (EOL)* of the decision. This means that the most you should be willing to pay for uncertainty reduction about a decision is the cost of being wrong times the chance of being wrong.

The EVPI is handy to know, but we don't usually get perfect information. So we could estimate the *expected value of information (EVI)*. This is the EVPI without the *perfect*. This is equal to how much the EOL will be reduced by a measurement. I won't go into further detail here other than to direct the curious reader to the www.howtofixriskmgt.com site for an example.

OVERVIEW OF INFORMATION VALUE

Expected value of information (EVI) = Reduction in expected opportunity loss (EOL) i.e., $EVI = EOL_{Before\ Info} - EOL_{After\ Info}$

Where:
EOL = Chance of being wrong × Cost of being wrong
Expected value of perfect information (EVPI) = $EOL_{Before\ Info}$
($EOL_{After\ Info}$ is zero if information is perfect)

The systematic application of this is why I refer to the method I developed as "Applied Information Economics." The process is fairly simple to summarize. Just get your Monte Carlo tool ready, calibrate your estimators, and follow these five steps:

1. Define the problem and the alternatives.
2. Model what you know now (based on calibrated estimates and/or available historical data).
3. Compute the value of additional information on each uncertainty in the model.
4. If further measurement is justified, conduct empirical measurements for high-information-value uncertainties and repeat Step 3. Otherwise, go to Step 5.
5. Optimize the decision.

This is different from what I see many modelers do. In Step 2, they almost never calibrate, so that is one big difference. Then they hardly ever execute Steps 3 and 4. And the results of these steps are what guides so much of my analysis that I don't know what I would do without them. It is for lack of conducting these steps that I find that analysts, managers, and SMEs of all stripes will consistently underestimate the following:

- The extent of their current uncertainty
- How much uncertainty reduction they will get from a sample of a certain size or set of data
- How much data is available
- How much useful observation can be obtained at a given cost
- The value of measuring the most critical data

I think the reasons for these underestimates are found in the research we discussed earlier. JDM researchers observed the extent of our overconfidence in estimates of our uncertainty. And Daniel Kahneman observes of decision makers that when they get new information, they forget how much they learned. They forget the extent of their prior uncertainty and think that the new information was no big surprise (i.e., "I knew it all along"). Researchers have also found that decision makers will usually underestimate how much can be inferred from a given amount of information.

I recently had a related conversation with a very experienced operations research expert, who had said he had extensive experience with both Monte Carlo models and large law enforcement agencies. We were discussing how to measure the percentage of traffic stops that inadvertently released someone with a warrant for his or her arrest under some other jurisdiction. The reason was that they needed to find a way to justify investments in building information technology that would allow easier communication among all participating law enforcement agencies.

After I explained my approach, he said, "But we don't have enough data to measure that." I've heard this many times before, including from people who had PhDs in OR or in the physical sciences. I said, "But you don't know what data you need or how much." I went on to explain that his assumption that there isn't enough data should really be the result of a specific calculation. Furthermore, he would probably be surprised at how little additional data would be needed to reduce uncertainty about this highly uncertain variable.

I've heard this argument often from a variety of people and then subsequently disproved it by measuring the very item they thought could not be measured. It happened so often I had to write *How to Measure Anything: Finding the Value of Intangibles in Business*, just to explain all the fallacies I ran into and what the solutions were. Here are a couple of key concepts from that book that risk managers should keep in mind:

- The definition of *measurement* is uncertainty reduction based on observation.
- It is a fallacy that when a variable is highly uncertain, we need a lot of data to reduce the uncertainty. The fact is that when there is a lot of uncertainty, less data is needed to yield a large reduction in uncertainty.

- When information value is high, the existing amount of data is irrelevant because gathering more observations is justified.
- The experience with computing the value of information is that you probably need less data, and probably completely different data, than you think. (See *measurement inversion* as discussed in Chapter 9.)

Introduction to Bayes: One Way to Get around That "Limited Data for Disasters" Problem

In risk analysis, it is often important to assess the likelihood of relatively uncommon but extremely costly disasters. The rarity of such events—called *catastrophes* or *disasters*—is part of the problem in determining their likelihood. *Bayes's Theorem* should be a basic tool for risk analysts to evaluate such situations, but from what I can tell it is rarely used in practice. Bayes's Theorem is the way to update prior knowledge with new information. We know from calibration training that we can always express our prior state of uncertainty for just about anything. What seems to surprise many people is how little additional data we need to update prior knowledge to an extent that would be of value.

Bayes's Theorem

$$P(A|B) = P(A) \times P(B|A)/P(B)$$

Where:

$P(A|B)$ = The probability of A given B

$P(A)$, $P(\text{NOT } A)$ = Probability of A and NOT A, respectively

$P(B)$ = Probability of B = $P(B|A)P(A) + P(B|\text{NOT } A)P(\text{NOT } A)$

$P(B|A)$ = Probability of B given A

One area of risk analysis where we don't get many data points is in the failure rates of new vehicles in aerospace. If we are developing a new rocket, we don't know what the rate of failure might be—that is, the percentage of times the rocket blows up or otherwise fails to get a payload into orbit. If we could launch it a million times, we would have a very precise and accurate value for the failure rate. Obviously, we can't do that because, as with many problems in business, the cost per sample is just too high.

Suppose your existing risk analysis (calibrated experts) determined that a new rocket design had an 80% chance of working properly and a 20% chance of failure. But you have another battery of tests on components that could reduce your uncertainty. These tests have their own imperfections, of course, so passing them is still no guarantee of success. We know that in the past, other systems that failed in the maiden test flight had also failed this component testing method 95% of the time. Systems that succeeded on the launch pad had passed the component testing 90% of the time. If you get a good test result on the new rocket, what is the chance of success on the first flight? Follow this using the notation introduced in the previous chapter:

$P(T|R)$ = Probability of a good test result given a good rocket = .9

$P(T|NOT\ R)$ = Probability of a good test result given a bad rocket = .05

$P(R)$ = Probability of a launch success for the rocket = .8

$P(T)$ = Probability of a good test result = $P(T|R) \times P(R) + P(T|NOT\ R) \times P(NOT\ R) = .9 \times .8 + .05 \times .2 = .73$

$P(R|T) = P(R) \times P(T|R)/P(T) = .8^{*}\ .9/.73 = .986$

In other words, a good test means we can go from 80% certainty of launch success to 98.6% certainty. We started out with the probability of a good test result given a good rocket and we get the probability of a good rocket given a good test. That is why this is called an *inversion* using Bayes's Theorem, or a *Bayesian inversion*.

Now, suppose we don't even get this test. (How did we get all the data for past failures with the test, anyway?) All we get is each actual launch as a "test" for the next one. And suppose we were *extremely* uncertain about this underlying failure rate. In fact, let's say that all we know is that the underlying failure rate (what we could measure very accurately if we launched a million times) is somewhere between 0% and 100%. Given this extremely high uncertainty, each launch starting with the first launch tells us something about this failure rate.

Our starting uncertainty gives every percentile increment in our range equal likelihood. A 8–9% base failure rate is a 1% chance, a 98–99% failure rate is a 1% chance, and so on for every other value between 0 and 100%. Of course, we can easily work out the chance of a failure on a given launch if the base failure rate is 77%—it's just 77%. What we need now is a Bayesian inversion so we can compute the chance of a given base rate given some actual observations. I show a spreadsheet in www.howtofixriskmgt.com that does this Bayesian inversion for ranges. In Exhibit 11.1, you can see what the distribution of possible base failure rates looks like after just a few launches.

Exhibit 11.1 shows our estimate of the baseline failure rates as a *probability density function (pdf)*. The area under each of these curves has to add up to 1 and the higher probabilities are where the curve is highest. Even though our distribution started out uniform (the flat dashed line), where every baseline failure rate was equally likely, even the first launch told us something. After the first launch, the pdf shifted to the left.

Here's why. If the failure rate were really 99%, it would have been unlikely, but not impossible, for the first launch to be a success. If the rate were 95%, it would have still been unlikely to have a successful launch on the first try, but a little more likely than if it were 99%. At the other end of the range, an actual failure rate of 2% would have made a success on the first launch very likely.

We know the chance of launch failure given a particular failure rate. We just applied a Bayesian inversion to get the failure rate given the actual launches and failures. It involves simply dividing up the ranges into increments and computing a Bayesian inversion for each small increment in the

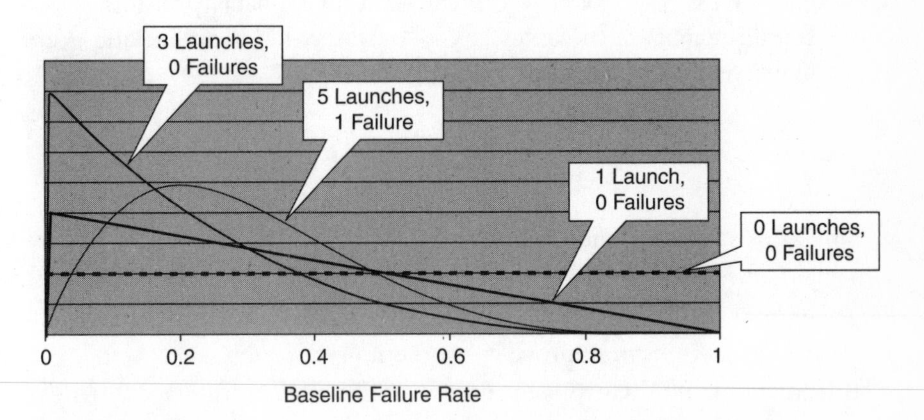

EXHIBIT 11.1 Application of Robust Bayesian Method to Launch Failure Rates

range. Then we can see how the distribution changes for each observed launch.

Even after several launches, we can compute the chance of seeing that result given a particular failure probability. This comes from a calculation in statistics called the *binomial distribution.* In Excel it is written simply as =binomdist(S,T, P,C), where S = number of successes, T = number of trials (launches), P = probability of a success, and C is an indicator telling Excel whether you want it to tell you the cumulative probability (the chance of every number of successes up to that one) or just the individual probability of that result (we set it to the latter). After five launches we had one failure. If the baseline probability were 50%, I would find that one failure after five launches would have a 15.6% chance of occurrence. If the baseline failure were 70%, this result would have only a 3% chance of occurrence. As with the first launch, the Bayesian inversion is applied here to each possible percentile increment in our original range.

BINOMIAL PROBABILITY IN EXCEL

The Excel Formula for the probability of a given number of successes after a given number of trials:

=binomdist(S,T,P,C)

Where S = number of successes, T = number of trials, P = probability of a success, and C = 0 if you want the probability for that specific number of successes or C = 1 if you want the probability of that number of successes or less.

Since this starts out with the assumption of maximum possible uncertainty (a failure rate anywhere between 0 and 100%), this is called a *robust Bayesian* method. So, when we have a *lot* of uncertainty, it doesn't really take many data points to improve it—sometimes just one.

But for the truly disastrous events we might need to find a way to use even more data than the disasters themselves. We might want to use near misses, similar to what Robin Dillon-Merrill researched (see Chapter 6). Near misses tend to be much more plentiful than actual disasters and, since at least some disasters are caused by the same events that caused the near miss, we can learn something from them. Near misses could be defined in a number of ways, but I will use the term very broadly. A *near miss* is any event where the conditional probability of a disaster given the near miss is higher than the conditional probability of a disaster without a near miss. In other words, P(disaster|with near miss) > P(disaster|without near miss).

For example, the failure of a safety inspection of an airplane could have bearing on the odds that a disaster would happen if corrective actions were not taken. Other indicator events could be an alarm that sounds at a nuclear power plant, a middle-aged person experiencing chest pains, a driver getting reckless-driving tickets, or component failures during the launch of the Space Shuttle (e.g., O-rings burning through or foam striking the Orbiter during launch). Each of these could be a necessary, but usually not sufficient, factor in the occurrence of a catastrophe of some kind. An increase in the occurrence of near misses would indicate an increased risk of catastrophe, even though there are insufficient samples of catastrophes to detect an increase based on the number of catastrophes alone.

As in the case of the overall failure of a system, each observation of a near miss or lack thereof tells us something about the rate of near misses. Also, each time a disaster does or does not occur when near misses do or do not occur, tells us something about the conditional probability of the disaster given the near miss. To analyze this, I applied a fairly simple robust Bayesian inversion to both the failure rate of the system and the probability of the near miss.

When I applied this to the Space Shuttle, I confirmed Dillon-Merrill's findings that it was not rational for NASA managers to perceive a near miss to be nearly as good as a success. I also confirmed it was not rational for managers to perceive a reduction in risk in the belief that the near miss proved the robustness of the system. Exhibit 11.2 shows the probability of a failure on each launch given that every previous launch was a success but a near miss occurred on every launch (as was the case with the foam falling off the external tank). I started with the "prior knowledge" stated by some engineers that they should expect one launch failure in 50 launches. (This is more pessimistic than what Feynman found in his interviews.) I took this 2% failure rate as merely the expected value in a range of possible baseline failure rates. I also started out with maximum initial uncertainty about the rate of the near misses. Finally, I limited the disaster result to those situations where the event that allowed the near miss to occur was a necessary

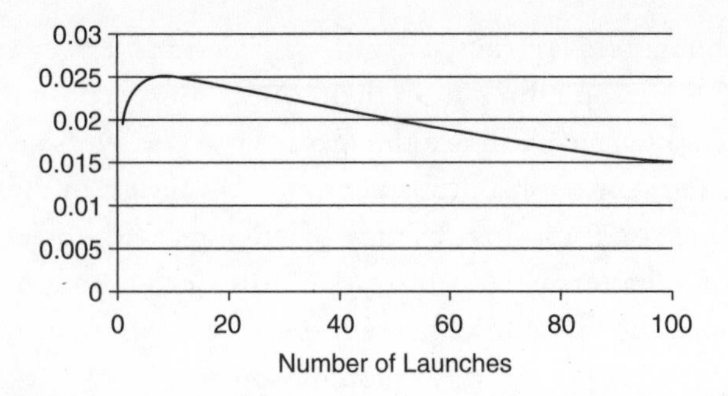

EXHIBIT 11.2 **Conditional Robust Bayesian Method: Chance of Shuttle Disaster after Each Observed Near Miss (e.g., Falling Foam, O-Rings Burning Through) with an Otherwise Successful Launch**

precondition for the disaster. In other words, the examined near miss was the only cause of catastrophe. These assumptions are actually more forgiving to NASA management.

The chart shows the probability of a failure on the first launch (starting out at 2%) and then updates it on each observed near miss with an otherwise successful flight. As I stated previously, I started with the realization that the real failure rate could be much higher or lower. For the first 10 flights, the adjusted probability of a failure increases, even under these extremely forgiving assumptions. Although the flight was a success, the frequency of the observed near misses makes low-baseline near-miss rates less and less likely (i.e., it would be unlikely to see so many near misses if the chance of a near miss per launch were only 3%, for example). In fact, it takes about 50 flights for the number of observed successful flights to just bring the adjusted probability of failure back to what it was.

But, again, this is too forgiving. The fact is that until they observed these near misses they had no idea they *could* occur. Their assumed rate of these near misses was effectively 0%—and that was conclusively disproved on the first observation.

The use of Bayesian methods is not some special exception. I consider them a tool of first resort for most measurement problems. The fact is that almost all real-world measurement problems are Bayesian. That is, you knew something about the quantity before (a calibrated estimate, if nothing else) and new information updates that prior knowledge. It is used in clinical testing for life-saving drugs for the same reason it applies to most catastrophic risks—it is a way to get the most uncertainty reduction out of just a few observations.

The development of methods for dealing with near misses will greatly expand the data we have available for evaluating various disasters. For many disasters, Bayesian analysis of near misses is going to be the only realistic source of measurement.

Self-Examinations for Modelers Who Care about Quality

Constantly testing your model by seeing how well it matches history and by tracking forecasts is absolutely essential. These tests are necessary to have any confidence in modeling at all. However, even though this testing is not difficult to implement, it is rarely done. There is simply very little incentive for analysts or management to go back and check models against reality.

Tracking: Documenting forecasts in your model (including variables forecasted within the model) so they can be compared to real outcomes when they occur

Back testing: Running models to compare them to existing historical data

In the course of conducting research for this book, my biggest challenge was to find strong, convincing evidence that using quantitative, probabilistic analysis methods (such as Monte Carlos) is superior to qualitative alternatives. To be fair, I have to apply the same measure to this method as I would to any other. I need to see evidence that decisions are consistently improved. I did find a couple of good examples. But the more interesting finding is that almost nobody measures the performance of their models now.

I try to routinely go back and check forecasts against reality. Of all the variables in all the models I've forecasted, I can easily get real data to compare to forecasts for only a small percentage. But it still adds up to over 100 variables.

We can validate forecasts of binary probabilities in the same way we validated the results of true/false calibration tests in the previous chapter. That is, of all the times we said some event was about 10% likely, it should have occurred about 10% of the time. To validate ranges, we can apply a test that is just a bit more detailed than the test we used to validate 90% confidence intervals. To get a little bit more data out of the actual observations, I separated all the original range forecasts into multiple "buckets":

- 50% should be in the *interquartile range* (the middle half of a distribution).
- 5% should be above the upper bound of a 90% CI.
- 5% should be below the lower bound of a 90% CI.
- 20% should be above the interquartile but below the upper bound of a 90% CI.
- 20% should be below the interquartile but above lower bound of a 90% CI.

The buckets are arbitrary and I could have defined a very different set. But, as with the true/false tests, things should be about as frequent as we estimate. In this case, the actual data should fall in these sections of a range about as often as would be implied by the forecasts. And ranges don't have to be all the same type. Some separation of buckets can always be done for any distribution of a range, no matter what its shape. No matter how I define a distribution, only 5% of the data should be above the 95 percentile of the forecast. Also, forecasts don't even have to be about the same topic in order to compare them (as is the case with calibration exams).

When I go back and look, I find that, within a statistically allowable error, the forecasts of most types of data were distributed as we expected. For those, the forecasting methods were working.

But, in 2001, just as I was reaching 30 projects in my database, I was also finding that there were certain variables the calibrated estimators still didn't forecast well, even though they had shown their ability to assess probabilities in the calibration tests. The two areas where I found that even calibrated persons failed to perform well were the estimation of catastrophic project failures and business volumes.

In the case of project cancellations (stopping a project after beginning it), the assessed probabilities were far too low to account for the observed rate of cancellations. Calibrated estimators never gave a chance of cancellation to be above 10% and the average estimate is 5%. But observation of those same projects after they got started showed that the cancellation rate was 6 out of 30, or 20%. According to the binomial distribution we discussed earlier, it would be extremely unlikely, if there were only a 5% chance of cancellation per project, to see 6 cancellations out of 30 (less than 1 in 1,000). One of the cancellations was a project that was thought to have no chance of cancellation, which, of course, should be impossible.

I saw a similar inability for people not directly involved with tracking business volumes to forecast them well. For many of the operational investments I was assessing for companies, the return on investment had to be partly a function of sales. For example, if an insurance company was trying to increase the efficiency of new policy processing, the value had to be, in part, related to how many new policies were sold. At first, we would ask IT managers to estimate this and, if the information value justified it, we would do more research.

But, again, I found that too many of the actual observations were ending up in the extremes of the original forecast. Unlike project cancellations, where there is only one such variable per project, there were multiple forecasts of ranges per model and there was more data to work with. Still, in the forecasts of business volumes I saw more than 15% ending up in the lower 5% tail of the original forecast.

The good news is that because of this tracking and testing, I found that the historical data for project cancellations and changes in business volumes was more reliable than the calibrated estimators—even if the data came from the industry, and not that particular firm. And now we know better than to ask managers to estimate business volumes if tracking them is not in their own area of expertise. Even more good news is that for every other kind of forecast I was asking estimators to make (e.g., project duration, productivity improvements, technology adoption rates, etc.), the calibrated estimator did as well as expected—about 90% of the actual fell within their 90% CI. The bad news is that I couldn't collect the data for more variables on more projects. The worse news is that almost nobody who builds Monte Carlo models does even this much tracking.

But, using historical data to validate models and tracking forecasts to compare them to actual outcomes is fairly simple. Don't worry that you can't get all the data. Get what you can. Even though I had limited data, I still learned something useful from tracking results. Here are four things to keep in mind (if these items sound a little like what we saw earlier, it is because the same principles apply):

1. Don't assume that because each model was unique, you can't assess their outcomes in some aggregate fashion. All forecasts of any type can still be assessed by comparing the chance you gave the event to the outcomes. For example, you can look at the 5% lower tails of all your forecasts of any kind and see whether about 5% landed there. Also, don't commit the *Mount St. Helens fallacy* (from Chapter 9). Just because there are unique aspects of two different systems doesn't mean that we can't learn something from one about the other.
2. Don't worry about not having enough data to track because you only have a few models. Almost *every* variable in your model is a forecast that can be checked against observation whether that forecast was based on other historical data or calibrated estimates. Even a single medium-sized model will have several forecasts you can attempt to track.
3. Don't worry about the fact that there is some data you can't easily get—because there is data you *can* easily get. If you don't know whether the forecast of some productivity improvement was accurate without doing a big study of operations, don't worry. You can easily check the actual project duration or widgets produced.
4. Don't presume that the few data points will tell you nothing. First get the data, then determine how much can be learned from it. In the case of the IT project that had a 0% chance of cancellation, I proved the original estimators wrong with one data point of a failure. If you find that events that were estimated to have less than a 1% chance of occurrence happened 3 times out of just 10 forecasts, then you have all the data you need to indicate that the event is probably more likely than 1%.
5. Change your time scales. There is a habit among some analysts to look at five years of data, as if that were a magic number. But, as 2008 proved, events that happen only once every several decades can be much more impactful. Consider an event that has only a 5% chance of occurrence in one year. In a 5-year period, it still only has

a 23% chance of occurrence but will have an 87% chance some time during the typical 40-year working career. Even showing management the chance of an event occurring in a decade as opposed to a year puts impactful events in a better perspective.

6. If you use history, use *meta-history*. If you are looking at the history of the price volatility of a stock, ask yourself "Historically, how often has this history predicted an outcome within a given range?" It is common for financial analysts to use the volatility of the previous 5 years of a stock to estimate the volatility for the next quarter. If we look at each day in the history of Dow Jones, how well does the previous 5 years match the volatility of the following quarter? We would find that it varies by a factor of about 2—the volatility of the next quarter could be anywhere between half as much and twice as much as the previous 5 years. Likewise, as we found in Chapter 9, don't just accept a historical correlation between two variables as immutable fact without asking how often previously correlated variables change their correlation.

Whereas such practices are hard to find, I did find some who attempt to evaluate the performance of their forecasts. Ray Covert works for MCR, LLC, a contractor that provides budget, tracking, and management services in government and industry. Covert spends most of his time building sophisticated cost and mission analysis models for NASA using the Monte Carlo method with the Crystal Ball tool.

Covert also routinely tracks his results against reality. He finds that whereas his Monte Carlo–based method for cost analysis still slightly underestimates mission costs on average, he does better than the deterministic methods based on point estimates of costs. A slight majority of his estimates are within 10% of (and some are slightly over) the actual, whereas all estimates from the standard accounting methods underestimate by 25% to 55%.

NASA offers another interesting opportunity for tracking the effectiveness of different methods. For over 100 interplanetary space probe missions, NASA has evaluated risks with both the 5-by-5 "risk matrices" (yes, the type debunked in Chapter 7) as well as probabilistic methods. Covert finds that the 5-by-5 risk matrices do not match well with observed reality when results are compared with facts. He says, "I'm not a fan of the 5-by-5 methods. Both Shuttle disasters and other satellite failures never show up on those charts."

Instead of 5-by-5s, Covert uses a mission failure model developed by David Bearden of Aerospace Corporation.[2] This is a historical model that produces a very good fit with actual mission failures of planetary space missions. Bearden developed a type of *complexity index* using 37 factors, such as how tightly the trajectory has to be managed, whether a foreign partnership was used, and the number of unique instruments. He finds, when he looks at actual, historical data of mission failures, that all failures are for missions where the schedule and budget were very tight for a given level of complexity.

Complexity alone is not a good predictor of a mission failure, but if a complex mission had tight budget and time constraints, mission failure is not only much more likely but can be overwhelmingly likely. When Bearden looks at the distribution of mission schedules for a given level of complexity, he finds that almost all of the partial or complete failures occur in the bottom third of the distribution. Missions that are in the top half for length of schedule and amount of budget for a given complexity never had any failures whether partial or complete. Bearden calls the area where there is not enough time or money to develop a system with a given complexity the "no-fly zone." By looking at historical data, most modelers could probably find similar no-fly zones for projects or investments of any kind.

There is an interesting moral of the story here for modelers in general. When NASA missions are under tight time and budget constraints, they tend to cut component tests more than anything else. And less testing means more failures. The same is true with your model of your organization's risks—the less testing, the more failures. The problem is that since testing almost never occurs in risk models, failures of risk models are much more likely than any space mission failure.

There is a direct correlation between cutting tests of components in NASA space missions and mission failure. The same applies to risk models.

NOTES

1. S. Wolfram, *A New Kind of Science,* (Wolfram Media, 2002).
2. D. Bearden, C. Freaner, R. Bitten, and D. Emmons, "An Assessment of The Inherent Optimism in Early Conceptual Designs and Its Effect on Cost and Schedule Growth" SSCAG/SCAF/EACE Joint International Conference, Noordwijk, The Netherlands, May 15-16, 2008.

CHAPTER 12

The Risk Community: Intra- and Extraorganizational Issues of Risk Management

Take calculated risks. That is quite different from being rash.

—George Patton

Prediction is very difficult, especially about the future.

—Niels Bohr, Nobel Prize–winning physicist

Most of this book is primarily focused on methods for the analysis of risks and decisions. That is certainly a key to answering why risk management is broken and how to fix it. The continued use of methods to assess risks in ways that are no better than astrology would make any improvement in risk management impossible. But if you were to implement better methods for measuring risks, then you would have much better guidance for managing risks.

To achieve an improvement, however, your organization has to have a way to deal with barriers that are not part of the quantitative methods themselves. You need to break organizational silos, have good quality procedures, and incentivize good analysis and good decisions.

The management side of the issue requires some larger-scale solutions that involve collaboration within the firm and may eventually need to go beyond the borders of the firm. Fixing risk management will involve a level of commitment from your organization that goes beyond superficial measures such as declaring that you have a "formal risk process" or even appointing a "risk czar."

Getting Organized

Dr. Sam Savage sees the organizational management and quality control issues to be at least as important as the risk assessment methods he and I both promote. According to Savage, "The big failure of risk management is the lack of consolidating individual risk models and the lack of being able to audit them." Christopher "Kip" Bohn of Aon agrees: "There's a huge silo effect at organizations. Nobody takes the big view of risk at organizations and therefore risk mitigation capital is not spent effectively." Without addressing issues such as these, the sophistication of the risk analysis method would be irrelevant.

Let me reiterate a previous clarification of *risk management* and the *chief risk officer (CRO)*. As I mentioned earlier, risk analysis is only part of decision analysis and analysis is only part of any kind of management—risk management or otherwise. As Chapter 5 pointed out, the position of some is that risks should include uncertain benefits as well as losses, but risk analysis with benefits is already called *decision analysis*. (Numerous analysts such as myself have just been calling it a *risk/return analysis*, where risk is only half the problem.) It seems awkward to arbitrarily carve out one important part of analyzing decisions under uncertainty (risk) and give to it another title. To me, that seems like separating accounting into even and odd numbers or classifying sales managers according to the first letter of the client's name.

Don't we really want analysis of all uncertainties, including risks, done in a systematic way that supports the objectives of the organization? The best choice on all big decisions is one that follows a tradeoff between risk and benefits—the risk/return analysis. Whatever title this person should have, someone should be given responsibility for the overall assessment of uncertainties of all types in the firm. Accounting doesn't deal with quantitative probabilistic uncertainties at all. Even the CFO would be too narrowly focused since we need to address uncertainties under the COO, the CIO, marketing, and everywhere else. Whomever it is, this individual should be given charge of the following:

1. *Document the risk aversion of the firm.* Someone needs to be the keeper of the *investment boundaries*, the utility curve that explicitly describes how much risk the organization is willing to take for a given set of benefits. This first item on the list may be conceptually the simplest, but it is absolutely critical. In Chapter 7, Exhibit 7.6 showed an investment boundary—a curve that shows the tradeoff between benefits and risks. There are many ways to draw this chart, but however you make it, it's *the* official position of your firm on risk tolerance. It is a version of what some have called the *risk appetite* (only more unambiguous and quantitative).
2. *Manage the model.* Someone needs to manage the initial development and continuous evolution of a simulation of all of the organization's key uncertainties (including opportunities as well as risks). This is not a divergent set of separate risk models for different problems. It may start out focused on specific immediate problems, but it will eventually become what I will refer to as the *global probability model (GPM)*. More on this later.
3. *Track and improve forecasts.* Someone needs to set up and monitor all forecasting efforts in the firm so that future assessments of uncertainty gradually improve. This person will be in charge of designing and overseeing the system for tracking individual predictions, reporting actual results, and incentivizing better forecasting.
4. *Network and expand the scope of the GPM.* Someone is needed as liaison with other organizations whose risk models feed into or use the risk models of the firm. This person may also be an independent source of guidance for a CEO, board of directors, stockholders, and even regulatory agencies for assessments of uncertainty.

This sounds like Sam Savage's recommended *chief probability officer (CPO)*. But, I have to admit, *CRO* is a much better cover-your-ass designation. Putting someone in charge of *risk* makes it sound more like management is "taking the bull by the horns" than would putting someone in charge of probabilistic modeling in general. The CPO may be less confused about his or her role in the firm but, as Savage sees it, "Risk management has already poisoned the well," and there may be no going back. So let's proceed from here.

The first item in the previous list is an important step for getting started and should be fairly straightforward. Defining the investment boundary of the firm is merely a matter of asking management the following:

- How do you want to define *return*? It could be an annualized IRR over a five-year horizon, a net present value at a 5% discount, and so on.
- How would you like to define *risk*? This could be the chance of a negative return on investment, the one percentile worst-case scenario (equivalent to a *value-at-risk*), or some other measure that could be applied to a variety of investments.
- How much risk are you willing to accept for a given return? This is done iteratively with several combinations of risk and return. For example, "Would you accept an investment of $10 million if we could show the average return of all scenarios was 40% but there was a 5% chance of losing part or all of the investment with no return?" If they say yes, increase the risk until they say no. Then increase the return and repeat.

After getting management to answer these questions, a chart like the one in Exhibit 7.6 can be developed. It is a simple process that could be done on a flipchart.

Now, let's discuss items 2 through 4 in the previous list: managing the model, tracking and improving forecasts, and extraorganizational issues. I finish out with some thoughts on other methods and the direction in which this should take us.

Managing the Global Probability Model

The idea of a model that reaches across organizational silos to combine several models seems daunting. But it can just start with some "seed" models and each new risk/return analysis made for the firm. Or it can start as a top-down design of the entire model for the organization. The technological home of this model could be any of the Monte Carlo tools described earlier.

The idea is that if two different areas of the firm are assessing a risk/return model that considers, for example, uncertainty about revenue, then they can both be using the same model for revenue forecasts. The uncertainty about revenue should come from marketing (or whoever is closest to the issue) and it shouldn't be reinvented by every modeler who needs to simulate the same thing. Likewise, individual analysts working on models for the risks and returns of big technology investments, new products, and supply chains should not be reinventing models for the weather, the stock market, and currency exchange rates if these uncertainties affect all the models.

Exhibit 12.1 shows how the GPM can evolve based on ongoing modeling efforts and external events. The right side of the process is, in effect, the *Applied Information Economics (AIE)* method I developed in the 1990s. This originally focused on major, specific decisions that involved a high degree of uncertainty, risks, and intangibles. I show a two-way interaction between the individual modeling effort and the evolving GPM. Each time a

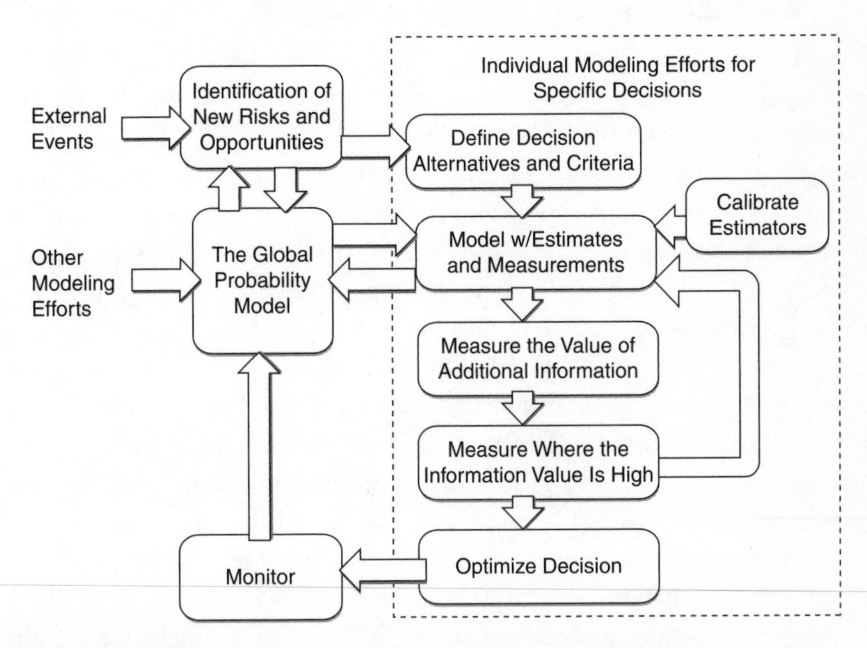

EXHIBIT 12.1 **Evolving Global Probability Model**

new decision requires additional modeling, that model becomes part of the GPM.

I also show interactions that represent other sources of updating the GPM besides a single modeling effort in one part of the organization. Other modeling efforts (possibly from other organizations) can be included in the GPM. Also, external events and new sources of risks can drive additions to the GPM even without supporting specific decisions. The GPM itself also becomes one of the ways of identifying new risks for the organization.

Sam Savage has developed a solution that nicely facilitates this sharing that a GPM requires. Savage created the technology for keeping *scenario libraries*. These are a database of 100,000 scenarios each for a variety of problems. They include variables that already have correlations with variables such as holiday sales and cost of part-time labor or energy costs and steel costs. He calls these *Stochastic Information Packets (SIPs)* and *Stochastic Library Units with Relationships Preserved (SLURPS)*.

This approach of keeping standard scenario libraries allows for an audit trail that is not usually feasible with Monte Carlo tools. These are part of what Savage refers to as *certified distributions*, which are validated for particular uses. His goal is a level of quality control and standardization that has not previously existed. This is not a product but a *standard* that Savage has championed. Crystal Ball and Risk Solver already support this standard and Savage is seeking more participants among the Monte Carlo software firms.

Perhaps the enterprise applications already used by an organization can contribute significantly to a GPM. There may soon be a way to include probabilistic modeling in all the major applications of the firm. Jim Franklin, who runs the Crystal Ball division at Oracle, explains that Oracle is integrating Monte Carlo simulation tools in all of its major enterprise applications. "Anywhere in the enterprise where Oracle has a static input, they will have an option of a stochastic input. Think of CRM with pipeline forecasting and being probabilistic." Several other enterprise applications produce forecasts of some sort for planning, budgeting, and so forth. Right now, these forecasts are deterministic, but they could be part of a Crystal Ball simulation.

This might seem overwhelming, but it is no harder than starting any Monte Carlo–based decision-making process. I've done stochastic analysis of risks in a variety of organizations (including some not very large) on a variety of decision problems. The only difference here is that I would try to keep each model and add it together with other models. Below are a few items to keep in mind for developing any simulation, which are also important in developing a GPM.

Start by standardizing a few model components that should not be reinvented each time you need to assess the risks and returns of some new decision. Some items that can be standardized early are:

- The sales of your firm (or other measure of output if it is a not-for-profit or government agency) and how they might be tied to other economic indicators
- Fairly routine risks, such as weather, accidents, or network and power outages

Then use these risks as part of your next big risk return analysis—for example, investments in a manufacturing facility. The model developed in that analysis then becomes part of the GPM. This continues with each new decision being analyzed, which, for most firms of moderate size or bigger, should be frequent. This could happen in conjunction with top-down design methods independent of individual decisions. But several of the same model development methods that would be used on individual risk/return analysis should apply to top-down modeling

Modeling should be an interactive process with the subject matter experts (SMEs) and, I find, some interactive processes are better than others. Many analysts start with a brainstorming session to identify all the things that could go wrong. I, too, start with this but I find that it reaches a point of diminishing returns fairly quickly. At about three hours, it is time to take a break from that process and move on to something else. Below are some ideas to keep that process going.

Ideas for Generating a List of Risks and Modeling Them

- Systematically work through the four "completeness" perspectives in Chapter 3: Internal, External, Historical, and Combinatorial.
- Pretend you are in the future looking back at a failure. An interesting method I found that changes the pace in brainstorming is from Gary Klein, the chief scientist of Klein Associates, a division of Applied Research Associates, in Fairborn, Ohio. He calls his approach a

premortem, which he describes as "the hypothetical opposite of a postmortem": Unlike a typical critiquing session, in which project team members are asked what *might* go wrong, the premortem operates on the assumption that the patient has died, and so asks what *did* go wrong. The team members' task is to generate plausible reasons for the project's failure.[1]

- Look to risks from others. Rick Julien of the management consulting firm Crowe Horwath proposes a way to look to other firms for ideas for generating a list of risks. For all the firms in your industry that are publicly traded you should look up their Form 10-K, the annual financial report. In Section 9 of this form, firms must disclose to the public the risks they see. Julien finds this to be a constructive addition to thinking of risks that his clients might not have otherwise thought of. I would also recommend looking up the reported risks of your key suppliers and even customers. I might even suggest sampling Forms 10-K from companies in related industries that are not competitors (other service industries, other durable goods manufacturers, etc.).
- Include everyone. Your organization has numerous experts on all sorts of specific risks, and chances are that many of them aren't in management. Some effort should be made to survey representatives of just about every job level in the firm.
- Ask business insurance consultants about potential risks. Sometimes their advice might be narrow, but it tends to be practical. Some risk management firms like Aon and Protiviti approach the problem from a fairly broad point of view and they are often quantitatively proficient in topics of risk analysis and risk management.
- Do peer reviews. John Schuyler (from Chapter 9) says, "The biggest improvement I've seen in my 30 years is the peer review. Everything goes through this rigorous filter before it goes to management for decision making." This is wise at several levels. First, it is always a good idea to check assumptions in models by showing them to someone who isn't immersed in the model. Second, spreadsheet errors are a virtual pandemic in decision analysis, and spreadsheet-based risk analysis tools are no exception. Research has shown that the extent

of errors in spreadsheet calculations is probably far beyond what most managers would like to believe.[2,3]

- Use a dynamic online source. Go to www.howtofixriskmgt.com for growing lists of risk categories and their considerations. There is a discussion group that will be expanding a list of risks. This will allow the readers of this book to be up to date regardless of what has happened since this book was purchased. I'll also include links to other good sources and free downloads of tools.
- Finally, the structural Monte Carlo approach to modeling also makes the best use of the knowledge of your own SMEs. While some of the heavy lifting in the model building might have to be done away from the experts, I like to conduct at least some of it in real time with the experts and managers in the room. I think it facilitates the brainstorming of risks (things that can go wrong) by periodically revealing to the analysts things that they would not have thought of on their own. I find that modeling a system will reveal many risks even without deliberately trying to name them.

Another tool evolving to aid in the GPM approach is the *Distribution Strings (DISTs)*. DISTs, as conceived by Sam Savage, pack thousands of scenarios for a particular variable, say oil price, into a single data element in a spreadsheet or database. They provide three benefits:

1. Unlike traditional representations of probability, DISTs allow for modular risk modeling. That is, the DIST of the sum of two or more uncertainties is the sum of their DISTs.
2. DISTs reduce the number of data elements in the scenario library by a factor of 1,000 or more.
3. DISTs speed up access to the data by orders of magnitude.

To ensure a practical and interchangeable standard for the DIST concept, Savage initiated a collaborative effort among academicians and software engineers, including Harry Markowitz, Nobel Laureate in Economics, and John Sall, co-founder of the SAS Institute. The specifications for the DIST 1.0 format have been published as an open source standard at www.probabilitymanagement.org.

Incentives for a Calibrated Culture

A *calibrated culture* is one in which managers and subject matter experts know that predictions will be documented and reported and that good predictions will be incentivized. It is also one where actions that change risks are considered in compensation plans as much as actions that improve one quarter's profit.

To make a calibrated culture, you will have to do more than taking your estimators through a calibration process. You need to track predictions, report results (i.e., show whether the predictions turned out right), and incentivize performance for forecasting.

One method for generating incentives is the use of the *Brier score*, originally developed in 1950 for weather forecasters.[4] The Brier score is a way to evaluate the results of predictions both by how often the estimators were right and by the probability they estimated for getting a correct answer. Getting a forecast right should be worth more if the forecaster was 90% sure than if she was 50% sure. And if the forecaster was 99% certain and she turns out to be wrong, there should be a bigger penalty than for being wrong if she said she was only 60% certain.

The Brier score is proven to be what decision theory researchers call a *proper* scoring method in that it is impossible to game; that is, it is impossible to get a better score by using a trick strategy other than giving the best calibrated answer for each prediction. An example of a method that can be gamed is our simplified calibration test of 90% confidence intervals. You could get a perfectly calibrated score by giving an absurdly wide range for 90% of the questions and a tiny range for the other 10%—resulting in a "perfect" score of 90% correct. But a Brier score would penalize that behavior.

Brier scores are averaged for a number of predictions for individual forecasted items and the lower the score the better (like golf). A perfect Brier score is, in fact, zero, and that can be obtained only by being 100% confident on each forecast and getting all of them right. The worst average score is 1, which is obtained by being 100% confident on each forecast and getting 'each one wrong. The score is calculated as follows:

Item Brier score (the score for a single forecast result) $= (P(T) - T)^2$

Where:

- $T = 1$ if a particular forecast turns out to be true and $T = 0$ if not

- P(T) = the probability, according to the forecaster, that T will be true
- Average Brier score = the average of item Brier scores for all of the forecast items of a given forecaster

Consider a forecast by an expert that this month there would be no injuries on the factory floor that required medical attention. If the forecaster were 90% confident that the statement "There will be no injuries next month" was true, then P(T) = .9. If the forecaster believed it was false with 80% confidence, then the chance it is true is believed to be 20% (P(T) = .2). If the former prediction was made (P(T) = .9) and it turns out to be true, then T = 1 and the item Brier score is $(.9 - 1)^2 = .01$. The average of several items Brier scores is shown in Exhibit 12.2.

Here are a few other items to keep in mind for incentivizing the calibrated culture:

- Brier scores can be computed for ranges just by decomposing ranges into a set of individual true/false predictions. For example, a range for the cost of a new building could be stated as a percent confidence it is over one amount, another percent confidence it is above another amount, and so on.

EXHIBIT 12.2 BRIER SCORE EXAMPLE FOR FORECASTERS

This Year the Following Events Will Happen	Assessed Probability Event Will Be True = P(T)	Event Was True (T = 1) or Event Was False (T = 0)	Item Brier Score = $(P(T) - T)^2$
New product will be available	0.95	1	0.0025
Labor strike	0.25	0	0.0625
Key competitors merge	0.5	0	0.25
COO will retire	0.6	1	0.16
Illinois factory will have layoffs	0.4	1	0.36
		Average Brier Score	0.167

- Some predictions, such as the completion date of a project, will be easily confirmed once the event occurs. Some predictions might be verifiable only with deliberate measures. For example, a forecast that a productivity improvement from a new technology will exceed 10% might require a deliberate survey. It might not be economically feasible to measure all such forecasts. But a random sample of forecasts could be measured in this way so that forecasters know than any prediction they make has at least a chance of being verified. They cannot know, of course, which predictions will be used in the score. Predictions such as this that happen not to get measured would be excluded from the score.
- You might want to consider compensating forecasters for volume as well. You could convert item Brier scores so that the best score is 1 (just subtract the result of the item Brier score in the calculation from 1) and add them up instead of averaging them. This means that the score will be high not only for being well calibrated but also for the number of predictions made. For this, you might want to limit predictions to a particular list.
- You might also want to consider different bonus structures for more important forecasts. For example, forecasting the successful completion of a major project could be more important than forecasting the successful completion of a small project.
- Forecasts from several SMEs on the same issue can be aggregated when the estimates are used in the GPM. JDM researchers Bob Clemen and Robert Winkler found that a simple average of forecasts can be better calibrated than any individual.[5]
- You might want to entertain the use of prediction markets as an alternative to Brier scores. Prediction markets allow individuals to buy and sell "options" on given claims. For example, if you are trying to forecast whether two competitors will merge, ask your SMEs to participate in an online market for options that pay $1 if the event occurs. The bid prices for these options historically show that they are a very good indicator of the probability the forecasted event will occur. For example, if the option for the merger of the competitors is selling at $0.65, then the market is estimating there is a 65% probability that the option will be worth $1 (which happens only if the

merger occurs). The option is worth nothing if the event does not occur. Sites such as www.intrade.com trade options on events such as who will win an election. But organizations can also create their own internal markets. Several firms currently sell software for this and already there is a large and growing community of users.

But perhaps the biggest issue for creating the calibrated culture is not incentives for forecasts, but incentives for risks. If we measure risks in a quantitatively meaningful way, then management bonuses could be based as much on risks as near-term profits. Fund managers who earn high profits only by taking highly leveraged positions that expose the entire firm to ruin would have the increased risk—as computed by the GPM—considered in the calculation of their bonuses.

Most risk analysts I talk to who have any relationship to the financial market, banking, or insurance have all pointed their finger to inefficient incentives as a common cause for many of the problems the market saw in 2008. "Incentives are a main culprit" says Andrew Freeman, a risk expert with McKinsey&Company, "Without proper incentives, risk management becomes boxes that management just ticks off to feel more comfortable." Usually, bonuses can be taken without regard to whether risk exposure was increased or decreased under the direction of management. Once the bonuses are calculated and paid, they are never garnished in the future if catastrophes occurred as a result of the risky positions that executives took.

If investors, boards, and regulators want a solution to this, they will have to start measuring risk while the executive is still there and before bonuses are paid. The risk can be considered in a number of ways for this purpose. For one, any probability distribution of gains and losses has a *certain monetary equivalent (CME)* for decision makers. Suppose I told you that you could choose between the following: (1) I will roll two dice and pay you the result times $1,000 for a payoff of between $2,000 and $12,000 or (2) I pay you a fixed amount of money. How much would the fixed amount have to be for you to be indifferent between the choices? If you are averse to risk, it would be some amount less than the expected payoff ($7,000). If you consider a certain payoff of exactly $5,500 to be just as good as taking the roll, then your CME for that range of possible payoffs with the dice is $5,500.

You can reduce any uncertain payoff or loss to a CME in the same way (although most people assign different values to possible gains and avoiding possible losses, the same principle applies). Suppose a manager makes a $5 million profit for one division. But the GPM says that the future losses from the decision expose the firm to a 25% chance of losing $500,000 to $4 million. What is the *risk-adjusted profit* on which the manager's bonus should be based?

It is a function of the CME of the board (or some high-level executive) for that probable loss. The board could also decide to defer part of the bonus and make it contingent on future gains and losses, possibly even after the manager retires. If the manager prefers a lump sum now, the amount would have to reflect this uncertainty. If the manager had an option of selling those future contingent bonuses, then presumably the buyer would price the future contingent bonuses with those same considerations in mind.

Incentivizing better forecasts as well as better management of future risks is critical. Without this, no level of sophistication of risk analysis or modeling will be of any use.

Extraorganizational Issues: Solutions beyond Your Office Building

Some of the really big issues in risk management can't be solved by individual firms. Some of the most critical issues can be resolved only by better guidance from standards organizations, new professional associations, and, in some cases, changes in law. Here are a few of these necessarily longer-term issues:

- Societies of professionals in modeling should combine and share components of models that affect multiple firms. Some societies could develop GPM models that span multiple firms in one industry so that cascade failures among firms can be assessed. Unfortunately, the regulatory bodies have done little to consolidate disparate risk analysis efforts. Basel II, for example, seems to have different people working on different parts of risk management without much consideration for either the effectiveness of the methods or the issues of common mode failures among the different pillars. However, modeling of interorganizational risks is already being done by some firms that perform risk analysis in finance and banking. Dennis William Cox of Risk Reward Limited is a statistical economist who has been modeling cascade failures among investment banks for years. *He had told me in February 2008 that he was concerned about the cascade failure effects in investment banking, including specifically the exposure of Lehman Brothers (8 months prior to their collapse).* Collaboration of modeling efforts would allow organizations whose risks affect each other to make much more realistic models of their own risks and risks in their industry.

- Of all the professions in risk management, that of the actuary is the only one that is actually a profession. Becoming an actuary requires a demonstration of proficiency through several standardized tests. It also means adopting a code of professional ethics enforced by some licensing body. When an actuary signs his name to the Statement of Actuarial Opinion of an insurance company, he puts his license on the line. As with doctors and lawyers, if he loses his license, he cannot just get another job next door. The industry of modelers of uncertainties outside of insurance could benefit greatly from this level of professional standards.
- Standards organizations such as PMI, NIST, and others are all guilty of explicitly promoting the ineffectual methods debunked earlier. The scoring methods developed by these institutions should be disposed of altogether. These organizations should stay out of the business of designing risk analysis methods until they begin to involve people with quantitative decision analysis backgrounds in their standards-development process.
- Some laws and regulations are so vague about what counts as proper risk analysis that any of the approaches debunked earlier in this book would suffice to meet the requirements. Sarbanes-Oxley wrote a one-page guideline on risk assessment that mentioned nothing about what would qualify as a proper method. The FASB allows so much subjective interpretation of which "contingent losses" should even be reported that the entire guidance on this is meaningless. Regulatory bodies should likewise get on board with GPMs and develop unambiguous (i.e., quantitative) requirements regarding risks.

The impression one gets from reviewing the positions many organizations have taken on regulating and managing risks is that the emphasis is on simply "addressing" risk management in some way, *any* way—it matters not what or how. In these cases, it appears that whoever was thinking about risk management added it as an afterthought or simply developed the entire approach in isolation from all the quantitative research in the field. Including specific requirements about quantitative models of risks is the only way to keep risk regulation and risk management from being purely superficial.

Miscellaneous Topics

The topic of risk management and risk analysis is large and, even though this book ended up being larger than I had originally planned (about 80,000 words as opposed to 50,000), there are still several issues we didn't discuss in much detail. Some of these are central to risk management for some people, and others are more tangential. You can decide for yourself which of the following justifies further research:

- *Options Theory and real options theory*. Shortly after the 1997 Nobel was awarded to Myron Scholes and Robert Merton for their work in Options Theory, there was a surge in the interest of the application of the method not just to the financial instruments is was designed for, but to decisions internal to an organization. Consultants were addressing the option value to justify technology investments on one hand and the option value of deferring investments on the other. Two very important points are critical here. First, some have attempted to apply the original formula—the *Black-Scholes formula*—directly to real option problems. I rarely see this done in a way that is useful. Using this formula literally means that the analyst has to figure out what in a project or new technology translates into specific variables in the formula, such as the *strike price* or the *underlying instrument*. In the cases I've seen, the use of those terms is meaningless. What does *strike price* mean when applied to an IT project? Second, there is no way to apply Black-Scholes without knowing a probability distribution for future values, and in most of the cases I saw there was no probabilistic analysis of any kind. Whereas there are some sophisticated users who have used this correctly in some risk management contexts, I suspect many more managers put more credibility in the use of the term *options theory* than the proper application of the theory. The most useful application of what some people called *real options* usually turns out to be a classic application of decision theory dealing with decisions under uncertainty. "Options" have been around since the beginning of decision analysis. Don't feel you have to include a literal application of Black-Scholes to your problem.

- *Autoregressive conditional heteroscedasticity (ARCH).* ARCH and its numerous cousins are the standard model used by many financial firms to assess future volatility of financial instruments. Although ARCH won the Nobel Prize for Robert Engle 2003, it is (like MPT and Options Theory) only currently a Level 2 model (see Chapter 10) at best. If your firm uses this, be sure to back-test your results in your firm and for data in the related parts of the industry. Some studies find mixed results when comparing the models to historical reality.[6]
- *Neural networks and genetic algorithms.* These are more advanced mathematical methods that have generated a lot of interest in solving a variety of problems. If you haven't heard of these tools, I won't be able to explain them here; if you've heard of them, you probably know enough for me to make this point. I've met a few consultants and academics who get very excited about applying cool-sounding math to just about anything. But be skeptical and empirical. The measured performance matters more than mathematical aesthetics. These methods involve calculations in complex systems that aren't even understood by the people that develop them—they don't know exactly *why* they appear to work on some problems.
- *Fuzzy logic and fuzzy sets.* This is dealing with the mathematics of the kind of imprecision we are used to in the real world. Like *neural nets* and *genetic algorithms*, this is one of the more esoteric areas of mathematics and some analysts are very excited about applying it to everything. But I tend to find that those people are not yet familiar with the work in decision analysis. Probabilistic decision analysis already deals with the fuzziness of uncertainty. The other fuzziness they refer to is ambiguity, which I find is always avoidable.
- *Business intelligence and data analytics.* These are attractive names for certain kinds of enterprise software (if you haven't heard, *enterprise* generally means it's more expensive). Data analytics and business intelligence both start with the basic assumption that the path to better

information is via better analysis of your existing data. This can be helpful, but is part of a larger program of implementing better decision analysis.

- *Influence diagrams, fault tree analysis, and failure modes and effects analysis (FMEA).* The first two items are good standard tools used in probabilistic models of risks, but I consider them rather obvious extensions of what we have already discussed. FMEA involves listing and working out consequences of several components in a system, so it may sound like a probabilistic risk analysis (PRA). But I've seen uses of FMEA that involve ineffectual scoring methods, so be on the lookout.

Final Thoughts on Quantitative Models and Better Decisions

I mentioned earlier that finding firms that tracked the performance of their models was difficult—but I found some. It was even harder to find research that showed how quantitative models actually contributed to overall performance of the firm. Thompson Terry, a modeler who works at Palisade Corporation (the makers of the @Risk Monte Carlo tool), recently offered some anecdotal evidence of the effectiveness of better quantitative modeling. He pointed out that Goldman Sachs, Morgan Stanley, and Deutsche Bank were all @Risk users and they all survived the 2008 financial crisis. He then pointed out that Merrill Lynch, Bear Stearns, and Lehman Brothers were not customers. This is interesting, but obviously not conclusive.

I did find one piece of research that measured a real strategic advantage for users of more advanced quantitative methods. Fiona MacMillan, now with Palantir Economic Solutions, wrote her PhD thesis on a survey of oil exploration firms and their use of quantitative methods. She later coauthored a paper on it in journal of the *Society of Petroleum Engineers*. It showed a strong correlation between several measures of financial performance and the maturity of the firm in the use of more quantitative risk analysis methods.[7] She was also able to show that the improvements in financial performance occurred *just after* they began to adopt more quantitative methods.[8] This is about as good as evidence gets in this field since so few other firms use quantitative methods at all.

Most of the users of quantitative methods in MacMillan's study probably were not even using many of the methods I discussed in this book: calibration, incentives for forecasting, global risk models, and so on. Still, the findings indicate what the potential could be for all firms. And, as interesting as the findings were, what I liked most from MacMillan's study was the observation made by one participant in it.

For the past several years, many firms have focused on information technology as necessary for growth and being competitive. But what Kahneman referred to as *quality control of decisions* was not necessarily a focus. MacMillan felt that many respondents in her study thought the primary objective of these quantitative methods was simply the reduction of risk, not optimizing decisions in general. But one participant in the study stood out as taking a more enlightened view about risk management and decision analysis and the key challenge for all businesses and governments:

> There is no longer any sustainable competitive advantage to be gained through technology, but only through making better judgments on whether each opportunity has the right amount of risk, neither too much nor too little.

NOTES

1. G. Klein, "Performing a Project Premortem," *Harvard Business Review,* September 2007.
2. T.S.H. Teo and M. Tan, "Quantitative and Qualitative Errors in Spreadsheet Development," *Proceedings of the Thirtieth Hawaii International Conference on Systems Sciences*, 1997.
3. R.R. Panko and R. Sprangue, "Hitting the Wall: Errors in Developing and Code Inspecting: a 'Simple' Spreadsheet Model," *Decision Support Systems* 22(4), April 1998, 337–353.
4. G.W. Brier, "Verification of Forecasts Expressed in Terms of Probability," *Monthly Weather Review* 75, 1950, 1–3.
5. R.T. Clemen and R.L. Winkler, "Combining Economic Forecasts," *Journal of Business & Economic Statistics* 4(1), January 1986, 39–46.
6. C. Starica, "Is GARCH(1,1) as Good a Model as the Nobel Prize Accolades Would Imply?," *Econometrics*, 2004.
7. G.S. Simpson, F.E. Lamb, J.H. Finch, and N.C. Dinnie, "The Application of Probabilistic and Qualitative Methods to Asset Management Decision Making," *Society of Petroleum Engineers*, 2000.
8. F. Lamb (Now MacMillan) et al., "Taking Calculated Risks," *Oilfield Review,* Autumn 2000.

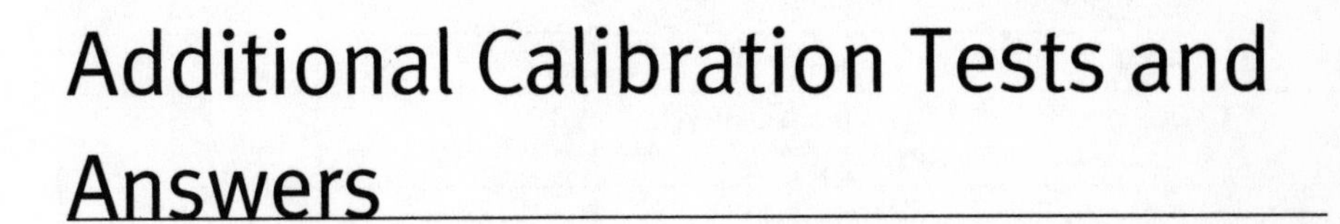

Additional Calibration Tests and Answers

CALIBRATION TEST FOR RANGES: A

#	Question	Lower Bound (95% Chance Value Is Higher)	Upper Bound (95% Chance Value Is Lower)
1	How many feet tall is the Hoover Dam?		
2	How many inches long is a $20 bill?		
3	What percentage of aluminum is recycled in the United States?		
4	When was Elvis Presley born?		
5	What percentage of the atmosphere is oxygen by weight?		
6	What is the latitude of New Orleans? [*Hint:* Latitude is 0 degrees at the equator and 90 at the North Pole.]		
7	In 1913, the U.S. military owned how many airplanes?		
8	The first European printing press was invented in what year?		
9	What percentage of all electricity consumed in U.S. households was used by kitchen appliances in 2001?		
10	How many miles tall is Mount Everest?		
11	How long is Iraq's border with Iran in kilometers?		
12	How many miles long is the Nile?		
13	In what year was Harvard founded?		
14	What is the wingspan (in feet) of a Boeing 747 jumbo jet?		
15	How many soldiers were in a Roman legion?		
16	What is the average temperature of the abyssal zone (where the oceans are more than 6,500 feet deep) in degrees F?		
17	How many feet long is the Space Shuttle *Orbiter* (excluding the external tank)?		
18	In what year did Jules Verne publish *20,000 Leagues Under the Sea*?		
19	How wide is the goal in field hockey (in feet)?		
20	The Roman Coliseum held how many spectators?		

#	Answers to Calibration Test for Ranges: A
1	738
2	63/16ths (6.1875)
3	45%
4	1935
5	21%
6	31
7	23
8	1450
9	26.7%
10	5.5
11	1,458
12	4,160
13	1636
14	196
15	6,000
16	398°F
17	122
18	1870
19	12
20	50,000

CALIBRATION TEST FOR RANGES: B

#	Question	Lower Bound (95% Chance Value Is Higher)	Upper Bound (95% Chance Value Is Lower)
1	The first probe to land on Mars, *Viking 1*, landed there in what year?		
2	How old was the youngest person to fly into space?		
3	How many meters tall is the Sears Tower?		
4	What was the maximum altitude of the *Breitling Orbiter 3*, the first balloon to circumnavigate the globe, in miles?		
5	On average, what percentage of the total software development project effort is spent in design?		
6	How many people were permanently evacuated after the Chernobyl nuclear power plant accident?		
7	How many feet long were the largest airships?		
8	How many miles is the flying distance from San Francisco to Honolulu?		
9	The fastest bird, the falcon, can fly at a speed of how many miles per hour in a dive?		
10	In what year was the double helix structure of DNA discovered?		
11	How many yards wide is a football field?		
12	What was the percentage growth in Internet hosts from 1996 to 1997?		
13	How many calories are in 8 ounces of orange juice?		
14	How fast would you have to travel at sea level to break the sound barrier (in mph)?		

15	How many years was Nelson Mandela in prison?		
16	What is the average daily calorie intake in developed countries?		
17	In 1994, how many nations were members of the United Nations?		
18	The Audubon Society was formed in the United States in what year?		
19	How many feet high is the world's highest waterfall (Angel Falls, Venezuela)?		
20	How deep beneath the sea was the *Titanic* found (in miles)?		

#	Answers to Calibration Test for Ranges: B
1	1976
2	26
3	443
4	6.9
5	20%
6	135,000
7	803
8	2,394
9	150
10	1953
11	53.3
12	70%
13	120
14	760
15	26
16	3,300
17	184
18	1905
19	3,212
20	2.5 miles

CALIBRATION TEST FOR BINARY: A

	Statement	Answer (True/False)	Confidence that You Are Correct (Circle One)
1	The Lincoln Highway was the first paved road in the United States, and it ran from Chicago to San Francisco.		50% 60% 70% 80% 90% 100%
2	The Silk Road joined the two ancient kingdoms of China and Afghanistan.		50% 60% 70% 80% 90% 100%
3	More American homes have microwaves than telephones.		50% 60% 70% 80% 90% 100%
4	*Doric* is an architectural term for a shape of roof.		50% 60% 70% 80% 90% 100%
5	The World Tourism Organization predicts that Europe will still be the most popular tourist destination in 2020.		50% 60% 70% 80% 90% 100%
6	Germany was the second country to develop atomic weapons.		50% 60% 70% 80% 90% 100%
7	A hockey puck will fit in a golf hole.		50% 60% 70% 80% 90% 100%
8	The Sioux were one of the Plains Indian tribes.		50% 60% 70% 80% 90% 100%
9	To a physicist, *plasma* is a type of rock.		50% 60% 70% 80% 90% 100%
10	The Hundred Years' War was actually over a century long.		50% 60% 70% 80% 90% 100%
11	Most of the fresh water on Earth is in the polar ice caps.		50% 60% 70% 80% 90% 100%
12	The Academy Awards ("Oscars") began over a century ago.		50% 60% 70% 80% 90% 100%
13	There are fewer than 200 billionaires in the world.		50% 60% 70% 80% 90% 100%
14	In Excel, ^ means "take to the power of."		50% 60% 70% 80% 90% 100%
15	The average annual salary of airline captains is over $150,000.		50% 60% 70% 80% 90% 100%
16	By 1997, Bill Gates was worth more than $10 billion.		50% 60% 70% 80% 90% 100%

(Continued)

17	Cannons were used in European warfare by the 11th century.		50% 60% 70% 80% 90% 100%
18	Anchorage is the capital of Alaska.		50% 60% 70% 80% 90% 100%
19	Washington, Jefferson, Lincoln, and Grant are the four presidents whose heads are sculpted into Mount Rushmore.		50% 60% 70% 80% 90% 100%
20	John Wiley & Sons is not the largest book publisher.		50% 60% 70% 80% 90% 100%

#	Answers for Calibration Test Binary: A
1	FALSE
2	FALSE
3	FALSE
4	FALSE
5	TRUE
6	FALSE
7	TRUE
8	TRUE
9	FALSE
10	TRUE
11	TRUE
12	FALSE
13	FALSE
14	TRUE
15	FALSE
16	TRUE
17	FALSE
18	FALSE
19	FALSE
20	TRUE

CALIBRATION TEST FOR BINARY: B

	Statement	Answer (True/False)	Confidence that You Are Correct (Circle One)
1	Jupiter's "Great Red Spot" is larger than Earth.		50% 60% 70% 80% 90% 100%
2	The Brooklyn Dodgers' name was short for "trolley car dodgers."		50% 60% 70% 80% 90% 100%
3	*Hypersonic* is faster than *subsonic*.		50% 60% 70% 80% 90% 100%
4	A *polygon* is three dimensional and a *polyhedron* is two dimensional.		50% 60% 70% 80% 90% 100%
5	A 1-watt electric motor produces 1 horsepower.		50% 60% 70% 80% 90% 100%
6	Chicago is more populous than Boston.		50% 60% 70% 80% 90% 100%
7	In 2005, Wal-Mart sales dropped below $100 billion.		50% 60% 70% 80% 90% 100%
8	Post-it Notes were invented by 3M.		50% 60% 70% 80% 90% 100%
9	Alfred Nobel, whose fortune endows the Nobel Peace Prize, made his fortune in oil and explosives.		50% 60% 70% 80% 90% 100%
10	A BTU is a measure of heat.		50% 60% 70% 80% 90% 100%
11	The winner of the first Indianapolis 500 clocked an average speed of under 100 mph.		50% 60% 70% 80% 90% 100%
12	Microsoft has more employees than IBM.		50% 60% 70% 80% 90% 100%
13	Romania borders Hungary.		50% 60% 70% 80% 90% 100%
14	Idaho is larger (in area) than Iraq.		50% 60% 70% 80% 90% 100%
15	Casablanca is on the African continent.		50% 60% 70% 80% 90% 100%
16	The first manmade plastic was invented in the 19th century.		50% 60% 70% 80% 90% 100%
17	A chamois is an alpine animal.		50% 60% 70% 80% 90% 100%
18	The base of a pyramid is in the shape of a square.		50% 60% 70% 80% 90% 100%
19	Stonehenge is located on the main British island.		50% 60% 70% 80% 90% 100%
20	Computer processors double in power every three months or less.		50% 60% 70% 80% 90% 100%

#	Answers for Calibration Test Binary: B
1	TRUE
2	TRUE
3	TRUE
4	FALSE
5	FALSE
6	TRUE
7	FALSE
8	TRUE
9	TRUE
10	TRUE
11	TRUE
12	FALSE
13	TRUE
14	FALSE
15	TRUE
16	TRUE
17	TRUE
18	TRUE
19	TRUE
20	FALSE

Index